SIMON
SAYS

SIMON SAYS

SAYS

THE BEST OF
ROGER
SIMON

C O N T E M P O R A R Y
BOOKS, INC.
CHICAGO ▪ NEW YORK

Library of Congress Cataloging-in-Publication Data

Simon, Roger, 1948–
  Simon says.

  1. United States—Politics and government—1981-
—Addresses, essays, lectures. 2. United States—
Foreign relations—1981   —Addresses, essays, lec-
tures. 3. Simon, Roger, 1948-   —Journeys—Ad-
resses, essays, lectures. I. Title.
E876.S49   1985   973.927   85-17473
ISBN 0-8092-5243-0
ISBN 0-8092-4853-0 (pbk.)

Published by Contemporary Books, Inc.
180 North Michigan Avenue, Chicago, Illinois 60601
Manufactured in the United States of America
Library of Congress Catalog Card Number: 85-17473
International Standard Book Number: 0-8092-5243-0 (cloth)
                                    0-8092-4853-0 (paper)

Published simultaneously in Canada by Beaverbooks, Ltd.
195 Allstate Parkway, Valleywood Business Park
Markham, Ontario L3R 4T8 Canada

For Marcia

CONTENTS

PREFACE

I never wanted to be a columnist. What I wanted to be was a trumpet player in a bawdy house. I wanted to wear a purple derby and blow my trumpet while ladies sat around in their underwear sipping on mint juleps.

Needless to say, my mother was horrified by this idea. She told me that someday I would change my mind. And, of course, I did. And I remember writing to Mom to tell her that I had become a columnist for a newspaper.

She sent me a trumpet.

I have been writing columns for about 10 years and almost every one was done in a day, some in a few hours, some in less than that. That's not a complaint or a boast; it's simply what a newspaper column is like. History on the run, you might say.

The columns in this book range from South Africa to South Lebanon to the South Side of Chicago. They range from Ted Kennedy to Phil Donahue to John Wayne Gacy to Henny Youngman to a few score people you never heard of.

People always ask me where I get my ideas and I am never able to come up with a good answer because they come from everywhere. They come from what I see and what I hear and what I feel and what I think. They come from how things are and how they were and how I think they should be.

I cannot think of a better job. On some days, on days when you work and rework a line a dozen times to get it right or rush to a phone and make your deadline by five minutes and someone calls or writes or stops you in the hall to say, "Hey, that was a good one," on those days, I'd do it even if they didn't pay me.

A man who, I am happy to say, did pay me for many years is Jim Hoge, my former editor and publisher at the *Chicago Sun-Times*. Almost everything in this book was done under his direction and tutelage and I owe him a debt that can never be repaid. My gratitude also goes to Gregory Favre, my former managing editor; Joe Reilly, my former metropolitan editor; as well as Tom Gavagan of the copy desk.

Grateful acknowledgment is also made to Natalie DeZanek, my secretary, for her loyalty, hard work and tolerance; Jody Rein, my editor at Contemporary Books; Ward Just, who gave me my first column at the *News-Sun* in Waukegan, Illinois, when I was just a year out of college; and to the staff of the *Los Angeles Times* Syndicate, which distributes my work nationally, including Fred Dingman, Don Michel, and former editor Rick Newcombe.

Thanks also to Reg Murphy, my publisher at the *Baltimore Sun*, and James I. Houck, managing editor of the *Baltimore Sun*. Also Connie Wilkie, Tim Howard, Ken Greenberg, Diane Balk, and those who helped me track down what happened to some of the people who appear in this book: Larry Green of the *Los Angeles Times*, James Warren of the *Chicago Tribune*, David Devane of the Cook County state's attorney's office and Irving Paley of the Chicago Museum of Science and Industry.

But most of all my thanks go to the person who read, reread and organized the pieces that went into this book, my toughest critic, biggest supporter, best friend and wife, Marcia Kramer.

Choosing the 100 or so pieces that are included here out of the 1,600 or so that I have written was a little like deciding which child you love best.

All I can say is that I know they are in good hands.

3,000 Reasons
Reporters Are Suspicious

I now realize all reporters are beasts. I know this because I read it in *Time* magazine and saw it on Ted Koppel.

The press informs me that the press is under attack. So it must be true. Unless the press is lying again.

I have been as bad as all the other reporters. I have been much too suspicious of people, especially of politicians.

I am told this is the biggest mistake reporters make.

The lesson hit home yesterday when I got my hands on a police report filled out by a Chicago alderman.

The alderman is Wallace Davis, Jr., of the 27th Ward, and the report involves his stolen car.

A couple of weeks ago, Davis's 1983 Cadillac Fleetwood was stolen in Glenwood, a south suburb.

Davis reported the loss to police, saying he had parked the car around 3 A.M., and when he looked for it at about 9 A.M. it was gone.

He also told police there were some items of value inside the car.

There was a walkie-talkie, a bulletproof vest, and a brown case containing $3,000 in $50 bills.

Back when I was a typical, snooping, irresponsible reporter, this would have made me suspicious. I would have wondered what a Chicago alderman was doing in the suburbs at 3 A.M. with $3,000 in fifties.

But not anymore. I realize suspicion is a sickness and the press needs to get well. There are any number of perfectly reasonable explanations for what the alderman was doing there with all that dough at that hour.

Maybe he was going to a garage sale and wanted to be first in line, for instance.

I was going to forget the whole story. Why bother a man during his grief? So I can't really explain why I called Davis. Old habits die hard, I guess.

I learned there was good news and bad news. The good news is that the car has been found. The bad news is that it doesn't look like a car anymore.

"It has been stripped," Davis said. "All the seats were taken out and the bumpers ripped off and the sunroof ripped out and they even took the mag wheels. I bought that car in May for $27,000. It hurt my heart to look at it. I threw my hands into the air when I saw it."

And the bulletproof vest? I asked.

"Gone," said the alderman.

The walkie-talkie?

"Gone, too," said the alderman.

And, well, I don't know quite how to ask this, alderman, I mean I don't want to pry or anything, but what about that $3,000 in $50 bills in that brown case?

"There was no $3,000 in $50 bills in that brown case," Davis said.

There wasn't?

"No, the $3,000 in $50 bills was in a brown plastic bag stuffed under the front seat," he said.

I should have let the whole thing drop right there. I mean, how much badgering can one person take? But I plunged on.

Uh, alderman, I asked, could you tell me *why* you had $3,000 in $50 bills in your car?

"Well, yes, I can," he said. "I have nothing to hide. I am having some work done on my home, a considerable amount of work, and the money was for the contractors."

So what was it doing in a brown plastic bag in your car in Glenwood at 3 A.M.?

"Well, when I'm at home, I park my car in my garage," he said. "But when I drove to Glenwood, I just had the money under the front seat."

See what I mean about reporters being too suspicious? Here was a perfectly reasonable, completely understandable explanation. I wanted to kick myself for even disturbing the guy.

What was your first reaction when you found your car gone? I asked.

"Jesus Christ, my money's in there!" Davis said. "Then I was praying the thieves might not look under the seat. But when the thieves took the seat, they must have found the money."

And what were you doing in Glenwood at 3 A.M.?

"Yes, well," he said. "I have a friend there, a nurse, who hurt her foot and she needed to have somebody help her down the steps so she could get to the hospital in the morning. And that's what I was doing there."

I see.

"I know some people will be suspicious of this whole story," he said. "What with all the graft and extortion and everybody getting indicted. But I have nothing to hide. In fact, this may be a setup."

Really?

"Yes, some agency—I don't rule out the FBI—might have stolen my car in an attempt to trap me and smear me," he said. "I know my phones are tapped. But whoever is trying to get me has failed. My life is an open book."

And have you learned anything from your tragedy?

"I will never leave money in my car again," he said. "I have paid a heavy price."

Just one last one, alderman.

Why on earth would anybody leave $3,000 in a car overnight?

"Well," he said, "I thought the suburbs were safe. I thought the suburbs were supposed to be safer than the city."

You mean if you had parked in your own ward, you would not have left the money in the car?

"Of course not," he said. "Do you think I'm crazy?"

And just to show you how much I have grown as a reporter, I didn't even answer his question.

December 13, 1983

Yanks Get Thanks from Grateful Grenada

I had walked to work and had not listened to the radio that morning. When I got to the newsroom, Gregory Favre, the managing editor, was standing outside my office. "The United States has just invaded the island of Grenada," he said. "Would you like to go?"

"Sure," I said, "unless you want to send someone who speaks Spanish better than I do."

"They speak English there," he said.

"Then I'm your man," said I.

As I got in a cab for the airport, it occurred to me I had no idea where Grenada was. As I later found out, neither did most of the invaders.

ST. GEORGE'S, Grenada

The black thunderheads had just come boiling up over the mountains when Frecuente Freddie opened fire.

The Americans are almost getting used to it, but they scattered anyway.

"It's this one guy up at Frecuente," Marine Gunnery Sgt. Marv Price said, naming the area above the Cuban-built airport on the southern tip of this island. "I don't know who he is, but he sure is determined."

There are ways of dealing with Freddie, however. There are planes here filled with equipment that can see a man's body heat. The plane drops a phosphorus marker and then calls in the Cobras.

The Cobras are the black helicopter gunships that fly in formation all over this island like swarms of angry dragonflies. They carry rockets, .50-caliber machineguns, and something called a mini-gun, which fires so rapidly it can literally shred a man. In a way, this is symbolic: all the technology of a great nation brought to bear against one man with a rifle.

But one man and one rifle can do a lot. Quoting a line once heard in Vietnam, one soldier said: "It's not the bullet with your name on it you worry about; it's the one that says to whom it may concern."

Our C-130 transport plane came into Point Salines airport yesterday out of a dark sky and it came in fast and dirty to avoid the possibility of enemy fire. When it dropped its rear ramp, we could see that American bulldozers had just about completed the 10,000-foot runway the Cubans had started, a runway now handling some of our largest jets.

This is but one of the ironies of this war: We were afraid the Cubans were building a military airport, so we built one. We were afraid the Cubans were going to invade, so we invaded. We were afraid the people would not have a democracy, so we imposed martial law, at least temporarily.

But the Grenadians are not complaining.

Yesterday was the first day the press was allowed to roam the island without a military escort. And unless all the anti-Americans have taken to the hills, one must conclude the American invasion is genuinely popular here.

Dr. Barry Rapier, a native Grenadian educated in Edinburgh, Scotland, had only one complaint:

"This invasion should have come four years ago. The Americans should have come sooner." On the day of the bloody coup two weeks ago, Rapier closed his office, headed home, and locked his door. He did not come out until after the Americans invaded.

"I went back to my office in St. George's to see if it had been looted and when I came back home, I found the Americans had broken in looking for Cubans.

"Angry? Ah, what the hell, I'm just glad the Americans are here. They were very decent about it. I want them to collect the crazy fellows we've got running around with guns up in the hills.

"It will take a couple of years to go back to normal. But your Grenadian, all he wants is a job and a little money and you know the Yankees are pretty good at spending dollars."

Life is struggling back to normal here as Americans are busy painting U.S.A. on captured Russian trucks and removing machine-gunned cows from the ditches. Grenadians are slowly getting their electricity back.

The hills, which rise to breathtaking heights and are covered with a nubby green carpet of trees, still contain Cubans and members of the People's Revolutionary Army. The Americans are hoping that starvation and desperation will drive those forces to surrender.

Meanwhile, Grenada looks like an American outpost.

Offshore and clearly visible are gray American warships on constant patrol. And the roads are crammed with American soldiers on or in every conceivable vehicle.

Two paratroopers in full camouflage gear and carrying M-16s

buzzed by us on a tiny, orange minibike. Another two came by in a green Jaguar sedan.

Unfortunately, from a traffic standpoint, the Americans insist on driving on the right and the Grenadians insist on driving on the left. The results can be startling.

The road from Point Salines to the capital of St. George's passes artillery Fire Base Gater that has a big sign turned toward the hills: "You shell, we shell."

And along the same road, in front of Veronica's Tropical Wear, the first American checkpoint is set up.

"We found some people with a trunk-load of Spanish-English dictionaries," Gunnery Sgt. Price said. "That's the kind of stuff Cubans use. There are still Communists on this island and we have got to find them."

In St. George's, whose white-walled, red-roofed buildings rush off the hillside and up to the clear water of the harbor, there was calm yesterday.

But as I walked past youngsters who were gliding by on roller-skates, two tan jeeps, manned by Americans and mounted with .50-caliber machine guns, came screeching up to the Grenada Telephone Co. The soldiers had heard that there might be Cubans inside.

The Americans found no Cubans, but did uncover two green, wooden boxes full of ammunition and military clothing.

Down the street, Master Sgt. Jack Stroude stood at a fire hydrant helping to fill a water truck. As he stood there, armed to the teeth with a rifle, sidearm, and machete, Grenadian men and women walked by and waved to him.

Giving an "aw shucks" grin, Stroude said: "I'm just trying to help out, that's all."

Along the harbor where some boats were docked, a small boy, much smaller than his 11 years, stood holding his baby niece.

He was wearing tan shorts about three sizes too big and a tan shirt with a wild red pattern. His niece was wearing a brown blouse and a diaper.

He told me his name was Cosmos Simon, and when I told him we had the same last name, he thought that was the funniest thing he had ever heard in his life and convulsed into giggles.

He would not tell me his niece's name for fear I might say something equally silly.

He said he had been afraid of all the shooting, but he wasn't afraid anymore.

As we walked along, he took my hand as if we had known each other for years.

He pointed to a soldier from the 82nd Airborne eating out of a K-ration can with his bayonet. "Will he be staying here?" Cosmos asked.

I told him he would not.

"Will you be staying here?" he asked.

I told him I would not.

A V-formation of Cobra helicopters passed above us, moving with grim slowness across the rose and gold sunset.

"Will they be staying?" he asked.

No, I said, we will all go, all of us. And soon, perhaps.

"Well," he said, "I think I shall stay. But thank you all for coming."

October 31, 1983

The Gifts and Crimes of Freddie Martin

Just after Freddie Martin killed them, just after he plunged the knives into their chests and turned on the gas jets, he knelt over the body of Catherine Alferink and tore the wedding ring from her finger.

He took it home that night and tossed it to his wife, Gwenda. "Here," he said. "Have a present."

He would live to regret his generosity. Because a few days later the police would come and knock on Gwenda's door. And when she answered, one policeman would happen to look at her hand. And see the wedding ring catch the light and glow like a beacon in the dim hallway.

Stephen Connolly didn't have to drive down to the courtroom in Harvey yesterday. It was a bitterly cold day and Connolly isn't a prosecutor anymore. After the Freddie Martin case, he had left the office for a successful private practice and his days were no longer filled with the kind of pictures he now held in his hands.

"Take a look," he said, and shoved them across the desk. "It may help you understand."

The pictures showed a white-haired Herbert Alferink, 76, a retired janitor, lying on his kitchen floor. His hands and feet were bound with clothesline. His wife, Catherine, 78, lay next to him, looking terribly small and frail in her cotton house dress. A knife handle rose out of each of their chests.

So Stephen Connolly went to court. And he sat with his former partner, Cliff Johnson, to see how the court would sentence Freddie Martin. There was simply no other place he could be.

I looked at the pictures and tried to do what Connolly asked me to do. I tried to understand. But it's when you try to do that—when you try to understand the crimes of Freddie Martin—that it becomes so difficult.

By his own account, Freddie Martin did not have a tough time as a child. His father and mother worked; there was enough money in the house. He mowed lawns in the summer and played basketball in the fall. When speaking of his childhood he said simply that it was "good."

On August 11, 1969, he was sentenced on six counts of burglary, auto theft, and possession of narcotics. It was his 20th arrest in three years. He was 21 years old.

The judge gave him a relatively light sentence: one to eight years. He did not serve his full sentence, of course. No one does. If we believe in anything in this country, we believe in rehabilitation.

Twenty-one months later, a rehabilitated man, he got his parole. Freddie Martin was on the street.

Ten months after that he rang the doorbell of an 85-year-old woman and asked to use the phone. He said his car had broken down. The woman opened the door. There are a lot of nice people in the world.

Once inside, Martin began to choke her, demanding the location of her valuables. She was old and weak but when he threw her to the floor, she was still alive.

He was caught and sentenced to five to ten years for robbery. But of course he did not serve five to ten years. Not anywhere near it. Four years after he was sentenced, the parole board said he was rehabilitated again. And Freddie Martin was on the street.

On November 12, 1975—five weeks after Martin had been paroled—Gus Strombeck, 74, was murdered in a fashion so brutal that it shocked even the police. It would later become a very familiar story.

Strombeck was a retired painter living alone in a small house on Chicago's South Side. A neighbor testified that on November 12 she saw Freddie Martin stand in front of Strombeck's house and then move down the street.

Twenty minutes later she saw the smoke. When the firemen finally broke inside the home of Gus Strombeck they found him tied to a chair. A butcher knife had been plunged into his chest. The gas jets had been turned on. By the time they dragged him out, his face had been burned almost beyond recognition.

Gwenda—Freddie Martin's wife—got a present on the night that Strombeck died. It was two brooches that once belonged to Strombeck's wife. "These are for you," Freddie told her. Strombeck's cassette recorder turned up in a pawnshop. And Freddie Martin's name was on the pawnshop ticket.

Less than a month passed. On December 6, Edward Mullen, 86, and retired, was brutally murdered. He lived a block from Freddie Martin. When the firefighters got to Mullen's small home, the fire was already raging. They found Mullen tied to a chair in his living room. He had been stabbed with a kitchen knife in the chest. His watch was missing.

That night Freddie gave Gwenda a watch. He told her it was a present. He didn't tell her that it came off the wrist of Edward Mullen.

A month passed. And Freddie Martin still walked the streets. On January 15 he took a bus to the south suburb of Harvey, a place where many people have moved to escape the high crime of the city.

The bus took him past the small home of Herbert and Catherine Alferink. It was a Thursday night, the night that two of the Alferinks' daughters, Ruth Bronson and Agnes Golec, were supposed to visit.

The Alferinks lived alone and looked forward to the visits of their daughters. Herbert was retired and they pinched their pennies. Their last meal was macaroni.

"I always go to play pinochle with them on Thursday night," Agnes said. "They love cards. But I was going to take Mom shopping on Friday, so I told them I would see them on that day instead."

Ruth was going to visit them on Thursday night, too. "But I had a leg infection," she said. "I told them I would see them Friday with Agnes."

But Freddie Martin saw them first. He knocked on the door and said that his car had broken down. He said he'd appreciate it if he could come in and use the telephone. They opened the door.

Cliff Johnson, the prosecutor, described their last moments: the husband and wife, old and weak, begging for their lives, pleading as Martin lashed their arms and legs together, following his actions with frightened eyes as he searched the kitchen drawers for just the right knives.

"My father was so weak with emphysema that he literally could not walk across the living room without resting," Agnes said. "And my mother had cancer. She had leukemia."

You would think that prosecutors get used to these kinds of moments, but they do not. The good ones do not. And so it was with tears in his eyes that Johnson addressed the judge yesterday and described how Freddie Martin had tortured the old couple into revealing where their pathetically few valuables were. Where he could find the television and the watches and, of course, the wedding ring of Catherine.

"Then he held them by the throat," Johnson said, his voice breaking, "and he slaughtered them like chickens."

Freddie Martin sat in the courtroom. The only emotion he showed was when the judge sentenced him to 150 to 450 years for murder. That is when Freddie Martin smiled.

Judge James Sullivan made it clear that if Illinois had a death penalty for such crimes he would have used it. "No one knows if the death penalty deters," Sullivan said. "But it would have deterred Mr. Martin."

The judge said he hoped the parole board would read the transcript of this trial. Martin will be eligible for parole in 11 years and three months. He will be 39.

Agnes and Ruth sat in the front row. The relatives of murder victims always expect to feel joy or relief or triumph when they hear the sentence, but they hardly ever do. They usually just feel empty.

They could not speak for a while and sat on their chairs while the courtroom cleared. When they did speak, they looked at their hands.

"This was my mother's watch," said Agnes.

"And this was her wedding ring," said Ruth.

And then they walked home.

December 3, 1976

Grab Those Somedays While You Can

They say we need electronic games and video recorders and Walkman stereos to entertain us wherever we go. That is because, they say, we are a nation that is easily bored.

So as I drove along the two-lane blacktop in central Wisconsin on my way to a speech the other day, I wondered why some people still drive out to see the trees change color.

The trees will change next year just like they changed last year. And almost everyone has seen it happen again and again. Yet some come out to see it anyway.

It reminded me of that day Carl and I were sitting on the porch of the old gray house that had somehow managed to survive countless generations of college students.

Classes were to begin in just a few days and we felt they could not be returned to without an appropriate adventure first.

Florida, California, Texas, New York—all those places that spelled excitement to Midwesterners—were out of the question for reasons of time and money.

"What we should do," Carl said in one of those moments of pure inspiration, "is circumnavigate Lake Michigan."

It was the word *circumnavigate* that did it. And it did not matter that our vessel of exploration would be Carl's father's Buick and not a schooner. The word gave us a sense of drama and mission.

We got out the maps and plotted our course. We figured we could do it for $20 plus gas.

A few hours later, we were on the road.

That would be impossible now, even unthinkable, I realize. Now there are responsibilities to meet and arrangements to make and the putting of your house in order before you can just pack up and leave.

But back then, there was only us and the road. And the best part of it, really, was what happened when we left the road.

I was navigating that day—my lap was heaped high with maps and guidebooks—and I read aloud to Carl over the engine's roar the single map legend: "Gen. MacArthur Pine."

I do not remember our precise conversation, but since sarcasm is the universal language of college students, it must have gone something like this:

"And what do you suppose a Gen. MacArthur Pine *is?*"

"A tree that *looks* like Gen. MacArthur? A tree *whittled* by Gen. MacArthur? A tree in which Gen. MacArthur is buried?"

"In other words, a sight not to be missed."

"To be sure."

"Of course."

It was at least a hundred miles out of our way, maybe farther, but we turned toward it without hesitation.

The tourist season was ending and the two-lane blacktop was empty in both directions. The forest got denser and denser, growing up to the edge of the roadway. The pines formed a canopy over our heads and the sun was flashing briefly between the branches.

We fell silent in the car, almost as if we had entered a church, and soon all we could hear was the whisper of the trees in the wind and the hiss of our tires against the highway.

We came upon it suddenly; it rested on little more than a wide place in the road. We pulled over and walked across the pine needles to where it stood. There was no one else around.

The little sign said it was the tallest white pine in the world, 140 feet high. It had been discovered by a U.S. forest ranger in 1945 and he named it after Douglas MacArthur, the hero of the Pacific, who was also a Wisconsin native. It was thought to be 400 years old.

I had never thought of trees as something you could "discover" or how exactly you determined which tree is the tallest. But we looked at it for a long while.

It didn't do anything. Trees rarely do. But when, without a word, we got back in the car, we left with an odd feeling of satisfaction.

This happened more than a dozen years ago, and it was that trip to Wisconsin the other day to make a speech that reminded me.

No map I have still marks the MacArthur Pine—a taller tree has been discovered—but I remember where it is.

I could have driven to it again after the speech. But I did not. I had responsibilities now. There were columns to write and people to see and things to do. There always are.

You've seen the names on the map yourself. Places called Horseshoe Canyon or Crystal Cave or Indian Rock.

And I'll bet you've passed the turnoffs to such places a hundred times, telling yourself you'll make the trip someday.

Well, maybe you should grab those somedays while you can. You never know when it will be too late. You never know when you'll grow up.

October 27, 1982

Yes, Paul, Love Will Endure

It is funny what you remember in the end.

His mother remembers being on her knees, scrubbing the bathroom floor when her son, Paul, came in and sat on her bed and asked through the open door how long he had to live.

He knew he had cancer. He knew that, at age 17, he had it bad. He knew what the radiation and chemotherapy were doing to his 6-foot, 160-pound frame. He knew he would never play football or hockey again.

He did not care. He just wanted to live.

His mother knew he would not.

"The doctors had told me," Rayna Leib Jacobson said. "They told me he had no chance and that it was time to 'plant the seed.' That is what they said. 'Plant the seed.' "

So she picked her words carefully. Too carefully, as it turned out. She had told him a few weeks before: "Paul, your prognosis is poor."

Paul had taken it well. He did not cry. He was in and out of the hospital and it was not until a few weeks later, when he was at home, that he came into her bedroom and sat on the bed and spoke to her.

"So what does that mean?" he asked.

She looked up from the bathroom floor.

"What?" she said. "What does what mean?"

"What does it mean that my prognosis is poor," he said. "Exactly."

She froze. She thought she had gotten past this moment. She had thought he had understood.

He pressed her. "I want an answer," he said. "It's my life! It's my body! I have a right to know."

She could not speak.

"Am I going to die?" he asked. "Say it. Am I going to die?"

The tears streamed from her eyes and down her cheeks. "Yes," she told him with the sponge still wet in her hand and the soapsuds around her. "Yes, I think so."

"When you told me before about the 'prognosis,' I thought that meant I might live until I was 30 or 40," he said. "Will I live that long?"

She shook her head.

He stared at her and she stared at him, her beautiful, only son, the son who wrote poetry and was an artist and wanted to become a father some day because he liked children so much.

"Do I have two years?" he asked in a flat voice. "Even two years?"

She shook her head again.

"A year? Less?" he asked. "Even less?"

Her heart was a rock within her. "Less," she said softly. "Less."

He stood up suddenly. He still looked pretty good. Even with the cancer filling his chest, his lungs, invading the heart itself, he still looked pretty good.

"I can't cry," he said. "I have to hold back. I can't cry."

She put her arms around him, but he shook her off. "I have to be alone," he said. He left the house and did not come back until the next morning. They did not speak of that night again.

But from that night on, he knew. He really knew.

If you talk to his friends, his relatives, his nurses, the adjectives come easily: shy, quiet, independent, self-reliant, wonderful, artistic, strong. Strong is mentioned a lot.

He made the choices. He made the choice to stop the chemotherapy. He made the choice to die at home. He made the choice to have no life-support machines. He made the choices about an open casket and the memorial service and who would get his clothes.

Just days before he died, he picked up the phone and called people. He called his doctors and the X-ray technicians and the people who drew blood from him and all the others. "Thanks," he said. "Thanks for everything and good-bye."

He believed in love. He used the word a lot. He believed in different kinds: the love toward his mother, his father, Sanford, and his half-sister, Julianne. The love for his grandparents and godparents. The love for his friends. The love between him and his nurse in those last weeks.

Her name is Michele Akerman. She is 30 and an assistant head nurse at Wyler Children's Hospital. She has seen a lot of young people die.

"Paul was . . . special," she said. "He was one of the most sensitive people I have met. You could talk to him as an adult; he could handle things."

He could. But not always. Sometimes he was just a 17-year-old kid who wanted to make 18.

He ran from the hospital one night, outside onto the grass. He lifted his face to the sky and shouted: "It is unfair! Unfair!"

And, of course, it was. Life, they say, is like that.

There was a four-year-old on the ward, call him Teddy, and he became Paul's friend.

"Teddy would ask me if he could get in bed with Paul and watch television," Michele said. "And he would crawl in and they would just watch together. It was a neat relationship. They would play catch or just sit. It was a big deal to Paul. Little kids were special to him."

But Paul did not fool himself. He knew why Teddy was in the hospital. He knew how Teddy would end.

Paul went up to Michele one night and said: "If Teddy doesn't die tonight, I'd like to stay with him." Teddy died on Thanksgiving and Paul was there beside him.

Did he see in Teddy his own death? Was he watching Teddy for a glimpse of his own end? Perhaps, because Teddy's death filled him not just with sadness, but with anger. "There must have been something more that they could have done for him," he told Michele. "There had to be something."

Michele and her mother and Paul went for a trip up to Michigan where Paul went swimming. "He was weak," Michele said. "The chemo and the radiation had taken their toll, but he swam. I think he knew it was his last time."

He cared about his appearance. He had an ego and sometimes he would look into a mirror with a smile and say: "Whatever happened to that good-looking Paul Jacobson?"

He hated pajamas because they reminded him of sickness so Michele bought him a green jogging suit and he wore it almost every day. He was wearing it at the very end.

On December 10, his mother's birthday, he decided to stop the chemotherapy and die at home.

"I'm not a quitter," he told his mother, "I'm a fighter. I'll walk until I can't walk and then I'll crawl if I have to. I can take more pain than you can imagine. I only have one goal now. I'm going to make it to high school graduation.

"I hope it's a sunny day, because I'm going to be there. Maybe they will have to carry me on a stretcher, but I'm going to be there."

He would not be. And his mother knew it.

The cancer, non-Hodgkin's lymphoma, was growing in his body with an awful fury. After the autopsy, the doctors told his mother that continuing the chemotherapy would not have mattered much. It would not have kept Paul alive until his graduation.

Paul left the hospital and came home. There was an oxygen tank there, but nothing else. No tubes, no needles, no nurses, no doctors.

He told his mother to call me at the newspaper. He had some things to say. He would call himself as soon as he felt strong enough. I told his mother that would be fine; I would look forward to it. But Paul never got strong enough.

December 23, a Friday, was the first time he thought he was going to die. He wanted certain people at his bedside. He made a list: relatives, teachers, godparents, his old baby-sitter, and other friends.

His friends from Niles West High, Staci, David, Karen, Mitchell, and Tracy, had spent time with him both in the hospital and out. They had written and called. Staci wrote him a seven-page letter, in neat, careful printing on lined notebook paper. It was a letter of friendship and love, of pain and fear.

"There's got to be more," she wrote. "I wonder if there is a heaven or if people come back. There must, it can't be just over. Tell me there's more. If you come back, let me know it's you. Just give me some kind of signal or something, if you can."

Paul wanted his friends with him that Friday, but they could not bring themselves to come. They talked to him on the phone, but they could not come. It is impossible to blame them. Blame does not enter into it. To stand and watch someone die is not an easy thing.

Paul knew that, but he also knew he wanted to see them one more time. "I can't die without my friends here," he said.

His mother did not know what to do. Then the doorbell rang. Karen Bernstein, 17, stood there. She had come after all. She sat by his bed and held Paul's hand and sobbed for hours.

Paul hung on. On January 14, he slipped into a coma.

His mother became frantic. She grabbed a flashlight and shined it into his eyes, but the pupils were fixed. She ran a finger down the soles of his feet, but there was no reaction.

She called a doctor, but she knew death was at hand.

"You promised," she said to Paul's still figure. "You promised."

She had made him promise. She had made him promise to say good-bye before he died. "It was foolish," she said later. "It was a foolish thing to make him do, but I couldn't help it."

She could not rouse him. But she spoke anyway.

"I love you," she said to him. "I will love you forever."

In the corner of his right eye, she says, she saw a tear. And as she turned away from the bed, Paul made two sounds.

Perhaps he said good-bye. We do not know. Paul Eric Jacobson died at 3:50 A.M., January 15.

In a few weeks, his tombstone will be carved. The message will be brief, but it will say everything.

There will be his name. There will be the dates marking the terribly short span of his life. And there will be three words: Love Will Endure.

February 9, 1984

Finding a Message in a Coke Bottle

Coca-Cola has done a great thing.
   Not by bringing back the old Coke for us to drink. I don't really much care about that. People who get all excited about which soft drink they drink should re-examine their lives.

No, Coke has done something truly praiseworthy for an entirely different reason.

It has liberated us from the cult of the new.

For decades now, Americans have been led to believe that new is always better.

We all grew up believing that laundry detergents actually could be new and improved every six months.

"New and improved" even sort of ran together in our heads as one phrase.

And we believed, we honestly believed, that if something was new, it *had* to be improved.

Companies counted on this. It was called planned obsolescence.

Things were built to not last, because that way companies could always "improve" them with a new model.

People were convinced in the fifties and sixties that cars should be traded in every few years. And they were right. The way Detroit was building cars, they almost had to be traded in every few years.

And if you bought a video cassette recorder or a home computer five years ago, it is virtually an antique now, hopelessly outclassed by the new models.

But have you ever wondered how the biggies in commerce and industry know we will like their improvements?

They spend millions on marketing studies to make sure, that's how.

They have study groups and test markets and sample cities, and by the time the new product comes out they know people will like it.

Sure. Just like they liked the new Coke.

The Coca-Cola people just didn't mix the stuff up in a vat one day and put it on the shelves, you know.

Nope, they agonized over it. They experimented and experimented until they got the new formula just right.

And they tested it and tested it on people until they were sure the public would love it.

And they made only one mistake.

The stuff stunk.

Not everybody thinks so. Some people would like anything labeled "new."

You probably could put "New and Improved Coke!" on bottles of kerosene, get Bill Cosby to endorse it and do OK with some people.

But it stunk anyway. And Coke decided to bring back the old stuff, admitting, perhaps for the first time in marketing history, that new is not necessarily better.

I just hope we don't stop there.

I'd like to bring back the old phone company. Not only do I not know whom to call when the darn phone doesn't work, but I am not really up to 11-page phone bills.

And how about the old public schools? Can we get them back, too? Can we forget about set theory and independent study courses and go back to fractions and learning to read, especially learning to read without moving your lips?

And I sure wouldn't mind having the old service stations back either. The ones where they used to check the oil and clean the windshield. Without paying extra. Remember them?

And didn't there used to be banks where you could safely put your money without worrying whether it would be there in the morning?

The New York Times called bringing back the old Coke "one of the most stunning about-faces in the history of marketing."

I don't know why we should be so stunned that a company finally has admitted that something new is not necessarily something better.

More companies should face up to that simple fact.

How about the wizards who brought out peanut butter already mixed with jelly?

And how about bacon bits made without bacon? And how about flavored popcorn?

And anything made with soybeans?

Come back, America!

It may take a while, but if we all work at it, we can convince the marketing geniuses that old can be new again.

Because if you think some things were better in the old days, that isn't nostalgia.

That's the truth.

July 17, 1985

Exquisite Torture
à la French Train

I would like to remind you that I do not like trains.
   If I wanted to travel in something hot, smelly, and dangerous, I would drive my own car.
So how did I find myself on a train last week? And in a foreign country, yet?
Because I am weak. And because there is nothing I would not do for you. There, now you know.
For years, people have told me about the fantastic European trains. How swift they are and how modern.
"Take a train in France and you'll change your mind about trains forever," my friends told me. "They are ooh-la-la!"
I doubt it, I replied. The French have never been able to make good chili, so why should they be able to make good trains?
"You are not being fair to your readers," I was told. "You shouldn't knock something you haven't tried."
So I tried it. I flew to Europe on a superb Air France jet. It was fast, comfortable, and nobody across the aisle felt the need to tell me his life story. In other words, the perfect airplane ride.
After a few days in the south of France, I rented a double compartment for my wife and me on the night train from Nice to Paris.
It was not cheap. In fact, when I was told it was more than $300, I was ready to give up the idea.
"They must be angry because we made them pay us for World War II," I said.
In the end, I paid. Solely because I didn't want to let you, my readers, down. That's the kind of swell guy I am.
Finding the right platform at the station was easy. I have no trouble with foreign languages. If you speak English in the accent of the country you are in, everyone understands you.
"Where is ze train to Paree, Meester French-person," I asked the first guy I saw. He immediately pointed out the right train.

Once aboard, I asked the conductor for the dining car.

"Zere ees no car for ze dineeng," he told me.

I asked where we were supposed to eat.

"Eenside ze lovely compartment," he said, opening a door.

On the other side of the door was a coffin-sized closet, with two bunk beds folded down from one wall and exactly four feet by two feet of standing room.

"You make ze joke on ze silly American, no?" I asked the conductor. "Le ha-ha?"

"No le ha-ha," he said. "Zees ees eet!"

This, I told him, would be considered double-celling in America, a condition judged by the Supreme Court to be cruel and unusual punishment.

The conductor backed out and shut the door.

"If we call home, I think the governor may grant us early release," I told my wife.

After much experimentation, we found that for one of us to take off our coat, the other had to climb into one of the beds or go out into the hall.

But we did discover the most charming thing about French train compartments:

Snazzily built into the sink stand, which is not separated from the rest of the compartment, is a little panel with a handle. When you pull the handle, the panel folds down. Bolted to the panel is a chamber pot.

After fulfilling your responsibilities, you merely lift the panel back into place and the chamber pot empties—somewhere. Into Germany, if I know the French.

My wife looked at me. I looked at her.

"I think I can wait until Paris," I said.

"It's only 10 hours," she said. "And we won't talk about the Mediterranean."

We managed to get into our bunks, using techniques pioneered by the Mercury astronauts.

"Did you happen to notice if this train was named the 'Spirit of Klaus Barbie'?" I asked my wife.

She turned off the lights.

At about 2 A.M., there was a heavy pounding on our coffin door. I pulled on my pants and opened the door. An elderly French woman rushed in.

"Nobody is going to believe this," I told my wife.

"*I* certainly don't," she said.

The woman refused to leave. She kept waving her ticket in my face and babbling in a foreign tongue.

A guy from down the hall was drawn to my compartment by the loud shouting and the fact he had never seen a 35-year-old man aim a punch at the head of an 83-year-old woman.

He looked at the woman's ticket and informed her she was in the wrong car. She left.

"Merci beaucoup," I told the guy.

"Forget it," he said. "Happens all the time."

"I'd invite you in for a drink," I said, "but I'd have to climb into the chamber pot to make room."

I finally got back to sleep. At 3 A.M., the French national soccer team entered the compartment next to mine and began singing a medley of Beatles tunes.

"We all leeve in ze Yellow Zubmareen, Yellow Zubmareen, Yellow Zubmareen!"

I banged on the wall. "Shut les mouths!" I yelled.

"All we are zay-ing, ees geeve peese a chanse! All we are zay-ing. . . ."

I decided to give up. I went next door and joined them for Eleanor Rigby, the Octopus's Garden, and two choruses of Here Comes the Sun. Somebody passed around a bottle. Or maybe it was a goatskin. I forget.

I asked the goalie if he really liked the train.

"Mais non," he said. "But eet can be amuzeeng."

I asked him just how amusing it could get.

He clutched my arm, gave me a wink, and dropped his voice to a whisper.

"At dawn," he said, "zey let us drive!"

September 28, 1983

A Mother's Love—
and Loss—of Baby

I can tell you only what she said, not what it sounded like.
I cannot give you the sound of her tears or her silent moments that said so much.

Reporters hear tragedies every day and still are able to ask their questions: the whens and wheres and hows.

This story is not really a tragedy, I suppose. In a way, it is kind of a sad triumph. But at the end, I just couldn't ask anything for a little while.

Call her Terry. Her daughter was born a few weeks ago. We do not know her daughter's name.

This is not an antiabortion story or an antisex story or an anti-anything story.

It is a story of a mother who had a little girl and who gave her away and still loves her very much.

It begins on an overcast day last October on the shores of Lake Michigan, the day Terry told her boyfriend she was pregnant.

"I waited a couple of days to tell him," she said. "We went for a walk along the lake and then . . . I just told him.

"It was like a scene out of a movie, the sky was so gray and all. He was very upset at first, you know? Very angry. He began throwing stones into the lake.

"We had never talked very much about what we would do if . . . if I became pregnant. I got pregnant only the second or third time we made love."

They had been dating five months. They had not had sex for the first four. "We established a love and a trust for each other first," she said very firmly, very definitely.

She grew up in a wealthy suburb on the North Shore. She went to a public school where the girls talked about what high school girls always talk about.

"I didn't have sex in high school at all, though," Terry said. "I'm Catholic and my parents always taught me that sex was an expression of love and it belonged in marriage. I agreed with them. And none of my friends were doing it in high school. None whatsoever."

She graduated and went to college and things changed, of course. She was no longer a girl. She was a woman. And she made up her own mind about things.

She met a young man and she fell in love and now she was telling him she was pregnant.

"Within a couple of minutes he turned to me and held me," Terry said. "We spent the afternoon holding each other. And crying."

She thought about marriage, of course. He had not offered it, but he would if she insisted. She was sure of that.

"But when I really thought about it, marriage was out of the question," Terry said. "We just weren't ready. We just couldn't have handled it."

And so? What did that leave?

"Well, abortion," she said. "He had always been opposed to abortion. He is Catholic, too. And I had always opposed it, though I think it should be legal.

"But . . . well, you just don't know. You just don't know until it happens to you. So I went to the abortion clinic. I went to have an abortion."

Her boyfriend went with her. He stayed in the waiting room upstairs while Terry went to have it done.

She told him not to worry.

"I was on the table," Terry said, "and the doctor came in and examined me and sprayed me with antiseptic and I just sat up on the table and said: 'I can't do this. I can't go through with this.'

"I felt, I felt this child was the product of love. And I just couldn't do it for that reason.

"I walked through the recovery room and saw all those women with such sad eyes looking at me. The women who do this aren't vicious murderers, like some people say. It is not something they want to do.

"I went upstairs. My boyfriend's face was just gray. Now I know what he is going to look like when he is an old man. I told him I couldn't do it. He looked relieved."

So did you think about marriage again? I asked.

"Yes," she said. "I knew he would. And there was a lot I loved about him. But I had my doubts, too. He was not emotionally mature enough to handle this. In two years, our relationship could have really worked. We both would have been ready. But not now. Not now."

So she decided to have her baby and give it up for adoption. She contacted a well-known agency, the Cradle Society in Evanston, Illinois, which has been operating since 1923.

She did not yet tell her parents. What could she say? But she told a close friend what she was going through.

The parents of that friend asked Terry to come live with them until her baby was born.

"I didn't tell my own parents until the middle of January," Terry said. "They were really very supportive. Of course, they were disappointed, too. And hurt. They had raised me with a system of values that obviously I had not practiced.

"But they said if I wanted to keep the baby I could bring it home. Or if I wanted to marry my boyfriend, we could come live with them. Even though we live in that suburb, they are not wealthy people and this would have been a sacrifice for them."

But Terry told them she was going to live with her friend's parents and then give the baby up.

Were your parents upset that you were going off to live with strangers? I asked.

"Well, in a way, I think they were relieved a little," she said. "This way their neighbors and friends would not know. I can understand that. In a way."

She finished her fall term in college and then left school to have the baby. "The family I lived with was fantastic," she said. "The father is retired and we spent all day talking. We both like to cook. I learned how to make bagels and Irish bread.

"Everybody in the family was warm. Even the sons sat down and talked to me. It was not like I was an outcast or something. I felt like their daughter.

"I had the baby in May. At the Cradle, I got to look at profiles of the different families who want to adopt. You don't get to learn their names, but you learn a lot about them. I wanted a Catholic family, that was important to me. And I found one where the mother had taught Sunday school. I thought that was good.

"But most of all, when the mother's brother was out of work, they took him and his wife and their five children into their home. That showed me that not only could these people talk to my daughter about loving other people, they could demonstrate it."

Terry had her daughter in the final days of May.

I asked her what her daughter looked like.

After a while, Terry said: "I don't know. I didn't see my daughter. I knew if I saw her, I wouldn't be able to let go of her.

"See, I was very close to her. We had a lot of communication when

I was pregnant. She was kicking away one day and I rubbed my middle and she would stop. Then she would start kicking again and I would rub my middle. We sat there doing this for a half hour.

"I spent a lot of time touching what I could of her. I really loved her.

"And sometimes the reality hits me and I know I have a daughter somewhere and sometimes I want her so badly, I want to hold her and watch her grow and see her smile and know everything about her."

There was silence for a time.

"Two days after I gave birth, I said: 'Yes, I want this child.' I could have changed my mind. But I was only doing it for selfish reasons. I knew adoption would be best for her.

"I want my child to have a mother and a father. I want my baby to have parents who were certain about themselves. Who have more emotional stability than my boyfriend and I could have provided.

"And, well, we've broken up now. He just couldn't handle all this.

"It's funny, you know? At first, I thought I should never see my daughter when she grew up. But, well, she has a file at the Cradle and I'm going to write her a letter on every birthday and I hope someday she goes and sees them.

"It was a very terrible time in a way. I can't tell you how many nights and days I just cried. Even with all the support I had from many wonderful people, I was so very lonely.

"It is not an easy thing to give away your baby.

"But I'm sure her parents will tell her I exist. I'm sure. She may never want to come looking for me and that's OK. But I hope she does. I hope she knows I'm out there. And that I love her.

"And I wanted to talk to you because I just want other women to know it can be done. My life did not end. I'm going back to school. I have a whole lifetime ahead of me.

"And I made a contribution. I made some family very happy.

"I gave them the most beautiful little girl in the world."

I don't remember what I said to Terry when I said good-bye.

But I wish I had said that if the daughter turns out to be like the mother, everything is going to be just fine.

July 21, 1983

I, like Terry, had no idea who had adopted her daughter. But the couple recognized themselves from this column and called me on the morning it appeared. They told me they were going to place it in their daughter's baby book, so she could read it when she got older. And if she decided she wanted to find Terry, that would be fine with them.

"And one more thing," the new mother said. "Terry was right. Her daughter is the most beautiful little girl in the world."

In the End,
The Terrorists Won

A pang of guilt shot through me as I turned off the TV, but I just couldn't watch any more about the hostages.

We have had the aftermath and the after-the-aftermath and now we are into the where-are-they-after-the-aftermath stories.

I can't take it anymore. I cringe when they come on the screen.

It isn't that I don't care. It isn't even that I am bored. I am just burned out by it all.

It was all too much. It was like watching a telethon in its final, weary hours. The coverage was so relentless that I think many of us reached our saturation point pretty early.

At least with a newspaper, you can flip the pages and go on to Doonesbury. With TV, you've got to stare at what is set before you.

I grew especially tired of all the experts: the Mideast experts, the terrorism experts, the psychiatric experts.

I no longer care what Henry Kissinger and Al Haig think about it all. I am not sure I ever did.

They talked and they talked and I watched and I watched and it seemed nobody was saying what I felt:

The terrorists had won. And we had lost.

Yes, I share the joy of getting those 39 people back. But we lost someone this time.

A man was murdered. Finally, at the very end, after ignoring it for days, the networks decided to mention the fact that Robert Stethem was killed by the thugs who had captured him.

Throughout the whole, sorry 17 days, we rarely heard this. Instead, everyone was talking about how nice the captors were behaving, how "civilized" they all seemed.

The way some people are gushing about the Amal militia, you'd think they were a sewing society instead of a band of 7,000 gunmen who recognized no law but their own.

Sure they were nice to our hostages. The whole affair was brilliantly orchestrated.

Grab some innocent people. Kill one or two. Turn the rest over to "moderate" kidnappers and use this to get free publicity for your grievances. Endless free publicity.

And it is no wonder that some of the hostages seemed to become mouthpieces for their captors.

The hostages must have been terrified. They must have wondered, at least in the beginning, if they would live or die.

And then came these smiling, charming young men who comforted them and told them that—as long as America went along with their demands—everything would be all right.

Then they fed the hostages their official line. To some it was a revelation. Education at gunpoint.

And what could be a greater victory for the terrorists than to have the support of the victims themselves?

They were bright enough, of course, to have the TV cameras come in and record all of it, the press conferences and the banquets and the hugging and kissing.

A new era. Showboat terrorism.

And if one man was pistol-whipped and had all of his ribs kicked in and then was shot in the head and had his body dumped on the tarmac like a side of beef?

Oh, well. These things happen. Let's not let it spoil the show.

Let's not ask at the press conference: "What are the names of the murderers? Where are they?"

Nabih Berri, head of the Amal and, in any court of law, a kidnapper, knows their names. How about him telling us who the triggerman was before we bestow hero status and 10 more TV interviews upon him?

But Berri and Syria are the big winners in all of this and Israel and the U.S. the big losers.

To many, Israel seemed part of the problem, not part of the solution. And unable to strike out at the nameless, faceless hijackers, they struck out at Israel.

But the United States is the biggest loser of all. Make no mistake, there is but one reason we got those hostages back:

The terrorist demand was one we could grant. The release of the Shiite prisoners was something we could negotiate.

If the demands of the TWA hijackers had been tougher (let's say they wanted us to seize the Israeli ambassador and turn him over to them for trial) what could we have done?

Although we deny making any deals to free the hostages, nobody, including future terrorists, believes that.

Sure we made deals. We made deals like crazy. And I'm glad Ronald

Reagan did. But we were all lucky the terrorist wish list was something we could afford.

The price, however, was still high. For all the yellow ribbons and brass bands and brave speeches, the price was very high.

These hijackers murdered a young man and got away with it. The Amal militiamen kidnapped a bunch of Americans and not only got away with it, but today are considered saviors.

We are calling the hostages heroes because we feel a need for heroes.

But they were victims. They endured; they did not prevail.

As Winston Churchill had to remind his country after Dunkirk, rescues, no matter how glorious, are not the same as victories.

July 10, 1985

STORM OVER SOUTH AFRICA

Going to South Africa was Jim Hoge's idea. He was my editor and he knew I had a lifelong ambition of being a foreign correspondent in Moscow.

"Go to South Africa instead," he said. "The story is better there."

I was 29; this was my first foreign assignment and after a month there, I discovered an amazing thing: Editors can be right.

My stay in South Africa changed me as a reporter and as a person. I was amazed at the number of people there who risked prison or worse to help me tell these stories. It wasn't because they knew me or even because they knew of my newspaper—they did not—but because they had a fierce desire to make the truth known to the world.

If there is any theme that runs through these pieces like a drumbeat, it is the theme of impending violence. I did not want to write that, but I had to.

Sadly, as the years have passed and South Africa has slid deeper into the abyss, the violence has come. Today, as I write this, hundreds of blacks in that country are being arrested and scores killed.

What improvements have come since these pieces were written have been minor, grudging, and cosmetic. They are, as Alan Paton, the great South African author, told me, "like the face of death done up nicely to look in the pink of condition."

But if there is any hope, it is that the people of America will continue to care about what happens in that faraway place at the end of the earth.

'Spilling Blood Will Make Us Free'

SOWETO, South Africa

T he red dirt road stretched before us like a strip of flesh torn from the body of the land. Over the low rolling veldt, the houses and huts of Soweto spread like a creeping growth upon the earth.

They do not know how many live in this place. Some say a million. Some say more. They know only that all who live here are black. They did not always live here. Years ago they lived near the great city of Johannesburg and their homes were near the homes of the other races.

But 30 years ago, the white man made all the races live apart. And where the homes of the black man once stood, now stand the suburbs of the white man. And in return, the black man was given Soweto. The name stands for South West Township. But it is not really a township.

Soweto is a prison.

The crime is to be black.

The sentence is for life.

The room was small. So small that our knees almost touched as we talked. The roof was tin and the floor was wood. Like almost every home here, there was no electricity. There was no hot water. There was no toilet. As we talked, the shadows deepened and stretched along the floor and made their way up the wall.

The man, Benjamin, was calm now and had stopped shaking. He laughed, wagging his head slowly, trapping his hands between his knees. It had been a bad joke and one for which I was sorry. The man who took me here, John, had decided to do it.

"You will stand in the doorway of his house," John said. "And I will knock on the door and he will see you. Oh my, how Benjamin will jump."

White men do not come to the homes of Soweto unless they are the police. No white is allowed in Soweto without a permit. No white is allowed in Soweto after 4 P.M. But it was long past that now and John was showing me he was unafraid.

"They will catch us up and lock us away!" he shouted, pounding on the steering wheel as he drove me into Soweto. "Oh, man, how brave we are! How you will tell them in America what we are doing!"

John knew, in truth, that there was little danger for me. A fine if I was caught; at worst, expulsion. But for John, it would go worse. John was black.

And so he decided to play the joke. He had me stand in Benjamin's doorway as he stood to one side and banged hard on the doorframe. "Benjamin, we have come for you!"

The top part of the door was screened and I saw Benjamin rise from his living room chair and saw the paper he had been reading slip to the floor. I saw the fear in his eyes as he looked at me in his doorway and I understood for a moment what it was to be a black man in South Africa.

John leaped into view by my side, hooting with laughter. "It is I," he said. "Did you think we were the police? Did you think that Benjamin's day had finally come?"

Benjamin moved his hand to his heart and closed and opened his eyes. "Come in, come in," he said, "Do not stand where they all can see you."

We came into the home where Benjamin's wife, Mary, had just prepared the food. There was a dish of corn mush and a cup of coffee. Dinner. "We were just thinking that the police had come back," said Mary.

And then Benjamin told us how the police had just been there and had taken him down to the Protea police station in Soweto and put him in a room and questioned him.

"They said I had been telling the children to stay home from school," he whispered hoarsely. "I said: 'You are wrong. Not this man. Benjamin would not do this.' "

To say such a thing in Soweto is to risk prison. And to risk prison is to risk death.

In June of 1976, the schoolchildren of Soweto had erupted into a violence that stunned the country. Armed with rocks, they took on one of the best trained and best armed police forces in the world.

The demonstrations spread across the country. Several hundred were left dead in the streets. About 6,000 were arrested, and about 400 were imprisoned without a trial.

The violence continued into 1977. Railway lines were dynamited. Police cars were stoned. More students were killed. Four days after the prison killing of Steven Biko, leader of the Black Consciousness movement, the citizens of Soweto gathered in St. Matthew's Anglican Church for a memorial service. Using tear gas and riot batons, police charged into the church. Once inside, they opened fire with shotguns, wounding several persons and killing a small child.

The Soweto school system again collapsed with both students and teachers striking. The police looked upon the strike as an act of revolution.

There were more arrests and more shootings by police. On November 24, a bomb containing between two and four kilograms of high explosive went off in the posh Carlton Centre in downtown Johannesburg, injuring 17.

The bombings continued into 1978. A few weeks ago, an opposition member of parliament asked the minister of police how many children under the age of 10 were being held in prison without trial. He declined to answer.

Benjamin stood suddenly in the center of the room. "They have got the wrong man," he said. "Would I tell the students not to go to school? Would I do such a thing?"

To do such a thing would be foolish. In South Africa, to be foolish and to be black is to be very foolish.

Benjamin sat heavily in his chair and rubbed the palms of his hands over his knees. Mary sat in the corner and followed us nervously with her eyes. "The wrong man," Benjamin said. "I am not political. I am a clerk."

At 48, a clerk in Johannesburg, Benjamin has gone as far as he will go in life. He owns a suit, the one he was wearing. It was brown with wide lapels and he wore it with a yellow shirt and tightly knotted brown tie. His shoes were good and worn smooth with many polishings.

The living room of his home was 10 feet long and 6 feet wide. It is the largest room of the house. There is a tiny kitchen and two tiny bedrooms. Twelve people live here.

Benjamin is one of the few blacks who owns his home, but he cannot own the land it rests on. That is forbidden to the black man. "If they tell me to leave tomorrow, I must go," he said. "And I must leave all that I have."

On the wall was Jesus on the cross and on a low table was a weaving with the head of Jesus. There were two chairs and a couch. In each bedroom, one bed. The 12 who live here sleep where they can.

Those who live in Soweto cannot choose in which home they will live. The white board of governors decides that. The blacks cannot leave their home without permission or sell their home without permission. They cannot be in Johannesburg without permission. They cannot stay in the home of the white man without permission.

The family of the black man cannot come and live with him in Soweto without permission. If Benjamin loses his job, he cannot remain in his home without permission. The home will be given to someone else.

The blacks cannot be in a white area after curfew, or eat in a white restaurant, or go to a white hospital or swim at a white beach, or dance where whites dance or buy liquor where whites buy liquor.

The black man is forbidden by law to hold certain jobs and in many jobs the law states he must receive less than the white man for the same work. The black man may not join a recognized union, he may not join a white political organization, he may not join a black consciousness movement. He may not supervise the work of a white man. He may not vote.

He may not marry outside his race or have sexual intercourse outside his race. To do so is a crime punishable by fine or jail. In 1976, 268 persons were arrested for this crime.

For whites, schooling is free. For blacks, the parents must pay a yearly fee. The government spends on the white student 17 times more than it spends on the black student.

The government does allow the black man one great freedom: It allows him the freedom to be ignorant. Schooling is compulsory for whites. The black child does not have to go to school.

Out of a black school population of 4.5 million, only 2 percent finish the eighth grade. Only two in 1,000 will get a high school degree. Out of 18.6 million blacks, there are 400 black doctors and 100 black lawyers.

"It will be better for my children," Benjamin said. "Oh, my. Of course, yes. Look here now. We did not always have a home of brick. Twenty years ago this was a shanty town and they gave us a site and we built a shack of iron. The flies were thick around us and it was very bad.

"But is it not better now? I have improved this with my hands. I built the floor and the doors. Electricity? No. It cannot be. But I earn very good money. I earn $55 per week, which is very, very good here. I started as a sweeper and now I have worked my way up."

He went over to the window and looked out into the fading light. There are more than 100,000 homes in Soweto, all low, and they spread and spread over the plain. Horse-drawn carts drag coal through the streets past the weed-choked fields where "markets" have been set up on the ground to sell meat and meal.

"Fun?" Benjamin asked, not believing the question. "Oh, my. Oh, my. There is no such thing as fun."

At night, sometimes neighbors will gather in each other's homes, but Benjamin and Mary do not go out at night. "It is not safe in the darkness," she said. "Never."

The white police of Soweto watch for political crimes and the black police, the dreaded "Blackjacks," drag off people who do not pay their rent. At night, the streets belong to the "tsotsis," the Zulu word for gangsters. A dozen deaths a weekend through fighting and paid assassination are not uncommon.

Besides the regular settlers of Soweto, Johannesburg needs the labor of hundreds of thousands of others. These blacks are shipped in from the countryside and put in migrant labor camps. Their wives and children are forbidden to join them. The men rarely return home. The family life in the countryside is shattered. Alcoholism, venereal disease and casual violence are epidemic in the city life.

"But there is progress," Benjamin said firmly. "It is my hope that my son will be a pharmacist. And today, the African (black) is getting promotions he never would before. We must be fair. Today I can go to the movies with the white man."

"You cannot!" John shouted violently. "You lie to this white man!"

"Special movies!" Benjamin yelled back. "Once there was a special movie and it was said that we could go with the white man. And the big hotels, now we can go to the big hotels."

"You can afford the big hotels?" John howled. "You can afford the special movies?"

Benjamin looked at his shoes and brushed away some dirt that was not there. "No," he said quietly. "No, we cannot."

But the agony of South Africa and the storm that is breaking there is not just the government-enforced segregation or black poverty. The agony is that for 30 years the government has made sure that the black man knows the white man only as his overlord, and the white man knows the black only now through fear.

And the fear is turning to hatred and the hatred to violence as the young have taken over. And Soweto is ruled by its young.

"Mix with the whites?" Mary said. "No. Never. It is not allowed. It is not of our lives. At work, well, they are your baas." She used the Afrikans word, the word that old blacks still call the whites as they tip their hats on the street. "The white man leaves Soweto at 4 P.M. After that, we do not see him."

"I do not blame the policeman today," Benjamin said suddenly. "He was an old man and very, very sorry for involving me. The informers are everywhere, but the informers can make mistakes."

John snorted his contempt from his corner of the room.

"Do not mock me!" Benjamin said pointing a finger. "Everyone says the change will come. The Communists say the change will come. You think in Soweto there is anyone who knows what a Communist is? There is not. I will tell you who will change things: God will change! Not me, not you, but God. And the change will not come for Benjamin or Mary or even for John. The change will come for our children."

Mary did not look at the Jesus on the cross when Benjamin pointed to it. For she does not believe as he believes. "The whites," she said slowly, "the whites, I think, fear the children. The whites, I think, know what will make the change. The whites, I think, know what the children will do."

A silence fell over the room and the shadows deepened into darkness and a coldness came in from the windows. "How will the change come?" I asked. "What will make it come? What will make the white man give up what he has?"

And in the dark corner, Mary sucked on one knuckle and said something low and melodic in Zulu, something people say in the dark that they would not say in the light.

And after she said it, John got up quickly and looked into both their faces and said, "We will go now." And I followed him out into the night.

The coal smoke hangs low and thick over Soweto at night and moves like a gray beast up and down and over the houses and down the dirt roads and over the fields. At night, the children move in and out of it, coughing against the coal smoke that robs them of life. Later, I will look it up in a book. For every white child who dies of tuberculosis in this country, 72 nonwhite children will die. Tuberculosis was cured in 1947. But not in Soweto.

In the shadows, the children of Soweto moved, and under the few street lights they would run past quickly, their bare feet making a gentle slapping sound against the dirt. John held me by the arm and said, "It is night and you are a white man. We will drive out and you will get down on the back seat and we will hope the police do not see you. And if the children come up to you, you will say nothing and you will follow me quickly."

I pulled my arm away, frightened by the new sound in his voice and of the darkness and the shapes of the children in the gray fog of the coal smoke. "What did she say in there?" I demanded. "What did she answer, when I asked what would change the white man?"

But John would not say and we got back into the car, with him in front and me in back and he drove quickly. And then it came suddenly as if he could not say it and yet he could not hold it back.

"The spilling," he said. "The spilling of blood. The spilling of the white blood. That is what will make us free."

March 12, 1978

The White Man 'Will Always Be the Boss'

CAPE TOWN, South Africa

Below them there is only the ocean and the ice. And above them there is only the fire. The fire of black Africa. And the white man remains here, clinging to the pale tip of a dark continent. And he remains because he has no place else to go.

He stood in the doorway of his home, in the shadow of his mountains, looking out onto land as sweet and happy as his life is sweet and happy.

"Oh, the coloured," the white man said. "The decent coloured don't want to mix with the white man. Only the trash do."

His wife stood with him and he put his arm around her and they stood among the white pillars of a home that has been here for 285 years, which is nearly as long as the white man has been here.

"Have you heard of the white swans of London?" she asked. "I read about them. A bunch of black swans landed among them and the white swans drowned the black swans. That is the truth."

"I went to Sweden," the man said, "and I saw the whites and blacks walking hand in hand. And they told me that they married together. And I said, 'My God, what about the children?' And they told me that in Sweden they thought the children were exotic.

"Well, by damn! By damn! In South Africa we do not consider them exotic!"

As we talked, the workers were getting in the red grapes to make the wine, for it was the time of the year for that. And beyond the garden of roses and palms stretched the vines and the grass of the low veldt, which runs up to the coastal plain and down into the sea.

In the winery, two men stamped the grapes with their feet, the dark purple juice glistening and clinging to the blackness of their skin. There are machines for this, of course, but it was a small crop and, where he can, the white man uses the old ways. For the old ways are always best.

"My workers are the descendants of slaves my ancestors owned eight generations ago," the white man, Nicolaas Myburgh, said. "They have stayed. And I have stayed. And now I am their slave." He laughed. "Yes, I care for them. And hold their hands. And I am there when their babies are born. I give them their homes and their clothes and they stay with me.

"Yes, I beat them. I give them regular hidings. Yes, I say that to you. And they thank me for it. The English, the English made them free." He laughed again. "The English are inclined to fraternize with them. But one minute you fraternize with them and the next minute they are calling you a bloody bastard. I do not fraternize.

"They call me baas. I do not ask the coloured to do it and I do not ask the black man to do it, but when they see me, they call me baas."

He is an Afrikaner. And he is the boss. His people came from Holland and Germany nearly 300 years ago and settled the land and fought for it. They fought the black man for it and they fought the English for it. And in many ways, they still fight both.

There were only the yellow Bushmen and the black Hottentot here when the Afrikaners landed. The Bushmen took up their small bows and poisoned arrows and left for the desert and left the land to the white. And to the Hottentot, the white at first gave glass and metal and cloth for his cattle. And then he gave them something else: He gave them smallpox.

Those who survived married with the white and married with the slaves that the white brought with him. And they formed a race fixed then and forever in the white man's law. And the white man calls these mixed people the coloured.

The white man moved farther into the country, away from the coastal plains and into the sweet grassland. And there he met the black tribes that had come down from the north and the white man fought again, as the white man in America fought the red man. And the white man won.

And when gold was discovered beneath the grass, the English came into the land of the Afrikaner and another war was fought. And thousands of Afrikaners died on the veldt, and thousands of their women and children died in the British camps. And to this day, the Afrikaner has not forgiven the English.

And now the Afrikaner is baas. He controls the law and the courts and the land. But the black man remains. And he numbers more than four times the white man. And the white man cannot forget that.

He is outnumbered and the world scorns his name and passes resolutions against him and he does not forget that either. But he is here and there is nowhere else for him. And he is staying.

"I have 75 workers here and I've got 101 children," Myburgh said. "They live in the homes I built for them. And the wives and children help to press the wine. They are mostly coloured. I have a few natives, but mostly coloured."

In the cities, the white man does not say "native" anymore when he speaks of the black man. It is near to saying "nigger" in America and it is not done. But this is the country, this is the land, and the ways are different on the land.

"The natives are not good with the vines," Myburgh said. "They are slow. Lethargic. The natives are better for the heavy work. And with the animals. The natives are good with the animals.

"The coloureds are all Christians and sometimes I think that is a shame. I once farmed in Rhodesia where the coloured are Mohammedans and they bathed three times a day. They didn't stink so bad. I think the missionaries made a big mistake when they made our coloured into Christians."

We went into the house, past a huge metal gong that was used for calling the slaves to the master's house. We went through an entranceway that could hold 100 ladies and their gentlemen and under the chandeliers of the dining room and into the living room. The walls were washed white and dark wood beams ran overhead. The floor was of red-fired tiles and across one wall stretched a giant fireplace of beaten copper that could hold a whole side of beef on a spit. We sat in chairs of heavy wood and leather and at our feet was a sea chest of teak, bound with bands of brass that had crossed the ocean with the first Myburghs and the first white men. There are 22 rooms here and it takes the servants two days to polish the brass doorknobs.

The farm is called "Meerlust," which means Seaview, and once it was nearly a country in itself. It stretched 150 miles and took eight days by ox wagon to cross. Now it has been divided among the sons and the sons of the sons, but this is the original house, the original land and the eldest Myburgh has always lived here.

"You from overseas think we all live in fear of the black," Myburgh said. "Do you think I bolt my doors at night? The doors of Meerlust have never been bolted. And they never will be.

"I am 55 and I walk among the coloured and the blacks and I am unafraid. I walk among them unarmed. They would never raise their hands to me. They would not ever.

"You think they are interested in politics? Do you think they want what you call freedom?"

"What they want," his wife, Eileen, said, "is their bottle of wine a day."

"I pay them a bottle of wine a day," Myburgh said, "and they get $4 in cash. And I have a store for them right here. I buy food and fish and meat and flour and coffee and tea and matches and I sell it to them—wholesale.

"And when they are old, they are allowed to stay if they have given me many years. And I even give them a burial. Right here. On the farm. Free."

Myburgh is a big man, with muscled arms that come from both his farming and his weekly golf. He has a face red and weathered from the Cape sun and he has a big laugh that is heard often.

"I'll tell you," he said, "I had a coloured man in here the other day. He was collecting for a charity and I sat him down to tea. And I said to him: 'Your trouble is that there are too many Hottentots among you.' I discriminate between a decent coloured and a Hottentot. Hottentot is slang for a rotten coloured."

"And do you know what?" Myburgh said, slapping the arm of his chair, "the coloured man agreed with me. He agreed."

"We don't associate with the poor whites," Eileen said, "and a decent coloured doesn't associate with a Hottentot."

To an American, the racial laws and divisions of South Africa are a bewildering, Alice-in-Wonderland kind of world. The whites, who rule, are divided into the Afrikaners, who hold the political power, and the English, who hold the financial power. The nonwhites are divided into the blacks, the coloured, the Indians and about a half-dozen others.

Each is kept separate in life and law by the official government policy called apartheid. But they share this tip of Africa and have shared it for centuries. And the white man, when he feels comfortable with his guest, will admit the truth.

"Well, when the white men landed, some of my ancestors were already here," Myburgh said with a wink. "There is a story that only two Myburghs came across from Holland. One married a coloured girl and the other was a bachelor. I am descended from the bachelor."

His big laugh filled the room, but, in truth, virtually every Afrikaner has nonwhite blood in his veins. But the mixing came hundreds of years ago and that makes no difference today. For a white man to sleep with a black woman is a crime and for a white woman to sleep with a black man is a crime. And last year, there was nearly one arrest a day for this crime.

"I know this coloured man named Johnny," Myburgh said. "And his daughter got involved with the white man. And Johnny went to the father of this white boy and said, 'I have given my daughter a hiding and you should do the same for your son.'

"This is the way it should be done. The only blacks who care about politics in this country are the ones who go to Oxford and come back and want a white wife.

"Well, I'll tell you. It is not going to be. It took the Afrikaner 300 years to get where he is and the blacks and the coloureds want it in five years. They say, 'Here. Give it to us.'

"You must understand, the blacks are a tribal people. If all the whites could leave and go to America for two or three years, we would come back and the blacks would have exterminated one another. That is why they like discipline. I can knock hell out of a coloured man or a black man and they appreciate it. If they deserve it, they appreciate it. The only law the coloured understand is a good hiding. European law is foreign to them."

We went from the living room to the dining room where a huge table had been set. Everything we ate, the mutton, the potatoes, the spinach, the onions, the tomatoes, and the milk had been produced on Meerlust. We sat and talked and in the middle of the meal, Myburgh turned to me as if he had just remembered something: "A few years ago, 10 or more, another American sat just where you are sitting. His name was Robert Kennedy. You know him?"

I said, yes, of course. "Well, he asked me what would happen if I got to heaven and I found that God was black," Myburgh said.

"And I said: 'Mr. Kennedy. What will you do if you go to heaven and find that God is a red Indian?' "

We sat for a while and then went out to the front of the house where the fabled mountains of Cape Town stood framed in the doorway. He asked me what I thought of it all and because he was an honest man, I gave him an honest answer.

"You think I am the master and they are still the slaves? That is what you really think?" he said. "Well, I will tell you. The whole world has condemned us. The whole world has condemned apartheid. And it will be a slap in your face if apartheid works.

"But you come back to me in 10 years. You come back to me in 20. Nothing will be changed. All the trouble, all the violence, will be for nothing. It won't make a bit of difference.

"There will always be a Meerlust. And there will always be the Afrikaner. And it will always be the same."

We shook hands and I drove away from the big white house. I drove out past the palms and the roses and past the vines and the grass and out from the shadow of the mountains. And as I left, I looked upon the last thing Nicolaas Myburgh had told me to look upon.

I looked upon the cemetery where eight generations of Myburghs lay, still part of their land. And not far away was the black cemetery. And near that was the coloured cemetery. And they, too, lay with their land. For this was South Africa. And from womb to tomb. From cradle to grave. In death, as in life.

All are separate.

And I thought that in 10 or 20 years, Nicolaas Myburgh will not have to worry if God is red or black or white.

He will have to worry that God is just.

March 13, 1978

Soweto's Proud Youth—
The Rage Simmers

SOWETO, South Africa

I n the city of the black man, the white man does not ask, "What is it that you want?" For he knows the answer: "What you have, white man."

They took me to the home of Lucas when it was very dark. There are high poles here with bright lights on them, but they are very few and easily avoided.

These were the young of Soweto, a city that is ruled by its young. A little more than a year ago, they left nearly 500 of their number dead in the streets after the riots with the white police. But there are many young here, and when one falls, there is another to take his place.

"Credentials? Do you think we carry cards?" one of them said and laughed a laugh that held no humor in it. "I will show you the credentials of Lucas."

They took me to a bottle store, which is where the white man sells the black man whisky. It stood under a white light, all burned out and scorched black. And the broken windows smiled a Jack-O-Lantern smile in the night. "Here are our credentials," he said, sneering the word. "Here are the credentials of Lucas."

They took me to his home and then waited outside, watching for those who watched for them.

He sat in the kitchen on a high stool. His arms were laid across his knees and his hands hung down loosely. He watched me come into the room, but said nothing. He rose and went to the sink and turned his back on me. He made some coffee and offered me none, but drank it where he stood.

"You want to know, of course, about the bombings," he said, with his back still toward me. "This is, of course, what your readers wish to read. But I will start where I want and end where I say. And there will be things you can say of me and things you cannot. And you cannot say where I live or who brought you to me."

I told him that, in truth, I did not know where he lived, for Soweto spills itself like a flood across the land. The roads turn and branch and branch again and there are no signposts. Only the blacks of Soweto know truly where they live, because, except for the police, the white man does not care.

Lucas began to speak, looking out of the window over the sink, holding the cup with both hands while sipping and speaking and staring straight ahead.

"At first, we wished to be like you. We wished to be white. We would say: 'How can I make the white man look at me? How can I make the white man love me?' And then we thought that we were white and we said, 'Here I am, I am white like you.'

"But it is very difficult to attain whiteness, is it not?"

It was not a real question, so I said nothing. "Yes," he said. "Very difficult. So we looked into ourselves and said, 'Let us look to our blackness and forsake the white man.'

"For we were oppressing ourselves. The white man made us want his whiteness. But no more. We no longer wish to be like him. Now we say: 'I am black. I am a proud black man.'

"And when I go before the white man, I do not go as a begger, I do not go as a beast. I go as a man. A man who numbers in the millions."

He is young, and he has already been in the white man's prison. But the white man did not know who or what he was and let him go. In this country, where most of the moderate and visible black leaders have been jailed or banned, the radical and invisible young fill the void. And so the white system sows the seeds of its own destruction.

"You think that I am very young, but there are those younger than me who stood before the white guns," he said. "They saw their parents bow before the white man and they saw that their parents looked up to the white man like he was the Lord, but they had enough and rejected this.

"Even I am too old. Those that come behind me will be true in their blackness."

Age is no protection in South Africa. Many that the police killed during the riots were young. Toward the end of 1976 and in 1977, there were many reports in the newspapers of children who had been blinded by the birdshot from police shotguns. A doctor at the St. John Eye Hospital in Soweto said he had treated many such patients for blindness and partial blindness. He said the average age of his patients was 12.

In Parliament, the minister of police was questioned about this. He said that "birdshot was not lethal, maintained the authority of the gun, and merely made victims itch for months afterwards."

But a member of Parliament produced a report showing that in the Cape Town area alone, 30 people had been shotgunned in the eyes and that 19 were either totally blind or suffered severe loss of vision.

But the minister said that the authority of the gun had to be maintained. And age was no excuse.

"When we began," Lucas said, "we never thought of becoming violent or becoming a liberation movement like the Palestinians. This was for a simple fact. We blacks in South Africa are mostly unarmed; it is not easy to obtain a gun permit.

"So it becomes very foolish to embark on something without the necessary equipment. So we said: 'We will not attack the white man, yet. We will concentrate on developing the black man.'

"But the white man would not allow this. He realized that the black man would be dangerous if he looked upon himself as a man and not a slave. And Soweto showed the white man how truly dangerous we had become.

"And the young saw it in the white man's eyes. He saw the fear! For the first time, he saw the fear."

He turned from the window and his face was alight with the memory of it. "The white man sees Angola and the white man sees Mozambique and he knows that he is all alone on this continent." He drew the words out, savoring each one. "The white man knows he is all alone.

"At first, we said that we would not drive the white man into the sea. We will all live in harmony. We need the white man to run the technology. But the white man will not agree to this.

"They say they have done us great favors. They came from Europe and they moved us out of the caves where we sat seminaked," he said, mocking the words. "They dressed us, you see. They gave us Western civilization, you see. And, oh, how nice they were to us. And how kind. And now we must be their servants forever and ever."

"And so the children burned down the buildings with their petrol bombs," he said simply. "Look out of the window. You see there are no white men in Soweto. You are the only white man in Soweto tonight. So because we could not burn the white men, we burned the symbols of the white men. We burned his liquor stores and the schools."

On March 31, 1977, the deputy minister of bantu (black) education, who is, of course, white, announced that $4,600 had been spent to repair damage to the schools of Soweto. He also announced that $35,800 had been spent to repair six liquor stores and 15 beer halls. Liquor stores produce revenue. Schools merely produce children.

"But the whites are tough," Lucas said. "Do not think they are not. They feel they owe it to their grandfathers to fight for this land and maintain the status quo. They would rather go down with the ship than share the ship with anybody."

He shrugged. "So now, whatever the white man gets, whether we kick him out of the country or whether we do worse to him, it is what he asked for. He kept us slaves. And when a slave turns on a master, and when a slave slays a master, he is not to blame."

I asked him of the young men who had left Soweto and left South Africa to be trained in the black countries of the north in the ways of the gun and the ways of the bomb. But he would not speak of them.

"They have gone and they have come back and that is all you need to know," he said. "They were forced to this violence that they have come back to make and that is all."

His people had gathered at the door to take me out and as he stood in the doorway I asked him what he, himself, wanted for the future. "As for me," he said, "I would let the white man live and stay. You see I am not a violent man. But the white man will not do this and so what is left but violence?"

His people gathered me up and as we left the home of Lucas and left the light of his doorway for the darkness, one turned to me.

"You must understand that Lucas is a moderate and likes the white man too much," he said. "And therefore he is irrelevant."

And so I left Soweto that night and I did not go back.

March 15, 1978

◆

Zulu Warriors Are Dancing

UMLAZI, South Africa

The Impi warriors danced slowly in the mist, shuffling forward and back, beating their feet against the matted grass. The mist rises just after sunup here, drifting out of the ground as the fearful African sun rises huge in the sky and sucks up the moisture from the earth.

They had been dancing for hours and would dance for hours more. They would beat their short spears against their shields and sing in low, haunting voices. Then there would be a silence and they would dance again, shuffling forward and back.

Some were dressed in skins and furs and woven grass and others in denim work pants and cotton shirts. Some were barefoot and others wore work shoes or sandals. They see no conflict in this. There is no separate past and no separate future. There is only the now.

They are Zulu. And the Zulu were always the Zulu. And the Impi were always their warriors. And if the white man rules them today, well, it was not always so. And perhaps it will not be again.

We sat on the ground in the shrinking shadow of a green 1960 Buick that had somehow made its way from Detroit to this place in Zululand. I had stood too long in the sun without a hat and had gone fuzzy and had sat down hard on the ground.

I found myself propped up against the warm metal of the Buick with a Zulu woman patting water on my forehead. When I thanked her, she slipped her hand into mine, gave me a black power hand-shake, and said, "Amandla Awetu."

She left and I asked those sitting next to me what she had said. They said it meant "Power to the People" and that I would hear it a lot this day, for here in the land of the Zulu, a black man can say it without fear.

There are 5 million Zulu in this country, which is many more than the white man and larger than any other tribe. Even though the white man still controls them and their land, the Zulu have a fearsome past and nobody knows their future.

And if they wish to call out Power to the People, there is no one—yet—who will stop them.

The Impi danced as the people slowly came out of the hills of Umlazi into the place where the rally would be held. In the end, there would be 10,000 of them, but that would not be for hours and now we were waiting for their leader, Chief Gatsha Buthelezi.

I had heard his name the night before, far away in the city of Johannesburg, where a white family, an Afrikaner family, had invited me to dinner. We went to a quiet French restaurant, one with red checkered tablecloths and white candles in silver holders. They brought white wine and champagne and the woman told me how her people had come here in 1652 and her husband's had come in 1688. "I have been here as long as Buthelezi," she said. "Why must I step aside for him? Why must I be ruled by him? Why is that fair?"

Years ago it would have been impossible to imagine stepping aside for a black man, but that was years ago. And now Gatsha Buthelezi is being called the most dangerous and powerful black man in South Africa. And it is not only because of what he says, and not only because of what he does, but because he leads the Zulu and no one in this country forgets what happened at Blood River when the white man met the Zulu. The Afrikaners will tell you again and again that to understand them and their country, you must first understand Blood River.

In the restaurant the white woman explained it. She explained how it had started in the mist, 140 years ago, when the wagons of the Afrikaner had crossed into Zululand.

There were 64 wagons and they circled into a laager and in the hours before the dawn, the whites sang hymns and prayed.

And when the mist began to rise, the white men could see the fires of the Impi around them and knew there would be a fight. So on that day, the white man made a covenant with God. The white man promised God that if He would slay the Zulu, the white man would build a church and make the heathen land a Christian land.

But they were Afrikaners and did not depend solely on God. They also had two cannon and 500 rifles and when the day was over, it would be hard to say whether God or the cannon played a bigger part.

The Impi gathered up their spears and shields and their women warbled a cry deep in their throats to send their men to battle. At 5 A.M., 10,000 Impi marched forward against the white guns.

The Impi were forbidden to throw their spears, for it was the Zulu way to kill up close and the Afrikaner general had his men hold their fire from behind their wagons until the Impi were 10 paces away.

Within three hours, four waves of the Zulu had been killed. At 8 A.M., the Afrikaners rode out of the laager on their horses, which was a thing the Zulu had never seen and the Zulu ran in terror as the whites slaughtered them.

The Afrikaner killed more than 3,000 Zulu that day while losing only two white men. And the river ran red with Zulu blood and the day is still celebrated every December 16 as a national holiday.

The woman's voice broke with emotion as she told the story. For as the past is a living thing to the black man, it is a living thing to the white man in this country and both blacks and whites are prisoners of their history.

"What Blood River means is this," she said. "It means if it really gets down to our survival, it means if it really gets down to us against the black man, that God will save us."

That is why when Jimmy Carter talks of human rights and Andrew Young talks about freedom and the United Nations talks about embargos, the Afrikaner talks about Blood River.

It is not just a phrase to him, but a covenant with God, consecrated in blood, which promises that South Africa will always be white and Christian. And neither the white man nor the Zulu forget that the blood that turned the river red was black blood.

Ten thousand fists slammed against the sky, 10,000 voices shouted, as Gatsha Buthelezi entered the rally. The people of his liberation movement, called Inkatha, lined both sides of the grass and Buthelezi passed between them as they threw their fists again and again against the sky.

The women warbled that terrible Zulu cry deep in their throats and the men shouted again and again, "Power to the People! Gatsha to the People! Power to the People!"

Buthelezi stood in front of them, and then knelt on a cushion placed upon the ground as the ministers blessed him. The women sang and the Impi dashed forward and back, smashing their spears against their shields. Buthelezi wears the military uniform of Inkatha, just to show the white man that they do not have the only army in this country. He wears a black beret and gold-rimmed spectacles and carries his hereditary staff of office.

The white government has told the Zulu that he must live on certain chunks of land, chunks that do not even touch each other. And that this land, called KwaZulu, will be made a separate country and that the black will live apart from the white man forever.

"But I will not do this," Buthelezi said to me. "My land is South Africa, all of South Africa, and we are one people. Just like Americans are one people. I believe we have a common destiny with the whites. The whites reject this. Let them.

"Whether they like it or not, we have a common future. Why should I accept less? I come from a warrior people. It is not long ago that we conquered the white man. We do not forget that."

To American ears, Buthelezi's call for a common destiny sounds like moderation. To a white South African, it sounds like revolution. The law states that the black and the white and the other races must be separate and that the white man will not share power with the black.

"The violence is coming and I regret that," Buthelezi said. "But the bombs go off every day in the cities and I regret that, too. But the white man has brought the violence. The white man maintains his position and the status quo through violence.

"So black people leave and go elsewhere in Africa for military training and come back to plant the bombs and I regret that, for I am nonviolent. But I represent the people, many people, and I tell you this: The white man must share power. We must sit down and determine the future where all races in South Africa share power."

A few days ago, at the funeral of a black leader, Buthelezi was stoned by young blacks for being too moderate. Buthelezi advocates working with the white man instead of killing him and for some blacks in this country that day has passed.

Last year, frightened and angry by reports that Buthelezi was becoming too powerful, not only with blacks but also with the other nonwhite races, Buthelezi was called to a meeting with the white minister of justice, police and prisons, J. T. Kruger.

"Tell me what you people want to arrive at," Kruger said. "You say that we leave you with nothing but violence. What do you get with violence?"

Buthelezi gave him an answer that came from deep within him. It has been understood for years by the nonwhites of this country and now, slowly, it is being understood by the whites.

"We will all be destroyed," Buthelezi told him. "You will be destroyed, too."

March 14, 1978

Agony of Color: 'Our Skin Seals Our Fate'

JOHANNESBURG, South Africa

I handed him the newspaper article and he read it in silence. It appeared February 14, on page eight of the *Rand Daily Mail,* one of the city's biggest newspapers. Here is the entire article. Not a word has been changed:

"A total of 115 people were reclassified last year in terms of the Population Registration Act.

"According to the annual report of the Department of the Interior, tabled yesterday, nine whites were reclassified coloured, and 44 coloured became white at their own consent.

"Another coloured was reclassified as white on appeal, and 16 blacks were reclassified coloured on appeal.

"Sixteen Indians were reclassified coloured and 22 Malays were reclassified Indian. Three Indians became Malays last year and three coloured were reclassified Indians."

He shook his head when he had finished reading and handed the newspaper back. His throat worked for a few seconds, but he did not speak. "Well, you have discovered what we are, what the country of South Africa is," he said finally. "It is this. It is madness. And this is what we must endure."

His name is Windsor Shuenyane. He is black, middle-aged, middle-class and a business executive. In America, his life would be taken up with three-martini lunches and worries about crabgrass.

In South Africa, he worries about going mad.

His son played on the floor at my feet. I would record a few snatches of his voice on my tape recorder and play it back for him. He squealed in delight as his father watched.

"You know, I could have become coloured," Windsor blurted out. "I am light-skinned, and the little fellow there, he is light-skinned. As a young man, I could have crossed over. Maybe I should have." He stopped as his son continued to burble and play with the recorder. "But no," Windsor said. "I am black. And this is what I am."

No agony exists in the world as the agony of skin color in South Africa. To be white, or black, or Indian or the mixed-race they called coloured is to seal your fate forever. The government has set up Race Classification Boards to judge the race of every man, woman and child.

To claim you are of another race, to go from black to coloured or coloured to white is to gain a better job, better life, more freedom, more food, more future. More survival.

The race boards have a whole array of tools besides official documents like birth records. They have color charts to hold up to a person's face to measure darkness and they have been known to poke pencils through a person's hair to test the degree of kinkiness.

The boards are not only the most visibly repugnant part of South Africa race policy, but to the rest of the world they smack directly of Hitler's Germany.

Many whites deplore the boards, but they are trapped into supporting them. You cannot have a national policy based on race and allow people to choose which race they shall be in.

The tragic case of Johnny Nicholson cast worldwide attention upon both the system and the madness. In December of 1976, Johnny was born. Both his parents were officially white, but Johnny looked coloured.

"First the neighbors gossiped, then the whole town took up the story," a report on the case said. "And finally—when the pressure became unbearable—Mr. Nicholson cracked. He calmly picked up a gun, shot his wife dead, then committed suicide himself."

Little Johnny is now in an orphanage. For coloureds.

"You know, it was not always like this," Windsor said. "Before the Nationalists took power the races lived together. Coloured lived next to Indian, Indian lived next to black, we were all jumbled together. We lived fine.

"But then it came. And we heard the word apartheid. And all the signs went up. They erupted into signs. White, nonwhite, European, non-European.

"My God, my God. What a sadness was that day. It spelled out our hard times. It spelled out our doom."

Windsor Shuenyane's house is a beautiful house, even by American standards. It is large and airy, with white walls and wood beams. It has electricity and a television and a telephone. It is also in Soweto, the great black slum. For to be a black man who works in Johannesburg, you must live in Soweto no matter how much you make or how high you rise.

If you are black, it does not matter if you are a rich man or a poor man or a beggar man or a thief. For you, there is no exit.

Windsor took out the dreaded pass called a reference book that each black must carry on pain of arrest. Nearly 382,000 blacks were arrested for pass law violations last year. It is something the white government does not take lightly.

Blacks in South Africa look upon the pass the way Jews in Hitler's

Germany looked upon the yellow Stars of David they were made to wear. Their pass books list where the blacks may be and when.

Nearly 390 South African cities, including the capital and the major city of Johannesburg, have curfews demanding that blacks be off the streets during the night hours.

In February, a small town voted to end its curfew laws. The national government refused to allow it. Last year 30,000 blacks were arrested for being on the white man's streets after hours. In 1960, blacks protested the pass laws at Sharpeville, a black ghetto. The police opened fire, killing 69 unarmed persons.

"When I wanted to get married, I could not," Windsor said. "I was working in one town and my wife was working in another. The whites refused to let her come and join me. So I quit my job. And then the whites said, no, I could not join my wife.

"Can you imagine how I felt? Can you imagine the rage! I had to beg, I had to literally beg and say, 'Please, Whitey, please let me be married.' And finally, Whitey let me."

Windsor is the opposite of a revolutionary. He has a good job and has as good a future as a black man can have. But he knows a darkness is descending on his country. "I tell the kids, go slow, it will all be all right, but we are irrelevant to the young," he said. "My generation has failed and they know that. Their only solution is violence and it makes me so fearful."

But Windsor Shuenyane's agony goes deeper than that. It is the agony of the door that is permanently closed. And it drives peaceful men to violence, and sane ones mad.

"Look at me," Windsor said. "I have made something of myself. I come from the poorest of homes. But now I have made something. I have the money to go to a good restaurant and buy food, but I am not allowed. I am forbidden.

"In terms of my tastes, in terms of my cultural advancements, I have more in common with the whites than the blacks. But the law will not let me mix with them.

"And I will tell you a great truth," he said. "I will tell you the great truth of the successful black man. The more educated you are, the better off you are, the more bitter you are.

"In this country, we do not have hopes for the future. We have fears for the future."

March 17, 1978

'A Storm Is Coming, We Must Hurry'

LINTROSE, South Africa

We drove to the top of the mountain, which was not a mountain at all, but the rim of a great plateau that stretched to the horizon. And beneath our feet was the Valley of One Thousand Hills.

Jagged and green, the hills rose from the floor of the valley and spilled up against its steep sides. Here and there, chunks had been torn from the green to reveal patches of red earth, where the land had grown tired and would grow no more.

"The oxen of the Zulu were weak and old," Alan Paton said. "And so it was easier to plow up and down instead of with the contours of the land. And so now, they have the dust."

The dust blew around us, and bent the high grass down over our feet. It blew through the mango and mimosa trees and down into the valley of the Zulu. You could see the red dust eddy and swirl as it blew across the land and toward the sea.

He wore an old sweater and wrapped his arms around himself as the wind passed. "A storm is coming," he said. "And we must hurry."

He is 75 and the long, white strands of his hair fall forward over his face. His mouth is a hard line that is tugged down at the corners. It is a strong face and one that speaks even when the man is silent.

We got back in the car and he drove quickly across the dirt roads. I had come to him first in the study of his home, which is filled with the translations of his books and the books of many others.

"Wilder," he said. "Thornton Wilder. There was an author. My God. *The Bridge of San Luis Rey.* That was a book. I read it again this morning. I went to the *Encyclopaedia Britannica* to look him up, and do you know that Wilder is not in there? Me? Am I in there? Oh, no. Of course not."

I do not know why he said that. Or even why I looked it up, but I did. He is in there, of course. And the first line reads:

"Paton, Alan Stewart (1903—   ) The foremost writer in South Africa, and, through circumstances and conscience, an eminent but reluctant politician."

Through circumstances and conscience. Not a bad tribute when you think about it. For how many ever rise above the one to reach the other?

"I never met Wilder," he said. "I should have. But I never did. He was at New Haven, Connecticut, but every time I went to New Haven, he went to Italy. Not intentionally, I hope." His face yielded to a rare smile.

"But I suppose you came to talk about politics. Yes, I know. Politics is what you want. Not Huckleberry Finn or Faulkner. Or Melville. God, what writers.

"Well, I won't talk to you about politics. But I'll show you."

He got out from his chair and I followed him back out through his home. It is low, built of white painted brick with a red tile roof. It is designed so that the breezes come off the mountains and pass through the rooms.

We went out past his vegetable garden and got into his car and drove out along the quiet roads. "The people here are well-to-do," he said. "Many are retired. There are no blacks here, of course. They are forbidden. No matter how much money a black man has, he will never be allowed to live here."

We drove through the gates of a place called Kearsney College, which is like a U.S. prep school. The lawns were green and huge. The sky was so clear and the sun so bright, that the young boys in blue T-shirts and blue shorts seemed to shimmer in the light as they waved cricket bats and chased after soccer balls.

"This is for the privileged," Paton said. "This is for the whites. Some say violence must destroy this. Some say it must be ended. And if this kind of affluence does nothing to change the disparity between rich and poor in this country—then they are right."

We drove past a building of brick and glass that was very new. "See that building?" he said. "You could have built 10 black schools for what that one building cost. I come here and speak about the future to them." He shrugged. "They seem to listen more than they used to."

He drove over the landscaped driveways of the college and then back out of the gates. He took the road to the mountains that spread and formed the plateau. And at the top, we stopped and looked down into the valley and did not speak for a while.

"I will show you my other school," he finally said. "The other place where I come to speak." And we descended into the valley where the black children lined the road sides and touched their foreheads in salute as we passed. This was Nyuswa, where only the black man is allowed to live.

The road grew deeply rutted and then steep as we climbed over the jagged hills. On the hills were tiny huts where the people lived. And everywhere was the green of the growing things and the bright redness of the earth and the blackness of the people. And towering above it all was the plateau upon which the white man lived and above that the endless sky, which no man owned and no man could keep from another.

"I don't want to be sentimental about this beauty," he said. "To you and I this looks like paradise. To the Zulu, they must work very hard here just to survive."

We stopped to give a ride to a small, wide-eyed girl who could not believe she would ride in a such a car with two white men. Paton spoke to her in Zulu and she sat very tall in the back seat and then stood so her friends along the road could see her. Their mouths fell open as we passed and it was a thing that would be talked about.

We let her out and climbed again to yet another hill. And on that hill I saw Paton's other school. It was the lone building there and its once white walls were stained red by the blowing dust. A tin roof sat uneasily upon it and under its small windows cows grazed on the tall grass.

"This is the Bothas Hill Community School," he said. "This is where 500 students must learn. And so you see, I cannot tell you about politics. I can only show you. I can only show you where the white man sends his children and where the black child must go.

"Hope?" he said. "Hope is a very difficult word in this country. There is hope that comes because there is good reason to hope. And there is hope that comes of courage. And there is the hope that comes because we have nothing left but hope.

"South Africa is the kind of country where you hope on Monday and despair on Tuesday."

We drove back up and out of the valley and down the quiet streets to his home. Back in his study, I saw a plaque on the wall that had the statue of Lincoln from the Lincoln Memorial on it. It was his lifetime membership in the NAACP.

We sat down and he made tea. We drank it as the clouds continued to build in the sky, coming in from the sea on their way over the mountains.

"There is such a terrible disparity in this country," he said. "The disparity of wealth. The disparity of opportunity. The disparity of land. The disparity of power.

"You asked me about hope, but I'll tell you of my fears. My fear is that the Afrikaners, the Nationalists, are incapable of making change. They have so much power, they are muscle-bound with it.

"I know they say they have made changes, but they are cosmetic changes, like the face of death done up nicely to look in the pink of condition.

"I think America has every right to criticize us. If South Africa becomes a theater of war, you will not be untouched. If America took no interest in our affairs, it would be worse here.

"I will tell you the worst that can happen. If we whites don't make any changes that would make the black think there is something to hope for, then the whole country could be laid waste."

He sat in his chair behind his desk and looked out of the window. He looked out onto the land that he has lived upon and written about for so many years, since *Cry, the Beloved Country*, his first novel.

For 10 years his passport was suspended because the government did not like what he said when he traveled to other countries. He founded the Liberal Party, but the government disbanded that when they said that whites and blacks could not join together in politics.

But he is still involved in politics. Through circumstances and conscience. Through endless requests for articles and essays and interviews.

"How I would like to write just one more novel," he said. "I am trying to find the time to write a novel just once again. To leave this politics. And just write. Once more.

"You know, I am not Thornton Wilder. Not as good."

You are, I said, but he waved that away. "I am too old for compliments," he said. "Wilder would have written this novel. He would have done it. He would have left the politics."

And the country, I said, can you ever leave the country if war between the races comes? He has written about this, and quoted back some of his words to me.

"Have I a right to choose not to end my life in desolation?" he said. "Must I end here in disaster if disaster comes? Must I be trapped?

"My reason tells me that I have the right to go. But the heart has reasons also. And it is this conflict that is so painful."

He walked me back outside and waited in the roadway as I left, which is the custom here. Then he went back to the study to his work, and, perhaps, to think about the last novel that he may never write. And if it is not written, it will be one more thing the madness that rages in his beloved country has cost the world.

A storm is coming, he told me on the mountain. And we must hurry.

March 26, 1978

Simon Says

I wrote my first "Simon Says" column on June 21, 1978, and have done them about once a month since. The format is hardly original. Jimmy Cannon used it wonderfully. So did Benjamin Franklin.

You would not call it dignified writing, but the readers get an enormous kick out of it. And I have always believed that one thing in a paper should be intentionally funny—since so much is unintentionally so.

There are two types of people in the world: those who crack their knuckles and those who would like to kill those who do.

◆

Why is it that the saleswomen at cosmetic counters always wear too much makeup?

◆

I hate those parking garages where you have to drive all the way up to get down.

◆

Sitting side-by-side in those restaurant banquettes always gives me a crick in the neck.

◆

What did people do before remote control TV?

◆

No sport requires more strategy than the mile run.

◆

I guess I'm the only one in America, but I thought that in its last years "MASH" was boring, cloyingly self-important and not very funny.

I refuse to believe that Jon Voight and Michael Moriarty are two different people.

◆

Most men do not know their own hat size.

◆

You know the magic has gone out of your marriage if you no longer kiss your spouse in public.

◆

The only way to have fish is grilled.

◆

Don't even think twice about it: Bring a flower to a loved one tomorrow.

◆

Don't you just hate it when people use the phrase "loved one"?

◆

Next time you're in a fancy restaurant, check for gum under the table. You'll be surprised.

◆

I'd like antiques a lot more if they weren't so old.

Is it just my imagination or are fewer and fewer drivers using turn signals?

◆

People who check the coin return on vending machines and pay telephones even when they know they have no money coming back should be beaten with sticks.

◆

If you've never cheated at solitaire, I don't want to know you.

◆

Why is it that coin laundries attract such interesting people?

◆

Next time you are jealous of a beautiful woman or a handsome man, remember that the underside of their tongue is just as ugly as your own.

◆

People who raise little cactuses on their desks are strange.

◆

When is the last time you went into a person's home or office and saw a world globe?

◆

People who say "succumbed" instead of "died" are just kidding themselves.

◆

Bicycle riders over age 10 should be held responsible for their actions on the road.

I stay away from people who eat watermelon with a knife and fork.

◆

If you don't still get excited when you see a rainbow, you might as well pack it in.

◆

I've never met anyone who didn't like yes men.

◆

You know you're getting old when you can remember when the Chicago Seven were the Chicago Eight.

◆

I can't help myself, I always look for the hidden rabbit on the *Playboy* cover.

◆

I've never met a kid who could not open a childproof cap, or an adult who could.

◆

I'll bet being rich means never having to wait for the paperback.

◆

People with Ph.D.s who call themselves "doctor" are pathetic.

◆

Was there ever a holiday as overrated as St. Patrick's Day?

◆

People who clip their fingernails in public should be thrown down wells.

You can always judge a restaurant by its coffee.

True confessions:
- I have a library book overdue since 1965.
- I don't care how I treat rental cars.
- I watch public TV, but don't subscribe.
- I often tell people they look thinner when they don't.
- I have had unpure thoughts about Valerie Bertinelli.

Nothing is worse than a hotel shower that changes from hot to cold.

Next time, don't wonder about it. Just get up and give your seat to an elderly person.

If life was as nice as a McDonald's commercial, we'd all be better off.

◆

I liked it better when phone numbers began with letters.

◆

How come people who know the difference between misfeasance, malfeasance and nonfeasance always want to explain it?

◆

When shined shoes stopped being the sign of a well-dressed man, an era ended.

Never wear new shoes out of the store, nor leave your old ones behind.

Most bars that make their own Bloody Marys shouldn't.

Brooke Shields should seriously consider a convent.

The only bad part of traveling is the traveling.

Guys who roll up their sleeves to look like they are working real hard are the phoniest people I know.

It is nearly impossible to buy single-edged razor blades anymore.

A waiter who brings your food to the table and has to ask who ordered what is not doing his job.

People who wear mirrored sunglasses should seek professional help.

How come the people in the health club ads never look like they need a health club?

Seeing a Denver boot on a car makes my day.

Memories of Grandfather . . .

M ostly, I remember his hands. How large they were, how the big, blunted fingers would wrap around my own. When I was little, I would hold my palms up against his, feeling his hard callouses and measuring how far up his hands my own reached.

My grandfather's hands were a workingman's hands, a carpenter's hands. He would tell me how, when he was very young, it was decreed that he should become a blacksmith because that was what his village needed.

He would work over the forge, the heat and smoke blackening his young features, until one day he could stand it no longer and ran away. It was an act of unheard-of rebellion, shocking the entire community. But he won in the end and was allowed to become what he wanted to become, a carpenter.

"But why did they try to make you do something you didn't want to?" I would ask him. He would laugh, knowing the hopelessness of explaining 19th century village life in Russia to a child of America.

He came over by boat to Canada with his young bride. This, too, is something that can barely be understood now. It was an arranged marriage. I think my grandfather once told me he had never seen my grandmother before their wedding day. And yet he loved and cared for her with a single-minded devotion that lasted beyond her own death a few years ago.

They settled in the ghetto of Montreal and he built wooden railway cars for the Canadian Pacific. They paid him 13 cents an hour. He reared two sons and a daughter, my mother, and then came south to the land of unlimited promise, where he became an American citizen.

In Chicago, he built homes and stores. Nothing fancy, nothing famous, no landmarks. Just places where people lived and worked. He would carry his toolbox from job to job, from contractor to contractor, going wherever there was work.

For years I think he harbored the hope that one of his grandsons would become a carpenter, too. It was something he used to joke about, and I do not really know if there was seriousness behind the joking.

I remembered as a child begging him to show me his tools. And how he would go into the bedroom, carefully lift up the bedspread and reach beneath the bed to drag out his huge, wooden toolbox. He would lift it with one hand and give it to me. I would grab it with two hands and stagger around the room like a drunk, trying to keep it from crashing onto the floor.

Inside the box, carefully oiled against rust, would be his hammers and saws and planes and awls. He would let me hold them, let me breathe the sharp oil smell and run my hands over the smooth blueness of the steel.

When it became clear that none of us would follow him in his trade, that none of us would work with our hands for a living, he put the tools away for a final time. I do not know where they are today.

When I first became a reporter, he sat me down and asked me to explain just what I did for a living. "I talk to people, Grampa," I said. "Then I take what they say and I put it in the paper." He just looked at me for a while.

"Tell me something," he said, with the beginning of a smile, "for this they pay you?"

One of his own jobs became a story told to me almost every time we spoke together. I must have heard it first while sitting on his lap, and heard it again not many weeks ago. It was beyond a family joke and became a ritual.

The job was in the Drake Hotel, one of Chicago's fanciest establishments. My grandfather showed up in his workman's overalls, carrying his toolbox, and attempted to go through the front door. The doorman rushed up and stopped him, huffily explaining that "laborers" were to use the service entrance.

"Someday," my grandfather would tell me, "someday, do you know what I am going to do?" I would shake my head in wonder. "I am going to buy the Drake Hotel," he would roar, "and I am going to fire that doorman!"

The only picture of my grandfather and me was taken at my wedding a few months ago. In the picture, his hands are wrapped around mine, dwarfing them, like they did when I was a child. What astounds me is that in the picture I am taller than he, something that must have happened over the years without my realizing it. And now, looking at it, I still prefer to think that it is a trick of the camera, an optical illusion.

Two weeks ago at age 91 my grandfather had a heart attack. He recovered well, drawing his strength from a life of hard, physical labor. When I visited him in the hospital, he was sitting up and eating a large lunch. I showed him the picture of him and me, which he had not yet seen. "I would say very handsome," he said, holding it. "Very handsome." I told him that he looked handsome, too. "I was talking about me," he said, smiling.

Two days ago he died. I am writing this a few hours before his funeral. I have always hated stories like this one. It has always seemed to me that they glorify more the writer than the man written about. People admire the fine phrases and fine sentiments, which is merely a knack that writers learn over the years.

But I understand now why they are written. At some point, after spending your life building word upon word, you find that you cannot really feel anymore except through them. And those words haunt you until you put them upon a page.

My grandfather does not need these words for his memorial. His memorial is to be found in the homes of this city, homes that still stand, homes in which people still live.

When I was 10, my family decided to move to California for a while. We broke the news to my grandfather, who sat weeping at our kitchen table, sure that he would never see us again. I still remember seeing him wipe his eyes with the backs of those huge hands. I tugged at his jacket and asked him why he was crying. "Your grampa will miss you," he said, wrapping me in his arms. "He will miss you."

Today, I miss him.

November 8, 1977

Nixon Back?
He Never Let Go

WASHINGTON, D.C.

An explanation was in order.

After all, what was Richard Nixon doing as a guest speaker at the American Society of Newspaper Editors convention?

The hundreds of people cutting into their seafood crepes this day were among the most powerful men and women in America.

They were newspaper editors, editorial writers, and even a few publishers. These people may not shape public opinion in this country, but they at least fondle it a little.

So what was Dick Nixon, the man they hounded from office, doing here giving a luncheon speech? An explanation was clearly in order.

"We invited all three living ex-presidents," the moderator announced, "but only Mr. Nixon responded."

He could have said something else. He could have said what one organizer told me: "Thank God only Nixon responded," he said. "Can you imagine filling this ballroom if Gerald Ford had accepted?"

Which was, of course, the point. While there was some debate and complaint about having a disgraced ex-president as an honored speaker, it was a sellout crowd. Journalists, someone once wrote, are all just gawkers at a car wreck.

Nixon looked good. He felt good. This was his seventh appearance before this group, but his first since he had resigned from office in 1974. He was introduced as that "well-known and most unusual man, Richard M. Nixon." The applause was polite.

Nixon was even more polite. He spoke for nearly an hour on the Soviet Union. He didn't use any notes and though the level of analysis was not very deep, it was step-by-step clear. Perhaps he knew his audience.

Then he took questions. And, naturally, *the* question was the first one. Richard Nixon was asked what he had learned from Watergate.

Not much, apparently.

"I think 10 years of [questions about Watergate] is enough," he said. "I'm going to think about the future, not the past."

There was a smattering of applause. Then he was asked about Spiro

Agnew being a crook. And Nixon drew a distinction so fine, it was almost invisible.

Nixon pointed out that Agnew took bribes as governor of Maryland and not as vice-president of the United States, although "some of the payments were apparently made after he was vice-president of the United States."

"But as far as I'm concerned, he's suffered enough," Nixon said. "And I'm not going to stand here and kick him around."

This time there was no applause. This time there were some uneasy murmurs. Was this how Nixon really viewed history? That Watergate is not worth discussing? That a vice-president taking bribes in the White House is not a fit topic for conversation?

Nixon reacted to the murmurs by flashing one of his ice-water smiles. "I realize he [Agnew] is not a pinup boy for this press group," Nixon said.

The editors soon retreated to safer ground. They asked Nixon about the Democrats. And, here, Nixon wowed the crowd with the topic he loves best: politics.

"Mondale will be nominated on the first ballot," he said. "But I think Reagan will win because he is the better candidate.

"I wouldn't bet the ranch on it. But I would bet the main house. And, unless the economy goes down, I wouldn't bet the outhouse on Mondale."

Roars of laughter. What a guy! the editors seemed to be saying.

When it was all over and as his Secret Service agents led him away, Nixon stopped and mingled with the crowd.

"I thought there would be more questions on Watergate," he admitted with a smile. "I was surprised there were so few."

He asked one publisher how his mother was and the publisher promised to pass on Nixon's regards.

"I always get a good reception from this group," Nixon said. "Always."

His agents told him his plane was waiting, but he would not leave. He went up to one editor whose name tag indicated he came from Cincinnati. "The Reds will do well this year," Nixon said to the man. "I saw them beat the Mets on TV."

The crowd thinned. The TV crews packed up their equipment.

The vast room was almost empty as the busboys began removing the dishes.

But there, at the far end, was Richard Nixon, grabbing a hand, making a comment, telling a story.

Richard Nixon—unable to say goodbye, unable to be alone, unable to let go.

May 10, 1984

Playmate Unfolds a Diplomatic Coup

I was snoozing behind a stack of papers when the Chief yelled out my name.

"Kid," he said, for that is what they call me, "just what is it that you're working on?"

"Uh, those two series we talked about," I said.

The Chief ground out his cigar on my hand. "*What* two series?"

" 'Infrastructure: Threat or Menace?' and 'Canada: Friendly Giant to the North,' " I said.

The Chief opened a drawer and took out a newspaper clipping. "Remember this?" he asked.

It was my column from June 29 of this year. It contained a picture of a woman wearing a tiny bathing suit and squealing in delight.

"I can explain that, Chief," I said. "First of all, I was drunk. Second, she claimed she was a lieutenant commander in the Cuban Air Force and wanted to defect."

"Wrong," said the Chief. "This is the picture of a young woman named Penny Baker. She was one of 7,000 women from across the country who competed to become the 30th Anniversary Playboy Playmate. By dumb luck, you interviewed her months before she won and months before anyone else did. Do you know what that means?"

I thought about it. "It means I was present at an important sociological event," I said. "Back in June, I explored the American psyche and just what it is about our way of life that causes thousands of ordinary women to try to become a Playboy Playmate. Now, if I do a follow-up column, we can more deeply delve into the cultural mores of American life."

"Try again," the Chief said.

"It means we can run another sleazo picture in the paper," I said.

"Kid," he said, "there is hope for you."

I went back and looked at my old notes. Penny Baker, 18, had grown up on a farm, was a model, and had never posed nude before. She said she didn't know how her parents would feel about it.

That was June. Now, she was revealed to millions in the centerfold of the January issue of *Playboy*.

Ms. Baker was in New York taping TV shows and we talked by phone. She told me she had gone home for Thanksgiving and her parents had seen her nude photos and were delighted. Her neighbors in tiny Springville, New York, also were delighted, she said, that those pictures had put them on the map.

Ms. Baker also had reached another cultural summit: She had met Hugh Hefner.

"Hugh Hefner is a very nice man," she said. "Real sweet and very intelligent. When we met, he was wearing pajamas. He was drinking a Pepsi and smoking a pipe."

Which is a neat trick when you think about it. Fortunately, I had a few questions prepared.

"What do you think of American foreign policy vis-à-vis Grenada and Lebanon?" I asked.

"I am a Republican," Ms. Baker replied without hesitation. "I believe in Mr. Reagan and what he is doing."

Another national scoop. The Chief would be pleased. To say nothing of Mr. Reagan.

"No one will believe in America unless we stand up and face our foes," Ms. Baker continued. "That is what we are doing now. The Soviets mean business. And we should mean business, too."

"Nuclear disarmament?" I asked.

"I would not want a nuclear freeze because I don't trust the Soviets," she said. "They won't freeze, too."

"If invited to the Soviet Union would you go and would you meet with the Soviet premier to discuss the major issues of the day?" I asked.

She paused for a moment.

"Yes," Ms. Baker said. "I would."

The idea was stunning. A political and cultural exchange. America's 30th Anniversary Playmate for Russia's Miss Tractor or Miss Beet Borscht.

"I have only one condition," Ms. Baker said. "I would only agree to go to the Soviet Union if they would guarantee I could get back out."

I took another look at Ms. Baker's picture.

"Don't count on it," I said.

December 14, 1983

She Took
His Life for Hers

I n the late evening of November 11, Carol Sheridan plunged a steak
knife into her husband's chest, thereby ending his life and her
misery.

Leaving her husband on the floor of the kitchen hallway, she
walked to a nearby fire station and asked them to call the police. She
had been married less than five months.

The authorities responded with efficiency and Carol quickly was
charged with murder. Bail was set at $30,000. In such matters the
legal system works smoothly. Reports are written, bodies located,
suspects arrested, charges made, bail set.

But looking back at the events that led up to this extraordinary
killing, one finds a system that works well only after blood has been
shed. There were opportunities—many of them—to prevent this
killing. But it wasn't prevented. And three days ago, Carol Sheridan, a
very unextraordinary housewife, stood before a judge to hear him
pass judgment.

Carol, 21, was married to Vincent, 30, on June 23, 1979, in Chicago.
He was a security guard for the Metropolitan Sanitary District. It was
the first marriage for both of them. According to the sworn testimony
of witnesses he began beating her one week later.

The reasons will never be known for sure. They are as simple or
complex as human beings themselves. Carol, like most brides, wanted
the marriage to work. And Vincent, even though he beat her, probably wanted the same.

The first beating, done in front of one of Carol's girlfriends, both
hurt and frightened her. The police were called. They did not,
however, do anything about the attack. Instead they called it a
"domestic disturbance."

Those two words are among the most familiar and terrifying that
battered wives hear. There is an official Chicago Police Department
rule, Order 78-18, that states that all calls from females who have
been battered or assaulted are not to be treated as domestic disturbances. The order directs the police officer to treat such assaults as
serious crimes and to make arrests where appropriate.

Like all orders, it is worth only what the cop on the street wishes to make of it. On the day of Carol's first beating, the police, perhaps noting that the couple was newly wed, decided to make little of it.

The next beating came 13 days later. On July 12, while in the home of her girlfriend, Carol again was beaten by Vincent. Her lip and nose were bloodied. The police again were called.

This time, noting the blood gushing from Carol's face, the police took Vincent to the station. He was released without charge.

The next beating came 12 days later. This time Carol had to be taken to Christ Hospital, where skull X-rays were made and she was treated for bruises on her face and forehead. The doctors also noted that some of her hair had been pulled out.

The people at the hospital acted commendably. They not only treated Carol, but also advised her to go to the battered spouse clinic at the YWCA.

Unfortunately, the YWCA was too far from Carol's home and she could not attend. The next beating came 22 days later.

On August 15, Carol fled the house after Vincent beat her. She sought refuge in the home of her girlfriend, Wanda. But Vincent followed her, broke into the house, and beat Carol again.

The police were called. They said that this was clearly a domestic disturbance and they could not get involved. Vincent was not arrested. Perhaps feeling just a little guilty, Vincent didn't beat Carol again for a month and a half.

But he made up for lost time. On this occasion, outside a Berwyn restaurant and cocktail lounge, he took Carol into an alley, beat her head against a garbage can, and ripped off her blouse.

The beating was witnessed by a Berwyn policeman who decided it was not a domestic disturbance. After taking Carol to MacNeil Memorial Hospital, the policeman insisted that Carol sign a battery complaint against Vincent, which she did.

She also continued to live with Vincent because she felt that she had no place else to go.

The next beating didn't come for a month. After this one, on November 5, Carol ran from the house. She testified later that she wandered around all night and ended up at 46th and Cicero, where she was abducted and raped. She reported the rape to the police and was taken to Holy Cross Hospital.

At the hospital, she made contact with a social service counselor, who tried to help her. Six days after Carol left the hospital, her husband beat her for the last time.

It began about 7 P.M. Vincent began to taunt her about the rape and told her she got what she deserved and that if she tried to leave him again she would be raped once more.

Carol called her friend Wanda for refuge. But Wanda's husband didn't want a repeat of what had happened the last time and refused.

So Carol phoned her mother. Her mother told her to call the police. But Carol said the police had been called time and time again and she felt they would do nothing.

As a last resort, Carol phoned Holy Cross Hospital and tried to reach the social service counselor. Instead she got a nun and social worker, Sister J. (She asked that her name not be used.)

Carol began to cry and asked for help. Sister J. asked her if she could get to the hospital. Carol said no. Sister J. asked her if she feared she would be injured.

"Yes," Carol said. "He will hurt me. Please call the police."

At that moment, Vincent picked up the phone extension. "If you send anyone over, I will kill them," he said. "I'll kill anyone who comes to help her." Then Vincent pulled the phone from the wall and the line went dead.

Sister J. checked the hospital records and found two addresses for Carol, one of which was for Carol's mother. Sister J. then called her supervisor. The supervisor told her that the police might be harmed if they went to Carol's home, that both Vincent and Carol might have been drinking, and that it was really a domestic disturbance and it was best not to get involved. For those reasons Sister J. did not call the police.

At Carol's home, Vincent was beating her. He picked up a knife, threw it at her, and missed. She got to the knife, picked it up, and stabbed him to death.

The next day, when Sister J. heard the news on the radio, she called the police and told them what she knew.

Last week, Carol went to court for a preliminary hearing. Her friends and Sister J. testified on her behalf.

The judge, Maurice Pompey, found that there was no probable cause to try Carol for murder and released her.

If there is any point to the slaying of Vincent Sheridan, it is that it was pointless. If the beatings had not been treated as domestic disturbances, if Carol had gotten help or refuge, if Vincent had gotten help or incarceration, it might have all come out differently.

About one of every 11 murders in this country is the murder of a husband by a wife or a wife by a husband. It breaks down about 50-50.

And there is one thing that police and friends and relatives should keep in mind when they get a plea for help:

All those murders started as domestic disturbances. None of them ended that way.

January 6, 1980

Court Relief
for 'Burger King Terror'

The trial of the century took place yesterday.
I consider myself fortunate to have been there for all 12 minutes of it.

On trial was Susy Schultz, 24, a reporter for the City News Bureau. The City of Chicago had decided to prosecute Ms. Schultz for trying to use a washroom in a downtown Burger King.

And you wonder where your tax dollars go.

Last October, Ms. Schultz went into a Burger King in downtown Chicago intending to buy a sandwich and coffee. She wanted to use the washroom beforehand, but was stopped by a security guard.

The guard grabbed her, pinned her against the wall, and called the cops.

Ms. Schultz was tossed into a paddy wagon, charged with disorderly conduct, and thrown into a cell.

She later posted bond, though why we allow such dangerous criminals to roam the streets is beyond me.

Neither Burger King nor its franchiser, Chart House Inc., wanted Ms. Schultz prosecuted, they said. They said they were sorry the whole thing happened and wanted to forget about it, but they could not persuade the security firm, Award Security Services Inc., to go along.

The City of Chicago does not have to prosecute every dimwit case that comes its way. But yesterday, the city decided to bring Susy "The Burger King Terror" Schultz to justice.

The case was heard in Branch 46, which is located in the Traffic Court building at 321 N. La Salle.

Traffic Court used to be where the Gray Wolves hung out. These were lawyers who prowled the corridors looking for cases, promising their clients quick dismissals from friendly judges.

But that was before Operation Greylord and electronic eavesdropping. Now, it seems like every third lawyer is leaning over his lapel and whispering, "Testing, testing."

Some people say it is difficult to tell the criminals from the lawyers in Traffic Court. That is not true. The criminals dress better.

Branch 46, which deals in nontraffic cases, is a semidingy room with green vinyl walls and linoleum floors. Even the courtroom's American flag could use a cleaning.

The trial began without much fanfare. There are no witness chairs in Branch 46. You just stand up in front of the judge and talk.

I remember from my City News Bureau days that reporters are supposed to describe what the principal characters in a trial are wearing. I don't know why. I have never known a trial to set a fashion trend.

The security guard, Leon Roberts, was wearing a brown suit. Ms. Schultz was in tan corduroy. The judge, John J. McDonnell, wore black.

Roberts testified that in just over a year he had prevented exactly 675 people from using the washroom in the Burger King.

That is truly an awesome figure. Imagine denying that many people the ability to relieve themselves or wash their hands before buying food.

Roberts said he was only following policy and freely admitted he grabbed Ms. Schultz and "pinned her in a half nelson."

He said he did this because Ms. Schultz had poked him in the chest and called him a "low-life idiot bum."

Roberts is about 5 feet 8 and 190 pounds. Ms. Schultz is 5 feet 1 and 110 pounds.

But the City of Chicago said that Roberts had suffered an "ordeal" at Ms. Schultz's hands.

Ms. Schultz testified she had only poked Roberts very gently and only to emphasize her words and only after he had grabbed her arm.

Her attorney said her behavior was justified because she had a real need to use the washroom.

The City of Chicago disagreed, saying Ms. Schultz's behavior was exactly what disorderly conduct is all about.

Judge McDonnell stayed awake for the entire trial.

McDonnell made a big splash more than a decade ago when he was accused of waving a gun at a man in a parking lot. McDonnell later testified he did not wave a gun, but a cigar. Criminal charges against McDonnell were dismissed, but the Illinois Courts Commission suspended him for four months without pay.

McDonnell may not know a cigar from a gun, but he definitely proved yesterday he knows disorderly conduct from baloney.

He pointed out something the city has yet to learn: Disorderly conduct must provoke a breach of the peace.

In other words, disorderly conduct is not just two people yelling at each other or, as some cops think, somebody being a pain-in-the-butt loudmouth.

In fact, if every pain-in-the-butt loudmouth was guilty of disorderly conduct, all the aldermen and newspaper columnists of this city would be behind bars.

Which, now that I think of it, might not be a bad idea.

Judge McDonnell said there was no evidence of any disorderly conduct on Ms. Schultz's part and he found her not guilty.

With that, Ms. Schultz was allowed to rejoin decent society.

She was delighted. "Justice was done," she said. "This whole thing was ridiculous."

Outside the courtroom I looked around for the TV cameras and the cheering crowds, but the only guy I saw asked if I could fix a parking ticket for him.

Ms. Schultz, accompanied by her father, mother, and two sisters, went out to lunch.

They did not go to Burger King.

January 5, 1984

A Red Flower—
for the Infantry's Buddy

HONOLULU

There was a broken red flower lying there and you could see, if you thought about it, an aging vet standing above the grave for a silent moment and dropping the flower with an embarrassed shrug.

People do not flock here, but a few still come and some still remember.

The tour guide had been thinking of places to go and things to do. "Pearl Harbor," she said. "And, of course, a pineapple plantation."

We nodded. These are the things that tourists do here. "And you might want to go up to the Punchbowl," she said. "It's a military cemetery."

No, we told her. We didn't think so. We were on vacation and cemeteries were definitely not part of it. Once you've seen one grave. . . .

"Sure," she said. "But there's this guy buried there. I can't remember his first name. But his last name is Pyle."

Ernie Pyle? we asked. Ernie Pyle is here?

"Yeah," she said. "That's the guy. You heard of him?"

Yeah, we said. We've heard of him.

They named a ship after him and a bomber and a Marine company and a library and a journalism school and a 16-cent stamp. On the side of the stamp it says, "Journalist," which is what they call a reporter after he is dead.

They made a movie about him. His books were best-sellers. He made the cover of *Time*.

And one of the most often-asked questions of the students who wander through the library dedicated to him is: "Who was Ernie Pyle?"

He was born in 1900 and was mostly known as the Little Guy. He was short and skinny and restless and became a war correspondent at age 40. He covered the London blitz and then the invasion of North Africa.

That is where it happened for him. During the next two years, he became one of the best-known reporters in the country and maybe in history.

He wrote about the troops and how they lived and fought, and when he told you about a guy he told you his full name and where he came from and what he was like. He wrote about fear and agony with a sweet simplicity. War was not grand for him.

He was not a man of sweetness and light. He constantly doubted himself and his abilities. His achievements, like many reporters', came through a fear of failure.

He saw his friends die and feared death himself. He often spoke of it. In Naples, during the invasion of Italy, he felt he had lost his touch, that he could not write about war anymore.

Another famous war correspondent, Hal Boyle, later said that in Italy, during his deepest despair, Pyle wrote the best single article to come out of World War II.

It was about how a group of soldiers brought their dead captain out of the mountains on mule pack. This is a too small part of it:

"Two men unlashed the body from the mule and lifted it off and laid it in the shadow beside the stone wall. Other men took the other bodies off. Finally, there were five lying end to end in a long row.

"Then a soldier came and stood beside the officer and bent over, and he, too, spoke to his dead captain, not in a whisper, but awfully tenderly, and he said, 'I sure am sorry, sir.'

"Then the first man squatted down and he reached down and took the captain's hand, and he sat there for a full five minutes holding the dead hand in his own and looking intently into the dead face.

"Finally he put the hand down. He reached over and gently straightened the points of the captain's shirt collar, and then he sort of rearranged the tattered edges of the uniform around the wound, and then he got up and walked away down the road in the moonlight, all alone.

"The rest of us went back into the cowshed, leaving the five dead men lying in a line, end to end, in the shadow of the low stone wall. We lay down on the straw in the cowshed, and pretty soon we were all asleep."

"He was a marvelous guy," said Bill Mauldin, the cartoonist who became as well-loved as Pyle during the war. "He was salty. He was not a sweet guy. He drank a lot and he worked hard.

"He was conscious that he was a civilian around soldiers. He took more risks because of that. He took more risks because he was a reporter and not a soldier. After Europe, he felt that he could not refuse to go to the Pacific."

"I'm afraid," Pyle once said. "War scares the hell out of me. I guess it's because I don't want to die. I know the longer we stay with this, the smaller our chances are of getting out. But what the hell! We can't leave and we know it."

When he boarded the ship to cover the invasion of Okinawa, a bunch of correspondents shouted over to him, "Keep your head down, Ernie."

He replied, "Listen, you bastards, I'll take a drink over every one of your graves!"

A few weeks later, on the tiny island of Ii Shima, a Japanese sniper put a bullet into his left temple. They buried him in his helmet.

They put up a marker that said:

> *At This Spot*
> *The 77th Infantry Division*
> *Lost a Buddy*
> *ERNIE PYLE*
> *18 April 1945*

Later, they moved his body back to America, to the simplest of graves in a volcanic crater outside Honolulu. On each side of him is the grave of an unknown soldier. A few tour buses still pass and the guides will point out the sight.

And every now and then, somebody with a few free minutes and a lot of memories will stop and put a flower on the grave.

November 19, 1978

A Fine Line
for Indiana Jones

As faithful readers know, I like to go to movie screenings.
A movie screening is an advance showing of a blockbuster picture for an elite set of opinion-makers.

I go to them when I get Roger Ebert's mail by mistake.

This time I got his invitation for *Indiana Jones and the Temple of Doom*.

At first, I was a little afraid to go because I look so much like Harrison Ford [the light has to be just right] that I usually get mobbed at his pictures. But I had heard so much about this film, I decided to risk it.

I arrived outside the Esquire Theater where there were about 1,100 elite opinion-makers, some of whom had shoes on.

I like the Esquire Theater because it has a balcony, which, once in a blue moon, they actually open and let people sit in.

I don't know why theaters don't open their balconies more often. The very worst we could be doing up there is increasing the future movie-going population.

I got to the Esquire 20 minutes before the movie was to begin and the line already stretched a block.

Like most people, I am scared by lines.

I always wonder: Is this the line for the people who already *have* tickets or is this the line for people who need to *get* tickets? Is it the line for the right movie or have I made a terrible mistake and gotten into a line for *My Dinner with Andre*?

So I went up to a woman in the line and asked. She was wearing a business suit and jogging shoes. I figured she was safe. I was a fool.

"Is this the line for the movie?" I asked.

"No," she said with a sweet smile. "This is the line for Comiskey Park. The Yanks are in town and Seaver is pitching and that's why it's so long."

"Thank you," I said—she could have had a knife—and then I joined the end of the line.

After a few minutes, the doors opened, the line began to move swiftly and I watched for cases of Line Panic.

Remember when you were a kid at the grocery store with your mother and were in the checkout line and she said: "Sweetie, I forgot the butter. You wait in line and Mommy will be right back"?

Remember the awful panic you felt as the line crept forward and your mother was still not back? Remember how you were sure you were going to be arrested because you didn't have any money?

Well, we all grow up, but Line Panic never leaves us.

Adult Line Panic is when your spouse drops you off in front of the theater and says: "You get in line while I park the car."

And, of course, the line starts moving and the goof is still not back and you look up and down the street and you begin to get closer and closer to the doors and you get angrier and angrier and you wonder why you ever married such a slug in the first place.

There was a really good case of Line Panic right in front of me. This woman tried taking teeny steps to slow down the line, but that never works.

She got to the door and her husband still had not shown up and she stood there fuming. I'll bet she really belted him when he showed up 10 minutes later, sauntering down the street, and whistling.

Inside the theater, I looked for famous people in the vast crowd.

I saw only two. One was Rick Kogan, who writes books, and the other was Mike Lufrano, a sophomore at the University of Illinois, whose only claim to fame is that he recognized me from my column picture.

I don't want to say I was overly grateful, but I did promise to endow a scholarship in his name.

I found out later there were 1,173 people at the screening, which would have been great except the Esquire seats only 1,113.

Lufrano, his date, and I got the last three seats way up high in the balcony by hip-checking some senior citizens out of the way.

The people without seats had to sit in the aisles, which meant I spent about half the movie watching the fire exits.

Before the movie began, Larry Lujack, the WLS radio megastar, came out and said: "Don't puke or wet your pants at the scary parts."

Which brings up a good point. The *New York Times* did a very serious story Monday on whether this movie was too violent for children and whether it really deserved its PG rating.

Having now seen it, I think it's fair to say that unless your child had combat experience in Vietnam, he stands a good chance of getting screaming nightmares from this movie.

Not that screaming nightmares are a bad thing. In fact, they are good for kids. It prepares them for the job market.

As to my overall opinion of the movie, I know I am not a professional movie critic so I want to be measured in my judgment: I think "Indiana Jones" is the best adventure movie in the history of Western civilization.

The cockroach scene alone is worth the price of admission.

And Steven Spielberg, the director, is a genius in my book.

He is the same guy who made *Jaws, Close Encounters of the Third Kind, Raiders of the Lost Ark,* and *E.T.*

Remember where you read it first:

If Spielberg keeps this up, he's going to be a millionaire some day.

May 23, 1984

CAMPAIGN '84

Author and journalist Frank Simonds said: "There is but one way for a newspaperman to look at a politician, and that is down."

I am not sure that is entirely true, but just looking at them can be a lot of fun.

Every four years, grown men go tramping around the country kissing babies, wearing Indian headdresses, eating blintzes—and asking for our votes.

And every night, the American public stays glued to their TV sets to hear the latest poll tell them who's ahead.

I try to stay away from the horserace stories. Until Election Day, I don't much care who's ahead.

I care, instead, about the people who are running and why they do it: what drives them, what makes them do the things and say the things they do.

And I try to keep in mind those immortal words: No matter who we elect, he's the only president we've got.

God help us all.

Ron's 'America'— A Sneak Preview

DALLAS

It was four years ago in a high school gym in Racine, Wisconsin, that I first experienced the power of Ronald Reagan.

The band had finished up and the local politicians had said their piece and Reagan took the podium to deliver his standard speech.

It dealt very little with politics.

More than any other candidate, perhaps more than any other candidate in history, Ronald Reagan talks about traditional American values: family, home, God, work, faith, hope.

Deep down and up front, he is a romantic, with a romantic vision of American power and greatness and goodness.

But this day in the gym, at the end of his speech, he paused and began talking about World War II, about an American B-17 pilot whose bomber was badly damaged over France.

The pilot was trying to make it back to England, when his belly gunner got badly hit and was trapped in his gun turret.

The plane, smoking badly now, kept losing altitude, and the pilot announced that everyone had to bail out.

But the belly gunner could not move. And he knew he was doomed.

One by one the crew parachuted to safety and soon only the gunner and the pilot were left.

Here, Ronald Reagan's voice grew thick with emotion.

"The kid in the turret cried out with tears," he said. "And so the pilot sat down on the floor of the plane and said; 'We'll ride it down together, son.' "

"And that pilot," Reagan said, his voice actually breaking, "was given the Congressional Medal of Honor—posthumously!"

His eyes moist, Reagan looked out at the crowd and spoke no more.

There was a deathly silence in the gym. And then the house came down.

The applause was thunderous. People leaped to their feet, tipping over their chairs, beating their hands together, yelling, shouting, some with tears flowing down their cheeks.

They had understood. They had received the message:

No matter how bad things get, no matter if our plane is on fire and we seemed trapped, Ron Reagan will stick with us.

His face may be lined and he may not hear every single word that is said and he may like an afternoon nap or two, but he will be there when we need him.

He is our pilot. And he will show us the way.

Like the audience, I was moved. It seemed so fine, so unpolitical a moment. A moment of genuine warmth and feeling.

Yet, as we traveled to the next campaign stop, a typically journalistic thought struck me:

If the last two men on the plane were the pilot and the gunner, and if both men crashed and died, how on earth do we know what the pilot said?

I was mulling that over as we reached the next stop and Reagan began his speech. And, at the end, he began to talk about a B-17 pilot in World War II.

And, at exactly the right moment, his voice grew thick with emotion. And then it broke. And his eyes grew moist. And he grew silent. And the crowd went wild.

As it would at stop after stop after stop.

I wrote a column about all this and a few days later a Reagan staffer kidded me about it.

"You angry?" I asked him.

"Naw," he said. "It doesn't really matter. This is going to be the first president who doesn't need a good press. This guy goes straight to the people. They love him.

"And nothing you or CBS or the *New York Times* say is going to make any difference."

As it turned out, he was right. There is an entire book on the stands right now listing all of Reagan's gaffes and contradictions and errors of fact.

You think anybody cares? I doubt it. He has won too many hearts and too many minds for it to matter now.

At a lunch here yesterday while attending the Republican National Convention, Reagan referred to the "eccentric clique" that runs the Democratic Party.

It was an ironic statement. Just eight years ago, when he ran unsuccessfully against Gerald Ford for the GOP nomination, it was Ronald Reagan who was the eccentric, hanging way out there on the far right of his party.

His main issue back then was opposition to the Panama Canal treaties, and he would go from speech to speech saying: "We built it, we bought it, and we're going to keep it!"

Then, party leaders snickered. Today, nobody is laughing. Today, Reagan is his party's mainstream.

He has not moved. The stream has. The Republican Party is a right-wing party and Ronald Reagan is no longer at the edges of it but at the center.

He is, as someone recently said, America's truest Urban Cowboy. Western in dress and speech, he loves to be photographed riding a horse, wearing his ostrich-skin boots, and looking as if he was about to punch some cows.

It takes an act of will to remember that he grew up not in the West, but in an Illinois town where the boots were likely to be rubber and the only thing you punched was a time clock.

But Reagan realized early on that the West was the future, the place to which the population and the power would shift and where "fringe" ideas could flourish. From what other state but California, for instance, could a movie actor become governor and then president? But he never forgot what brought him first to attention and then to office. He never forgot his Hollywood past. He never forgot the power of performance, the power of romance.

The finest moment of this Republican National Convention did not come when Reagan accepted his party's nomination and the bands played and the balloons fell and those weathered and smiling features were lit by a thousand lights.

The finest moment came the night before in a short film about his wife, Nancy. There was a funny little clip of both of them in the movie "Hellcats of the Navy," and then Nancy said some nice things about him and called him "Ronnie."

Then, near the end, with violins playing in the background, the camera moved in tight on the president and he said gently: "I can't imagine life without her."

And then he grew silent and his eyes grew moist.

And it all worked.

Ronald Reagan. The Great Communicator. The Great Romantic. The Great Showman.

Coming soon to a town near you.

August 24, 1984

Hart Gets His New Ax Together

BERLIN, New Hampshire

Gary Hart is changing.

He is changing from his exquisite gray, double-vented suit to his exquisite blue jeans with their knife-edge crease.

He is changing from his pale blue shirt with the white specks and his navy blue tie with the white seagulls to his red and black checkered lumberjack shirt.

He has come to the edge of this north country factory town to participate in a woodsmen's competition. A few score lumberjacks, with their beer-sipping friends looking on from the backs of pickup trucks, have come out to chop logs, throw axes, and saw through trees.

The unseasonably warm air was heavy with the smell of fresh-sawn timber, and the ground had turned to a straw-matted swamp, but Hart slogged cheerily through the mud in his hand-tooled cowboy boots.

When one thinks of Gary Hart, one does not think of a brawny outdoorsman. But that, too, is part of the change.

He is changing his image, trying to prove that he is not one of those candidates who loves The People but hates the people.

So as he went through the crowd, taking a swig from a Miller beer can that somebody thrust at him, he shook hands and stopped and talked and was a regular Joe.

But there was something calculated to it all.

And as one watches the brilliant smile, the carefully tousled hair, the dramatically slashing movements of his hands as he speaks, one feels one is watching a clockwork Kennedy, a stainless-steel version of a presidential candidate.

One feels one is watching a man who has analyzed the mechanics of becoming president, who has staked out his territory, and is now pursuing his goal with relentless precision.

The comparison with Kennedy—any Kennedy—is not something the Hart campaign is embarrassed about. The advance text of a Hart speech to be delivered at a senior citizens' home here contained the line: "The time has come to pass the torch to a new generation."

That line is so close to a famous one from John Kennedy's inaugural address that one has to be either stunned or impressed by Hart's audacity in appropriating it.

Hart does not yet speak like a Kennedy, but he is working on it:

- "Sometimes a country doesn't need to move to the left or the right—it needs to move forward."
- "Your children are being sent to die in Lebanon for no purpose. They are being sent to be bodyguards for Latin American dictators."
- "It is time for our party to do what it did in 1932 with Franklin Roosevelt and in 1960 with John Kennedy and that is to break with the old traditionalists and elect Gary Hart in 1984!"

While Hart is charging hard, things have not yet come together for him. Impressive second-place finishes are no substitute for victory.

And I think that if a Kennedy had dressed up like a lumberjack in preparation for a woodsmen's competition, he would have remembered—unlike Hart this day—to remove his Cartier tank watch first.

But Hart has become the glamour candidate, and the press and crowds are flocking to him.

So he is being very careful to change his image from the icy intellectual to a man who picks up and talks to small children, who goes from shop to shop on Main Street after Main Street and speaks to the common man. He is even managing a small joke or two these days.

Finishing yet another recitation of his stock speech, he stopped among a gaggle of reporters and said wryly: "Can't stand the excitement, can you?"

Yet, beneath the smooth surface there is almost a Great Gatsbylike quirkiness to Hart:

The reason he changed his name from Hartpence to Hart is still a matter of dispute between him and his relatives, and a *Washington Post* reporter discovered that Hart has long fudged his true age by an insignificant year, claiming to have been born in 1937 when in fact he was born in 1936.

Neither of these is anything near scandalous, but Hart can be uneasy when pressed by reporters on these or other subjects.

Here in Berlin, he was asked if he really believed that his emphasis on high tech could actually do something for such a depressed town.

"As I have been patient to explain," snapped Hart, coming down heavily on the word patient, "my program is not exclusively dependent on high tech."

But at the woodsmen's competition, another side, perhaps the true side, of Gary Hart came through.

He picked up a large, double-bitted ax, raised it over his head, and aimed it at a target about 30 feet away.

If this were Gerald Ford making the attempt, the press would have scattered. But if Hart exudes anything, it is confidence and even ax-throwing does not seem beyond him.

The ax whirled end over end and hit one of the wooden legs propping up the target. There were a few laughs and some weak cheers from the crowd. Hart strode quickly over to the target.

"I can do better," he said, pulling the ax free. "One more try."

Again he poised the ax over his head. But this time, he sized up the target carefully and rocked back and forth on his heels before letting go.

And this time it flashed through the air and hit the target solidly, edging into the red center. Not a bull's-eye—but a close second place.

"I'm quitting while I'm ahead," Hart said with a smile.

For now. But he is not the kind to settle for second for long.

February 27, 1984

Jackson Pulling the Hopeful

HAMPTON, New Hampshire

J esse Jackson stands on the steps leading down to the church basement. In front of him are 15 women, arranged in a circle, dressed in leotards and leg warmers and snapping out their arms and legs to the theme from *Flashdance*.

Jackson smiles a dazzling smile. He places his hands on his hips. "This is beautiful," he says. "This is wonderful."

The dancers, without missing a beat, respond with shouts of "Jesse! Jesse!" They begin running in place, twirling their arms and shouting his name.

Would the candidate for president like to change into his jogging suit and join in? the organizer of this "Jump for Jesse" rally asks.

No, the candidate would not. Not while there is still the remotest chance that he might become the leader of the free world. There is such a thing as dignity, you know.

The music pulsates wildly, the bass notes palpable through the worn linoleum. The room is like every church basement you have ever seen: cinder-block walls painted a hopeful yellow, homemade curtains, hand-lettered signs announcing the latest uphill struggle against—take your pick: hunger, poverty, loneliness.

But, tonight, about 75 people have driven through the fog to see a man who says the uphill struggles are the only ones really worth fighting.

The crowd is almost entirely white—there are only a few thousand blacks in the entire state—but that does not disappoint the Jackson campaign people.

Black crowds for Jackson no longer impress the news media. Blacks for Jackson are a "given." But the story of New Hampshire, the reason the four camera crews are with him tonight, is to see Jesse among the white folk.

And if one judges campaigns by the enthusiasm of the crowds and by the energy of the candidate, Jesse Jackson is a smashing success here.

Real politics has a harsher test, however, and that is who gets the most votes come primary day, February 28. By that measure, the Jackson campaign is likely to be considerably less successful.

No matter here tonight. In the basement of the First Congregational Parish Hall, the beat goes on. The music pounds, the torsos twist, chests heave, flesh peeks from beneath pink leotards, and the air fills with the musky scent of healthy sweat and overheated body lotion.

Jackson rocks back on his heels, surveying the scene. Though it is the end of a long campaign day, he is immaculate in a three-piece blue suit, a gold chain stretched across his vest, a shirt of the palest blue, and a striped tie that would feel at home in any corporate board room.

Not since John Kennedy has a presidential candidate managed to make politics seem sexy.

A small white child comes up to Jackson and tugs at his pants leg. He looks down and picks her up. "Gimme a kiss," he says. She giggles. "C'mon," he says, "gimme a kiss." She giggles again, wraps her arms around his neck and kisses him.

Off to one side is Jesse Hoessler, tiny, white-haired, and 77. "He's different," she says. "You listen to him on the TV, and you get a charge. He doesn't seem like a politician. He does and says what he wants. And we need a change, you know?"

Danny Cantor is 28 and working for the Jackson campaign. "We're going to surprise some people here," he says. "It's not just the activists who are coming in. It's working people, seniors, students. I'm not saying we are going to win here, but we are going to be very close to the top. You can feel it; you can feel the energy."

Two dozen senior citizens, part of a dance club, also have come out to see Jackson this night. He moves through them, giving out hugs, posing for Kodak snapshots.

Later, he will say to me in a voice tinged slightly by wonder: "Those old ladies tonight—they trust me, do you know that? That puts an obligation on me. And little children miss school to come hear my speeches. They write me notes. They say: 'I can't vote for you, but I hope you become president.' That's an obligation, a real obligation.

"My supporters see me as a champion who fights against great odds. I will continue to fight those odds. I will continue to fight for them."

Except that they both want to be president, Jesse Jackson and Ronald Reagan may seem to have very little in common. They are, however, the two candidates who speak almost exclusively about American values.

Reagan speaks to Americans who sense their prosperity slipping away, slipping away because of high taxes, big government, welfare cheaters or whatever.

Jesse Jackson speaks to Americans for whom prosperity is still a dream, for whom the pie has yet to be sliced.

"There is room in this nation for everybody," he tells the crowd in the church basement. "Everybody is somebody. American life at its

best is not a building or a budget or a bomb. It is a welcome mat for
the alienated, the hurt, the despised. Open your arms. Make room for
the locked-out and the rejected."

Other candidates have spoken for and to the lower classes, but
Jackson came from that class. "When I speak of reaching out to the
locked-out, it is evident I have gone that way," he says later. "When I
speak of a quest for social justice, it's not a speech I had to memorize.
When I speak of the effort that is required to go up the rough side of
the mountain, it is something I know about."

But you made more than $100,000 last year, I say. You're not poor.

"I have never made money in proportion to my talent or to my
market value," he says. "John Kennedy was a multimillionaire, and he
was seen as a friend to the poor. You know a tree by the fruit it bears,
not by the money it makes.

"And what I do tells the locked-out, which is the majority of
Americans, that if Jackson can do it, you can do it, too."

We are in the back seat of his Secret Service car. Jackson sits stiffly
upright in the darkness as we barrel through the pine forests on a
two-lane blacktop. His features are lit only by the occasional flash of
oncoming headlights.

You kissed Yasser Arafat, I say, and ask him: Why? He shakes his
head. "They keep running that picture," he says.

"The pope met with Arafat, and they don't keep running that
picture. I met with Arafat one time. When you go to Japan, you take
your shoes off before entering the house. In the Mideast, you
embrace and exchange kisses. I embraced Arafat; I wasn't embracing
his politics.

"When I went to see Arafat, I challenged him to fight for a mutual
recognition policy with Israel. But that got lost in all the hype."

Then you're not writing off the Jewish vote in this campaign?

"Not at all," he says. "I am trying to expand my base of dialogue
with Jews. I am meeting with Jewish leaders whenever I can.

"I am fighting to see that no human being is made a pariah. I
support the ERA because women are given less than justice in our
social order. I support the B'nai B'rith Anti-Defamation League
because Jews have been violated. I support the Arab Anti-Discrimina-
tion League for the same reasons, and I support the civil rights
movement for the same reasons. People are responding to that."

How afraid are you of being assassinated, I ask, and I see the Secret
Service agent in the front seat stiffen. Although they will not talk
about it, Jackson drives the Secret Service agents crazy.

He likes to make unplanned marches. He will be making a speech
one minute and the next lead the audience through the streets to a

voter registration office as the agents make a hopeless scurry to check viaducts and alleys and roofs.

"I am aware of the perils and the dangers and the inordinate number of threats against me," Jackson says with an undertone of real anger in his voice. "But I come from a tradition where one is ready to bear the risk of tragedy on the way to triumph. I hope I will see the fruit of my labors. But I may not."

He runs a hand across his face.

"I am pulling a wagon," he says. "That is my focus. I am pulling a wagon full of hopeful people. It is a perilous and dangerous journey, but it is a necessary journey.

"It is a journey I will take as far as I am able to go."

February 20, 1984

◆

Jackson Can Earn Our Forgiveness

MANCHESTER, New Hampshire

Daniel emerged from the lion's den unscathed. I am not sure Jesse Jackson will be so lucky. I am not sure he deserves to be. Jackson was eloquent and passionate when he went to a temple here the other night and talked about his use of the term "Hymie" to refer to Jews and "Hymietown" to refer to New York City.

Although he never said he was sorry, he did say he was wrong.

Although he never said why such language was part of his vocabulary, he did say it was thoughtless.

But Jackson's apology, if that is what it was, raised as many questions as it answered.

"What disturbs me now is that something so small has become so large," Jackson said. "In part I am to blame and for that I am deeply distressed."

But why is an anti-Semitic slur a "small thing" to Jackson? If Walter Mondale or Gary Hart or John Glenn had made a racist remark, would Jackson have considered that small?

"Even as I affirm to you the term was used in a private conversation, the context and spirit of that remark must be appreciated," Jackson said. "In private talks we sometimes let our guard down."

What Jackson means is that he now regrets he let his guard down in front of a black *Washington Post* reporter. Jackson assumed the reporter would protect him and not use the "Hymie" quote. Jackson assumed wrong.

The reporter did what reporters are supposed to do: He printed the truth without fear or favor.

So what Jackson really regrets is that he got caught.

"However innocent and unintended, it [the "Hymie" remark] was insensitive and wrong," Jackson said at the temple. And then for the rest of the speech, Jackson praised himself for having the guts to admit he was wrong.

Throughout his talk, Jackson portrayed himself as the victim. He did this so often and so passionately, in fact, that it was easy to forget it was he who uttered the slur in the first place.

The opening line of his standard speech is always the same: "America is not a blanket of one piece of unbroken cloth, one color, one texture. America is a quilt of many patches, many pieces, many colors, various textures. But everybody fits somewhere."

Is it now fair to ask where Jackson thinks the Jews—or, as he used to say, the Hymies—fit? In Hymietown, I guess.

Did the press unfairly hound Jesse Jackson on this matter, as he now claims?

Jackson did not think the press was unfair when it revealed Earl Butz's racist slur and forced him from the Ford Cabinet.

Nor did Jackson think it was unfair of the press to print James Watt's insulting remarks and force him from the Reagan Cabinet.

Compared to them, Jackson has gotten off easy.

It is hard to imagine any other presidential candidate making the remark that Jackson did, lying about it day after day, and still being politically alive.

Jackson said he was outraged that people were attacking him for what he said.

But as people have a right to support him, they have a right to oppose him. As people have a right to march in his behalf, they have a right to march in opposition to him.

Jews have a right to speak out on this subject. They have a right to respond to slur, to threat, to attack.

Jackson is correct when he says that both Jews and blacks have suffered. And as his people have reached upward seeking freedom and security, so have Jews. They will not be anybody's patsies or whipping boys or scapegoats. Not anymore.

And if a presidential candidate wishes to refer to people with phrases of ugliness, can he then be shocked to get ugliness in return?

But Jackson is right about one important thing. There is the possibility and the need for dialogue between Jackson and Jews.

I do not pretend to know him as well as many, but I think I know him well enough to say he believes more in goodness than in evil, more in love than in hatred, more in peace than in fighting.

That he is imperfect is to say he is human. What Jackson has said cannot be forgotten. It can be forgiven. I choose to do the latter.

But I do so only if Jackson remains true to what he preaches. The pot of gold at the end of his Rainbow Coalition is not Jesse Jackson in the White House. He knows that will not happen.

The pot of gold he seeks is greater harmony and decency and understanding in this country.

If Jackson's campaign is to be filled with insult and hatred, then it will have been for nothing.

But if it is filled with a true reaching out to all Americans—black and white, Christian, Jew, and Moslem—then he may do greater good than whoever does get to the White House.

Love or hate. Harmony or fear. A true victory or a true defeat. The choice is his.

As a man, as a reverend, as a presidential candidate, Jesse Jackson should know the ultimate lesson of both life and politics:

Whatsoever a man soweth, that shall he also reap.

February 28, 1984

◆

Hope Orbits the Glenn Camp

MANCHESTER, New Hampshire

The question for the day, right here between Wong's Egg Rolls and Papa Gino's Pizza in the Mall of New Hampshire, is what did John Glenn do 22 years ago yesterday?

It is not as easy as it seems. Just about everyone knows that he did something. But what precisely he did is a little tougher to come up with. And it shows that Glenn, though a full-fledged presidential candidate, was more famous decades ago than he is now.

"I remember sitting in front of the TV and watching him," Eve Romagnoli of Laconia, New Hampshire, said.

Watching him do what? I asked. Exactly.

"Uh, well, it was something to do with that astronaut business, I know that," she said.

"He went up with them others," her husband, Rudy, said. "I know he didn't go up alone. There were three of them. Or two."

Wrong. Try again.

"The moon?" Rudy said. "He walked on there?"

"Naw, that's not it," said Eve. "I don't remember exactly what it was, but I know I was watching it on the TV."

Right next to the Romagnolis, crushed in the crowd that was waiting for Glenn to arrive, were four heartbreakingly fresh-faced young women dressed in puffy ski jackets, corduroy slacks, and jogging shoes with wild-colored laces.

They are all 17, but they will be 18 by Election Day and they intend to vote. They have seen numerous political commercials on TV, but they want to see the candidates on the hoof before making up their minds.

I asked them the Question.

"Beats me," Kathy Olsen said. "I wasn't even born 22 years ago. Did Glenn do something then?"

"Didn't he go up in a capsule?" Colleen Nealon asked.

"He was an astronaut," Judy Mullins said. "Or something."

"Is it important?" Michelle Rooney asked. "I mean, does it matter?"

That, perhaps, is the real question. John Glenn, the candidate from outer space, has accomplished many things. He was an air ace in the Korean War, a businessman, and is now a U.S. senator.

Yet the most important moment of his life came on February 20, 1962, when he became the first American to orbit the Earth. He went up 162 miles, made three loops of the planet, and came down with a splash.

How much of this will help him become president of the United States is not clear. He seems to be a star without star quality. The often-told joke is that Glenn once gave a fireside chat and the fire went out.

The movie *The Right Stuff* was a bomb at the box office, which is certainly not Glenn's fault, but the producer's explanation for the flop is instructive: "Astronauts seemed dull to people," Alan Ladd, Jr., said.

Even Glenn's friends and political allies concede that he has a wee problem on this point. Sherrod Brown, the young secretary of state from Ohio, came to New Hampshire yesterday to campaign for Glenn.

"I first heard him in 1969 when he spoke at my Eagle Scout award banquet," he said. "He gave us all pictures of him with an American flag in the background and his hand on a globe. I'll never forget that."

But do you remember what he told you at the speech? I asked.

"Well, frankly, no," Brown said. "He is not a speaker who excites you. But he is believable.

"It is like the story of Demosthenes. When others spoke, the audience said 'My, what a wonderful speech.' But when Demosthenes spoke, the audience said, 'Let us march!'

"When John Glenn speaks, nobody says, 'Let's march.' But he is believable as a human being, which is a lot different from the guy now in the White House."

Almost any excuse is used to pump life into the Glenn campaign. Here in Manchester, the Glenn people rented an office on the main street of town and hung a gargantuan American flag, 12 feet by 26 feet, down the front of the building.

When the city's building commissioner said the flag might constitute a sign and might have to come down, the Glenn people went a little batty.

"It's a sign all right," the Glenn press secretary thundered. "It's a sign of America and freedom. We didn't take it down for Ayatollah Khomeini and we're not taking it down for the building inspector!"

The building commissioner didn't know what the Ayatollah Khomeini had to with it, but he knew when he was beat. He said Glenn could keep the flag as long as it "didn't flap around too much."

Glenn came to the state yesterday so he could use the East Coast media to explain his finish in the Iowa Caucus. "New Hampshire is much more important than Iowa," he said. "Iowa was a caucus and New Hampshire is a primary. A caucus doesn't use the secret ballot and a primary does. In New Hampshire, people will be able to vote their consciences. People will be able to vote for me."

Glenn insists he is not discouraged. Not by the polls and not by a nagging cold that, like Walter Mondale, just won't go away.

"I feel better," he said, thrusting a hand into his trenchcoat pocket and coming out with a bunch of throat lozenges. "Here. You want a Sucrets? I'm not really sick, I just sound raw. But I'm not cutting back on the campaign schedule. I'm increasing it."

I asked him how he felt about the anniversary of his space flight. He looked at his watch and then said a little wistfully, "I was just going into my second orbit about now."

In space, all he risked was a fiery death. In New Hampshire, he faces something that for a politician is far worse: defeat.

So out at the Mall of New Hampshire, he worked the crowds hard and managed to shake the hands of not only the four 17-year-olds, but also of the Romagnolis.

"He's got a nice handshake," Eve said, "but that's not enough reason to vote for him. In New Hampshire, everybody who wants to be president shakes your hand."

The girls were considerably more impressed. In addition to the handshakes, they got autographs. Afterward they held a brief caucus and appointed Kathy Olsen their spokesperson.

"We decided. We're going to vote for Glenn," she said. "Or maybe Reagan."

February 21, 1984

◆

New Hampshire: Where Hopes Go Askew

NASHUA, New Hampshire

New Hampshire is a cruel place. It breaks the hearts of men upon its rocky soil.

The losers know that now.

Reubin Askew stood in the freezing rain, the pebble-sized sleet bouncing off his bare head.

There were no voters in sight at the Fairground Junior High polling place. There was only a low and dirty sky, four reporters, six Secret Service men, and the candidate.

"Any live ones?" Askew asked, looking around and stamping his unbooted feet up and down in the slush.

His aides did not know what to say. There were no live ones, no voters. But if there had been, how much difference would it have made?

After 350,000 miles of travel over two years, after hundreds of thousands of dollars spent, after endless cups of coffee and uncountable speeches, the truth had set in:

The candidate would not win. The candidate would not do well. The candidate would suffer a defeat of such magnitude that humiliating barely describes it. The candidate would come in last.

A young woman with a Gary Hart sign walked away from the side of the gym where she had been huddled and approached Askew.

"Senator," she said, although Askew is one of the two Democratic candidates who has never been one, "you're a great man."

A smile lit Askew's ruddy features. "I wish you could vote twice," he said. "I wish you could vote for both Gary and me."

She smiled back and shrugged her shoulders and walked back to the protection of the wall.

The sleet continued to bounce crazily from Askew's head and shoulders. Finally he turned to an aide and said: "Well, I think I can say I've been here now."

Reubin Askew, former governor of Florida, can say he has been here. He has been here longer than any other candidate, in fact, a total of 73 days dating back to April of 1982.

But it did not matter. Reubin Askew still came in last.

They say you can tell them even before the votes are counted. The phones in their headquarters are answered too quickly and the voices there are too eager.

They look too longingly down the snowy roads for the TV trucks that do not come.

They read the polls and they say they do not care.

They walk and they talk but they have gone dead behind the eyes.

As Askew stood in the filthy weather this primary day searching fruitlessly for a hand to shake, one wondered why he bothered.

But, in a sense, he had no choice. If politicians believe in anything, more than in God or country or apple pie, they believe in themselves.

Rejection, therefore, is especially hard to take. And the reason they give for the rejection is always the same: The voters do not truly know them.

It is never the candidate who is being rejected, never the policies and the platforms. It is never that the voters know them too well, only that the voters don't know them well enough.

"With good media, we could have made it, but we just didn't have the money," Askew said. "We had that personal contact, but you have to follow that up with media. With the media, we could have held on to them.

"It's like boxing: We gave them the left hook, but we could not follow up with the right cross."

Even without that, the voters are knocked out in this state. By now, they are sick of the whole thing and even though the candidates and media spend millions here, the citizens will be glad to see them gone.

Why didn't you catch on here? a reporter asked Askew.

"It's not a matter of not catching on," he said. "It's a matter of not getting my message across.

"Oh, I suppose I could have done things differently. I could have said one thing to one group and another to another. I could have tried to grab headlines.

"But I don't want to be president unless I can get there in such a way as I still know who I am."

He does not have to worry about that now. He is in no danger of being president.

Askew spent his campaign looking for what he called the forgotten majority of his party, a majority that was opposed to abortion, automatic cost-of-living increases for Social Security, and closed-shop labor unions.

"I called it the sensible center," he said with a smile. "But I found the center not only didn't hold, it didn't exist."

You are relatively young, only 55, I said. Will you run for president in 1988?

Askew looked down at his shoe tops and did not look up when he answered.

"I have very serious doubts," he said, "that I will ever do this again."

Perhaps we should not feel sorry for them, these losers. They are still powerful people who live comfortable lives.

But they do feel pain.

And New Hampshire is where they feel it.

February 29, 1984

◆

Mondale Campaign Starts to Unravel

MIAMI

The sun had burned away the morning mist over Lake Jackson outside Tallahassee and the morning birds had begun to twitter. Walter Mondale walked down the sandy beach up to the very edge of the lake.

The cameras whirred, the microphones readied, the pencils poised.

"You need water to live," he said.

Later he grew even more profound.

Seizing upon an innocent fisherman, Mondale asked him what bait he was using.

"Well, we been using some surface lures," Tom Myers said. "But we're thinking of switching to plastic worms."

Mondale, as he does when he starts talking "down home," began dropping his g's.

"Been doin' some fishin', have you?" he said. "Well, funny thing about fishin'. You try a yellow lure and then nothin'. Then you try a green lure and, wham!, they start bitin'.'"

If politics were fishing, one would be forced to advise Walter Mondale to switch to his green lure.

The first definite sign, we later decided, was when the socks didn't come back.

Or, to put it more precisely, when the socks didn't come back from the hotel laundry to their original owners.

To be sure, Walter Mondale was not to blame. A man running for president of the United States has better things to worry about than whether the reporters covering him have their proper socks.

But it was seen as a clear sign. The cool efficiency of the Mondale campaign had been legendary.

The Mondale staff is one of the few to recognize the press has a need for clean laundry.

So when, in Atlanta, the laundry was returned to the wrong people, and when the *Washington Post* correspondent, a poised and professional man, was forced to stand up on the campaign bus and complain that he had received someone else's socks, the antennae of the press quivered.

It was, some said, the first sign of disarray. More signs followed.

The campaign schedule, usually distributed well in advance, was suddenly impossible to obtain. Dates, places, and times became "fluid," which is to say the campaign did not know where it was going from one day to the next.

The faces of the staff turned gloomy. Rumors circulated: Mondale had written off Massachusetts, was very worried about Florida, was praying for Alabama, and hoping for Georgia.

The Mondale campaign chairman, Jim Johnson, gave a rare on-the-record briefing to the press.

Based on what was knowable and predictable, he said, Mondale was in great shape. But nothing was knowable or predictable. Any questions?

What do the numbers show? a reporter asked.

The numbers? Johnson said. We've got any numbers you want. They'll show whatever you want. Next question?

There was a slight buzz from the press corps. What was happening here? Where was the well-oiled, smoothly running political machine?

"Whether we can fully recover, I suspect we won't," Johnson said. "But if we can really get people to focus on who they actually want to be president, we will do very well."

Well, can you at least say why Gary Hart has been beating you? Johnson was asked.

He shrugged. "Hart seems attractive," he said. "He seems to have no negatives." Another shrug. "But his support is soft. His voters have no reason for voting for him."

That clear now?

Well, if it is, then try explaining why the press bus disappeared.

At the Lakeland, Florida, airport, there was no bus for the press.

We knew that because the person who always stands and says, "This way to the bus" even if the bus is only 10 yards away on an empty tarmac, was not there.

We had grown to love and respect these bus-pointers for their single-minded dedication, and now, we missed both them and the bus.

Mondale had his car and the Secret Service had their cars, but what of us, the recorders of history?

"Uh, well," a Mondale aide said, "I guess you'll have to take taxis."

Surprising as it may seem, there is not usually an excess of taxis at the Lakeland, Florida, airport, but three were found and the press was stuffed inside them for the 10-mile trip to Plant City, site of the Strawberry Festival.

By the time we arrived, our meter read $15.75. A *Newsday* reporter dropped a twenty on the driver and said, "Keep it."

The Mondale campaign may be in disarray, but the press is still on expense accounts.

At the Strawberry Festival, where wandering fairgoers kicked up clouds of hot dust, Mondale was greeted by the 1984 Tampa Bay Honey Queen, who gave him a "Honey, I Love You" button.

Mondale smiled but his biggest grin came in the cattle shed, where he spent a good amount of time patting a steer named Samson.

Mondale was asked why this particular hunk of beef was so special to him.

Mondale gave a knowing look.

"If you remember," he said, "Samson made a very big comeback."

March 9, 1984

McGovern Bows Out of the Race Memorably

H e wanted to be president; make no mistake about that. But he
wanted something else even more.

It was hopeless, some might even say foolish, for George McGovern to run for president this year.

Where this kind of urge starts, we do not know. Perhaps in the cradle. Perhaps later on.

Maybe for McGovern it started out of guilt.

In 1964, he and 87 other senators voted for the Gulf of Tonkin resolution and gave Lyndon Johnson a free hand to escalate the war in Vietnam.

McGovern never forgot that vote. And he never forgave himself for it.

In 1970, when he took the Senate floor in support of an amendment he had cosponsored to withdraw all U.S. troops from that war, he tried to make amends.

He gave an extraordinary speech that day. There, in the austere elegance of that chamber, he said the room "reeks of blood."

"Every senator in this chamber is partly responsible for the sending of 50,000 young Americans to an early grave," he said. "Every senator here is partly responsible for that human wreckage at Walter Reed and Bethesda Naval hospitals and all across the land—young men without legs, or arms, or genitals, or faces, or hopes."

His amendment failed 55–39.

Judging strictly by the numbers, it was a defeat. But McGovern and others always considered it a victory, a significant day when more than a third of the U.S. Senate voted to end the war.

Judging strictly by the numbers, McGovern has been defeated once again this year. He has withdrawn from the presidential race.

But once again, there are those who consider it a victory.

In the beginning, it was almost pathetic. His entourage was not merely small, it did not exist. The McGovern "campaign" was George McGovern and his suit bag.

He went from stop to stop, raising his issues. And he began to be heard by greater numbers.

He wanted more. Yes, he wanted to raise issues. Yes, he wanted to be the conscience of his party. Yes, in his heart of hearts, he wanted to be president.

But he wanted even more. He wanted to redeem himself.

He wanted to redeem himself for the crushing defeat he suffered at the hands of Richard Nixon in 1972—a defeat, it should be noted, in which 29 million Americans voted for him.

He wanted to be what Barry Goldwater is to the Republicans: a senior statesman who has suffered a great defeat but who is still treated with respect.

In the final analysis, what George McGovern wanted most was not to be forgotten.

They had not invited him to speak at the 1976 Democratic National Convention, nor at the one in 1980. His picture did not hang from the rafters when his party gathered.

It hurt. "You're on center stage for months," he once said of the presidential race. "Walter Cronkite and others talk about you daily. Of course, it's fun. You're the subject of conversations in every bar and beauty shop. You live on adrenalin for a year."

But when it is over, the cameras disappear and the people stop talking and it can be a painful thing for these men, these ambitious men, to bear.

So he ran not just for the issues, but because he had the hunger in his belly, the burning hunger that politicians have for the roar of the crowd.

"My friends say I'm the most soft-spoken egomaniac they know," he said.

Years ago, he told a little anecdote, a quiet anecdote, an anecdote that explained his entire race this year.

It involved another loser, Hubert Humphrey. Humphrey and McGovern had met in Humphrey's office in 1975 to go down the list of the Democratic candidates for the following year's election.

Neither was entirely pleased with the list and McGovern hit upon an idea. Let's run together, he said. Humphrey for president, McGovern for vice president. How about that?

Humphrey did not answer. The sun had begun to set and it grew dark inside the office. McGovern sat and waited for a reply and thought it odd that Humphrey made no move to turn on the lights.

Finally, McGovern drew closer and saw that Humphrey was sitting in his chair and weeping.

He was weeping because somebody had asked him to run again. Somebody had asked him to carry his party's banner. Somebody had remembered who he once was.

George McGovern ran this year. He lost again. He will not be president. Not now, not ever.

But history will record, however briefly, that tens of thousands of people went into polling booths and marked their ballots for him.

"If at the end of this," he said early on in this race, "the people say, 'Well, George made a lot of sense,' that's all I want."

Let the record show that, finally, George McGovern got what he wanted.

March 15, 1984

◆

Hart TV Ads Measure California's Pulse

LOS ANGELES

It was the hottest screening in town.

We all leaned forward in our seats as the television monitor flickered and sprang to life.

A man was walking along a beach. He was a handsome man, neither young nor old.

As he walked, the wind tousled his longish hair in an appealing way.

The man stopped and looked at the ocean. He watched as waves washed over giant rocks and threw up curtains of spray and foam.

The man bent down, picked up a rock, and tossed it into the waves. He looked out to sea in what seemed like a very private moment.

And then, as the camera pulled back, we could see for the briefest of moments that the man was standing in the surf with water up to his boot tops.

Normally, you would wonder why a grown man would get soaking wet in this fashion. But in this case, there was no need to wonder.

The man was running for president.

And that explains everything.

The room was silent as television monitors went blank. There was no applause.

A reporter lifted his hand. "Again?" he asked. "May we see it again?"

The screening had no official title, but it could have been called "Gary Hart and the Temple of Doom."

What was being screened for reporters were three new Hart TV commercials, the last commercials of this primary season and Hart's last chance to become his party's nominee.

California should be Hart's state, but the latest polls show that it just as easily could be Walter Mondale's.

The Hart brain trust is baffled. The liberal vote, the youth vote, the anti-whatever-the-other-guy-is-for vote are all here in California and that vote should go to Hart.

But there is something else here for Hart: the sneaking suspicion, the creeping fear that this is the end of the line.

There is the feeling that for Hart the game has been played and played out.

The charm, the grin, the Kennedy comparisons worked for him in the early days, but Californians get that as a steady diet from all their politicians.

So to make sure that the dream does not die here, Hart is turning to what politicians always turn to—television.

He has spent the last money he has—about $400,000—on buying time for three new TV commercials that are billed as being "uniquely Californian."

The three 30-second spots don't say anything, but they don't say it magnificently.

Called "Heartbeat," "Natural Beauty," and "Brilliant," the three all have the sound of a beating human heart as their theme.

The heart beats continuously in the background with an ominous lub-dub sound.

Hart at the ocean, Hart at a rally, Hart shaking hands, Hart playing with children—it doesn't matter. The heartbeat just keeps lub-dub-bing away.

In "Natural Beauty," Hart walks alongside—and in—the Pacific Ocean in his lumberjack shirt and jeans and then shows up at a rally in San Francisco where he says:

"Well, one thing's for sure! The old ways won't work. We need new directions. New visions. New ideas are the heartbeat of this country's future!"

In "Heartbeat," Hart shakes hands in a crowd and pats a little blond-haired girl on the cheek.

"Stand with us or not," Hart tells the crowd. "But choose! Your voice and your vote are the heartbeat of this nation's future."

After seeing the first two commercials, the brighter members of the press corps figured out that heartbeats were somehow the theme of the California campaign. But what did it mean? Except for the obvious play on Hart's last name, did it mean anything at all?

Fortunately, an expert was on hand to tell us.

Bill Zimmerman, a California campaign adviser, knew exactly what all those beating hearts meant.

"They mean energy," Zimmerman said, adjusting his aviator glasses. "It is a unifying theme. It builds excitement."

The third commercial was easy to figure out.

It shows a black-and-white photograph of Mondale and Hart shaking hands, though neither is looking the other in the eye. In fact, it looks as if both men are wondering whether to check and see if their wallets are still there.

The recorded voice of Walter Mondale is heard saying: "Gary Hart is one of the most decent and compassionate public servants I have ever known in my life. He is brilliant."

Then the announcer's voice says: "But now that they are opponents, Mondale, the politician, is attacking Gary Hart. Bitterly. Recklessly."

In fact, Mondale made his statements about Hart's brilliance in November, 1979, while campaigning for Hart's re-election to the Senate.

Now, Hart is using that against Mondale. In politics, this is known as gratitude.

Zimmerman saw it differently. "We hope to show Mondale's hypocrisy with this commercial," he said.

Because the commercials seemed to be very heavy on symbolism, somebody asked half-jokingly what it meant when Hart threw that rock into the ocean.

Zimmerman paused, as if considering the environmental impact of Hart's act. He considered what it might mean to Californians to have a rock removed from its natural habitat and drowned, just for a TV commercial.

Then he responded brilliantly.

"It was," he said, "an artificial rock."

May 30, 1984

Simon Says It Again

I haven't changed my vacuum cleaner bag in five years and now I'm afraid to.

◆

People who keep a pencil behind their ear don't look nearly as hard-working as they think.

◆

TV timeouts are ruining college football.

◆

Whatever happened to grocery store baggers who knew how to keep the pickles from crushing the bread?

◆

Why is it every time a train derails, it seems to be loaded with toxic chemicals? Don't trains loaded with oranges or cotton balls ever derail?

◆

There is nothing more humiliating than having the change machine reject your dollar bill.

◆

Do those buttons you push to change the traffic lights really do anything?

◆

As if abandoned babies don't have enough troubles, why do nurses always give them such awful names?

There is something about headbands on women that drives me wild.

◆

You know you're hooked when you'll watch the delayed-action telecast of a game to which you already know the outcome.

◆

How come only mothers know how to get stains out?

◆

There are basically two types of people in this world: those who twirl their pasta and those who cut it.

◆

Does anyone ever wear both sides of things that are reversible?

◆

People who use chopsticks are just showing off.

◆

I love car washes where you get to stay in the car.

◆

I panic every time someone asks me for directions, even though I know the way.

◆

I know what mince pie is, but I have no idea what a mince is.

Just once I'd like to see a woman on "Family Feud" refuse to kiss Richard Dawson.

◆

How come shoelaces break only when you're late for work?

◆

If a paralegal is almost a lawyer, what does that make a parakeet?

◆

The quickest way to lose your appetite for junk food is to find out the ingredients.

◆

People who creep up on the shoulder when the expressway is jammed and then merge in at the last moment are the second worst people I know.

◆

The people who let them in are the worst people I know.

◆

There's nothing wrong with the Moral Majority that a punch in the nose wouldn't cure.

◆

I never know what to do with that extra hour we get when we turn back the clocks.

◆

What do people mean when they say to a waiter: "I'll try the soup?" What are they going to do after they "try" it, give it back?

Long distance is *not* the next best thing to being there. Writing a letter is.

◆

I'm always suspicious of people who use a Rolodex.

◆

People remember movies that make them cry a lot longer than movies that make them laugh.

◆

How come the windshield wipers always work better on the passenger side?

◆

People who refuse to move to the back of a crowded bus should take cabs.

◆

I may be the only person alive who went to Hawaii and didn't see Don Ho.

◆

Both Jim Jones and Charles Manson were born in Indiana. Could it be something in the water?

◆

The next census will show that there are seven blow-dryers for every man, woman, and child in Southern California.

◆

People who press the elevator button more than once should seek professional help.

I don't believe they ever change the earplugs on airline headsets.

◆

If California wines get any more expensive, they might as well be French.

◆

Baskin-Robbins will never make a better flavor than chocolate mint.

◆

Can't we just pay somebody to end inflation?

◆

How did the Pilgrims get along without electric carving knives?

◆

I have never seen a judge use a gavel.

◆

People who order chili in strange restaurants have a great deal of courage.

◆

No one under 25 remembers what a pinwheel is. Give a kid a pinwheel today and he'll ask you where the battery goes.

◆

The only reason to bring kids to Las Vegas is to bet them.

◆

Do kids still go out for a Coke and french fries after last period?

When is the last time you treated yourself to the "Magic Fingers" in your motel bed?

◆

Anytime someone starts a sentence with "To be perfectly honest," it's time to start counting the silver.

◆

Don't you just love tearing the old month off the calendar? And feel guilty when you just can't wait any longer and do it two days early?

◆

I have never checked my antifreeze and I don't care who knows it.

◆

I am proud of the fact I have never worn anything with an alligator on it.

◆

If you like "Doonesbury," you would have loved "Pogo."

◆

Rocking chairs take more energy than they're worth.

◆

People whose checks have flowers, birds, or mountain lions printed on them should seek professional help.

◆

Anything advertised as a collector's item probably won't be.

It is a scientific fact that two coat hangers left alone in a dark closet will multiply to more than 400 in a single year.

How come a cigar smells good only to the person smoking it?

People who stop to chat at the top of escalators should be beaten with sticks.

It is truly said, a recession is when your friend is out of work; a depression is when you're out of work.

You know you're in a classy hotel when they turn down the bed.

People who wear sweaters draped over their shoulders and knotted around their necks should be deported to Club Med.

♦

Never eat anything that looks back at you from the plate.

♦

There is no excuse for an adult to chew gum.

♦

The greatest service Queen Elizabeth II performs is making everyone else feel a lot better dressed.

Never marry a man who owns his own tuxedo. He is either a gigolo or a band leader.

How come drive-ins don't have more matinees?

Making really good paper airplanes is a lost art.

Never eat in a restaurant where the waiters sing "Happy Birthday."

The only place you should wear a cowboy hat is on horseback.

How come left-handed people always say to other left-handed people, "Hey, you're left-handed!"

People who sneak across the hall every morning to steal their neighbor's newspaper are pathetic.

How come there are so few doubleheaders these days? Were the fans getting too much for their money?

People who prefer air conditioning to a nice breeze should reexamine their lives.

An All-American Life and Death

This is the story of the short life and sudden death of an all-American boy.

It begins in the small, one-high-school town of Clermont, Florida, and ends where a lot of stories end, Hollywood.

It is the story of David Bell, the cocaptain of his high school football team, the boy voted Most Talented, the young man who landed a part on "Quincy," who did a Kraft cheese commercial, who met Robert Redford, and who died a bizarre, horrid, totally American death.

It is not the story of a starry-eyed kid who went to the big city and got mixed up with evil people. It is the story of a handsome, sensitive, bright young man who knew what he wanted and was determined to achieve it.

It is also the story of the 70-year-old woman who shot him to death because she no longer understood what her neighborhood, her city and her country had become.

David Scott Bell was shot to death on the morning of December 27, 1980, in a dispute over a parking space. Death was caused by a .38-caliber bullet passing through the right lens of his glasses and crashing into his skull.

He died instantly. According to police, he was the 1,037th person killed in Los Angeles that year.

He was 6 feet 2 inches tall, weighed 185 pounds, had blue eyes and brown hair.

The day after he died, a casting agent for ABC called his mother and wept on the telephone. "That kid was going places," the agent sobbed. "He was up for two TV pilots! Two!"

He was 22 years, 6 months, and 3 days old. It was the first Christmas season he had ever spent away from home.

On Christmas Day, he called his mother. "Mama," he asked, "have I ever told you how much I love you?"

As a matter of fact, he had. "For a macho-looking kid, he was very affectionate," his mother said. "He was never embarrassed to put his arm around you and tell you that he loved you."

He told his mother he would be home in a few days. In Clermont, his family left the tree up so he could see it.

Clermont, Florida, is, in the words of David Bell, "the quintessential small American town." Now about 5,000 in population, it was nearer to half that when David was growing up in his modest tract home.

Orlando and Disney World are about 30 minutes away, but there is very little that is flashy about Clermont. It is citrus country and residents like to tell you that 17 million fruit trees surround the town.

Life tends to revolve around the churches, the Little League, the Clermont High Highlanders, and Lake Minneola. David swam it when he was 10.

There is a typical main street and a typical shopping center with a K Mart. A McDonald's came to town about three years ago.

There are no movie theaters. There is a single drive-in.

At Clermont High, David was a star athlete in a town where athletics count for a lot. He lettered in football—playing both offense and defense—baseball, track, and basketball, where he had a good outside shot.

He was president of the National Honor Society. He won the Talent Show award for a comedy routine. "When you can make your own mother laugh," his mother, Toni, said, "you are funny."

Toni Bell, 41, is a teacher at Clermont High. She is an uncommonly intelligent, self-possessed woman.

"David was not just a jock," she said. "Not just another pretty face. He knew about art. Philosophy. Literature. Sociology. I used to direct the high school plays and David would come to rehearsals when he was a little boy. One of his favorites was 'The Lottery,' based on the Shirley Jackson short story."

It seems a strange favorite for a little boy. A dark, eerie story, it is set in some future America where, every year, one member of the community is stoned to death by the others.

There is a physical, brooding quality to it, a theme that would appear again in David's life.

When he was 10, a neighbor boy was struck and killed by lightning on Daytona Beach while trying to herd younger boys to safety. A few years later, the dead boy's brother collapsed and died for no apparent reason during football practice.

Both deaths profoundly affected David. "He was not morbid, but the deaths traumatized him," his mother said. "He thought a lot about death. For a while he went around cursing God. At the first funeral, the body of the boy was on display in an open casket.

"I remember him coming to me and saying, 'Mama, don't ever do that when I die. I couldn't do that to my friends.' "

A dozen years later, his wish would be honored.

He was a methodical young man. He sent away for 50 college catalogs and studied them all. He wanted to major in journalism and finally chose Northwestern because he could begin his major as a freshman.

"As it turned out, though, he was more interested in the theater than in journalism," one of his roommates, Brad Hall, said. "He was in a number of plays during college. I remember 'Of Mice and Men' and 'Catch-22.'

"He was an incredibly charming, hilarious guy. A wonderful wit; a good musician. He did a few TV commercials while he was in college and some print ads."

He was a walk-on player for the Northwestern football team in his sophomore year and although he was issued a jersey, he was not listed on the team roster and probably never played in a conference game.

"That kind of thing was ending for him," another roommate, Rob Mendel, said. "He still jogged four miles a day and all. But his jock period was coming to a close."

He took private lessons in Evanston from Barbara Harris, the actress, and there met his hero, Robert De Niro, then known for his explosive, violent roles in "Taxi Driver" and "Raging Bull."

"He called me up to tell me he had met him," his mother said. "He called a lot. We had terrific phone bills. We would talk for two or three hours. The thing that impressed him about meeting De Niro was not that he was a star."

"Here's a man who studies his craft, who cares about it," David told his mother. "Money is not the most important thing to him. Acting is. That's what I want to study. That's what I have to learn."

At home on vacation, he took voice lessons and ballet. "After ballet class, he told me he hurt in places he never knew he had," Toni said. "He said it was tougher than football."

All his friends mention that he came extremely close to being cast in the role of Buck, the dead son, in *Ordinary People*. He met Robert Redford, the director, and Redford was encouraging. At the last minute, though, David was turned down.

His mother felt terrible for him.

"Don't," he told her. "You have to learn how to handle rejection in this business."

He was strangely shy, even awkward at parties. People tended to remember his smile. "His eyes would light up when he smiled," a friend said, "and this enormous dimple would form in his left cheek. He was some good looking kid."

In September of his senior year, he went to a two-person play and saw a pretty, blue-eyed, brown-haired young actress named Laura Innes.

After the play, he walked up to her and stuck out his hand.

"You're wonderful," he said. "I just love what you did."

And then he walked away.

"In the next week, I heard from friends that David really wanted to take me out," Laura said. "I said that would be fine. A lot of women used to moon after him, but he wasn't affected by that."

David Bell kept a journal, and during this period he wrote nearly daily about Laura.

"Mama, I want to marry her," he finally told Toni.

"That's the only girl he ever said that about," Toni said. "She would have fit into our family beautifully."

But Laura was a stage actress, soon to appear at the Goodman Theater in Chicago, and her rainbow was leading her to New York. David wanted to go into film. And Hollywood is where you go if you want that.

They both decided that a little separation might even do them some good. They would pursue their separate careers for a while. "We talked about marriage and a family," Laura said. "After David had a few screen credits he was going to join me in New York and seriously study acting."

But Hollywood came first.

"I wasn't worried that he was going off there," his mother said. "After all, he had been living near Chicago and he survived that. Besides, he was a big kid. Strong. I didn't worry about him that way."

After graduating in the summer of 1980, he went home before setting out for the coast. His parents gave him the perfect gift for life in Los Angeles, a car.

Even though his father, Richard Bell, was the president of the family business and well off, David had not been spoiled. The 1980, red-brown Toyota Tercel was the first car he ever owned.

He was very proud of it. As it turned out, he would die for it.

On the evening of December 27, Detective Jerry Blair knocked on the door of the Bell home. The Christmas wreath was still in place for David to see.

"I had taught Jerry Blair in high school," Toni said. "He was one of my pets. He had played Big Julie in 'Guys and Dolls.' "

"Hey, come on in, Jerry," Toni said. "What brings you here?"

"I have some bad news about David," Blair said, looking down at his shoetops. "You'd better sit down."

Toni Bell remembers that she did.

January 6, 1981

A Gun Speaks—
The American Way

They say his dreams ended in Hollywood, but that is not true. David Bell, a bright, athletic, all-American boy, was not a dreamer.

He planned. He had goals: to go to Los Angeles, to study acting, to get screen credits, to move to New York with his girlfriend, to marry, to perfect his skills, to treat his craft with honor and respect.

The apartment he found was perfect. Large, sunny, paneled in pine, it looked more like a fishing cabin than a bachelor flat. And it was in North Hollywood, close to the TV and movie studios.

Bell had been looking for it since August and now, a few months later, he and his roommate, Rob Mendel, moved in. At $350 a month, the two-bedroom place was a steal.

Things were going well for David. He already had an agent and was a member of both the Screen Actors Guild and the television actors union. His first real audition landed him a part on "Quincy."

His looks helped, of course. He was tall and blue-eyed, with an outdoors handsomeness. His athletic build didn't come from a Hollywood gym, but from years as a high school and college athlete.

He was used to success, but not smug about it. He realized his role in "Quincy" was tiny. But still, it was the big time.

He played a jock, a track star. His part consisted of two lines: "Coach, I . . ." and "But I . . ." He was paid $500.

Back home those two lines made front page news. The *South Lake Press* carried the headline: "David Bell Makes Acting Debut."

The show aired December 3, 1980. Precisely 24 days later, David Bell was shot to death by a 70-year-old woman who thought he had parked too near her driveway.

"I'll never forget flying out there and walking into the L.A. morgue to claim David's body," his mother, Toni, said. "I thought: 'Hey, I saw this place on 'Quincy.' "

The woman who shot him, Kay Marion Beach, lived just a car trip away from his apartment, but then everything in L.A. seems just a car trip away. Her home was in Hollywood, but not the Hollywood of movie studios and gold stars in the sidewalk.

Twenty-five years ago, when she and her husband first moved into the large, two-bedroom home, it was a predominantly white, well-off community, the kind they call "comfortable."

"It was a real nice neighborhood here once," one of her neighbors told a reporter after the shooting. "Everybody had roses and rose gardens and everything. Everybody knew everybody. But in the last 10 years, it's gotten really crappy."

Some homicide detectives in the Hollywood Division of the Los Angeles Police Department couldn't agree more. "If it's Hollywood," one detective said, "it's the pits."

The neighborhood started to decline about the same time Beach's husband died. During the next 10 years, she stayed in her neighborhood, and put a 7-foot chain link fence around the house and the postage-stamp front lawn.

Like other elderly people in the neighborhood, she felt she had become the target of kids and street gangs.

On July 10, 1980, Edward De Leon, 18, told police he was riding his bike in front of Kay Beach's home at about 10 P.M. when he stopped to ask her the time.

De Leon said she yelled, "Get out of here before I kill you!"

According to police, she then shot at him with a pistol.

Minutes after the gunshots had faded away, the L.A. Special Weapons and Tactical unit—the SWAT team of television fame—descended on Beach's house wearing black flak-jackets and carrying high-powered, telescopic rifles.

Beach was arrested and charged with assault with a deadly weapon. But perhaps because the witness was not considered good, or perhaps because Beach was 70, or perhaps because nobody much cared, the district attorney's office decided not to prosecute.

So Kay Beach marched down to the police station and demanded her gun back. The police gave it to her. They had no choice.

"It all comes down to one thing," Hollywood Division officer Robert Thomas said. "The last time, the DA and the courts dropped the ball. Now, someone's dead."

That someone is David Bell, shot down because he didn't want to be late for his last day of work.

Like a lot of actors, Bell worked at a restaurant to help pay rent. He was a "host and expediter" at Hampton's, a gourmet hamburger restaurant in Hollywood.

His roommate, Rob, worked there with him. "We were one step below the waiters," he said. "Our job was to tell people their burger was ready at the salad bar and then help them fit the salad on their plates." They made $4 an hour.

Although he liked the people he worked with, David was growing irritated at the near mindlessness of the job. Normally cheerful, his mood had darkened at the shooting of John Lennon.

The night he heard the news, he sat down at his desk and wrote out nearly a dozen poems. All of them had to do with loss or death. That night, he also wrote in the journal he kept in a cheap, white spiral notebook. Most of the journal was filled with thoughts of the girl he loved back in Chicago, Laura Innes.

That night he wrote: "John Lennon was shot by some maniac with a gun. Where are we all headed?"

It would be the last entry he would make.

But soon his spirits lifted. After Christmas he was going to Chicago to be with Laura, a 23-year-old actress. They were serious, had talked of marriage, and their relationship was sound even though it was separated by 2,000 miles.

After seeing her, David was going to go to Clermont, Florida, where his parents lived. He was going to bring back the news that he was up for two TV pilots. He had given notice at work. His last day was to be Saturday, December 27.

"He was running a little late," Rob Mendel said, "and he liked to be on time. He was up, though, happy. What can I say? He was a happy guy."

Few of us get to choose carefully our last words to our friends.

"See ya later," Rob shouted out to David as he left the house.

"Right," David said.

Had he known, David Bell, an actor, certainly would have picked a better exit line.

It was about 10:20 A.M. on a sunny, blue-skied day, when David drove his Toyota past the restaurant. As usual, there was no place to park. Employees were not allowed to use the restaurant parking lot. It was something they used to grumble about.

So he searched through the neighborhood and a few blocks away, he saw a space on the 1400 block of North McCadden Place, in front of the home of Kay Beach.

He noticed the large, hand-painted sign that said "No-No Parking" that Beach had posted in front of her driveway. He edged his car as far forward as possible so that no more than two or three feet stuck out into the drive.

The police would later say that David had parked legally, that he did not obstruct the drive. Besides, they said, Kay Beach didn't even own a car. She wasn't using her driveway.

There were people on the street that day, and witnesses told police this story:

As Bell got out of his car, Beach yelled at him from the house to move it. Her neighbors were used to her yells.

"Most of us stayed away from her," one told a reporter. "She was always mad at people, making threats to shoot them."

David was a big guy, but did not look threatening. He had an all-American, boyish look. He was dressed casually, but neatly, that morning in a button-down shirt, jeans, and sneakers. He was still wearing the glasses he used for driving.

"I'll only be 10 minutes," he shouted back to Beach.

Then he sprinted to the restaurant and punched the time clock. He made it on time. "I'll be right back," he told the people there. "I've got to move my car."

Many people, most people perhaps, would not have bothered to go back. After all, he was parked legally on a public street.

"But David was raised to be polite to elderly people," Toni Bell, his mother, said. "In Clermont, that's how you behave to old ladies."

But in Clermont, few old ladies pack .38-caliber revolvers.

When David got back to his car he was stunned and angry. The driver's side of his windshield was smeared with a soupy mixture of dog excrement and water. It was so thick that it was impossible to see out of the car to drive it away.

Neighbors told police that Kay Beach had done it.

David Bell walked across the sidewalk and up to the chain link fence. He grabbed it and was over in one smooth motion. The police don't believe he had anything violent in mind.

"Just like anyone would be, he was mad, " Officer Robert Thomas said. "He started banging on her door. He was gonna ask what her problem was."

There was no reply to David's knocks and he soon gave up. He walked over to where a garden hose lay and turned on the water. He was heading to where he could spray the windshield of his car when Kay Beach came out the door.

According to police, Beach would later say that when David turned around, he had the garden hose in his hand and she was in fear of her life.

Had Kay Beach gone after David Bell with a knife, a club, or even a hatchet, he could have either fended off the blows or run away. At most he would have been injured.

But Kay Beach came at David Bell with a handgun. The bullet hit Bell in the right eye. He fell instantly to the weed-choked front lawn. He may have been dead before he hit it.

Eight hours later, Beach was found sitting at a bus stop in Van Nuys. She was charged with murder. Bail was set at $50,000.

"When someone dies in Clermont," Toni Bell said, "people come to your home. They cook, they bake, they sit with you. I cried all night."

Laura Innes, David's girlfriend, got the news after she came home from the Goodman Theater where she was appearing in "The Christmas Carol." The next day, Sunday, she did an evening performance plus a matinee.

"I know it sounds trite," she said, "but David would have wanted it that way."

Rob Mendel has decided to stay in the apartment he used to share with David. "I'm going to have a hell of an Irish wake," he said. "Then I'm going to join a handgun control group."

On December 30, the Los Angeles City Council adjourned in honor of David Bell.

Toni Bell did not teach her classes at Clermont High this Monday, the day after Christmas vacation. "I could have faced it, but the kids need a day to talk about it," she said. "Otherwise they would just stay quiet for fear of upsetting me. I couldn't do that to them. They're such nice kids."

She spent the day reading letters from David's friends. He was a big man in high school and had a lot of them. One came from a Clermont girl who was not very popular.

"I'll never forget how nice David was," she wrote, "when I was just a little nobody and he was so popular and good looking and how he grabbed me at graduation and hugged me and kissed me and I was on cloud nine that day."

The most popular girl in his class also thought of David, but she did not write. She is Kristy Anderson, the blue-eyed, blonde-haired beauty who was homecoming queen David's senior year.

On every vacation from college, he would stop by her home and talk and joke for hours. Not many guys did anymore. Kristy Anderson developed encephalitis a month before graduation and is totally paralyzed. She cannot even speak.

"But I can hear her laughing, Mama," David would say when he got home. "I swear I can."

Marion Kay Beach pleaded innocent to the charge of murder.

David Bell was cremated.

He was one of about 10,000 people killed with handguns in 1980.

The all-American boy had come to an all-American end.

January 7, 1981

A jury refused to find Marion Kay Beach guilty of murder, instead finding her guilty of the lesser charge of involuntary manslaughter.

On August 6, 1982, in what he called the most difficult sentencing decision of his life, Superior Court Judge James M. Ideman sentenced Beach to six months in jail—all but 18 days of which she had already served while awaiting trial—and five years probation.

In addition, Judge Ideman ordered Beach to perform community service work and write a public letter of apology to David Bell's mother.

Beach also was deprived of the right to bear arms.

Crime of Hunger:
Sweet Roll Tab is Jail

Jimmy Lee Shanks, 35 and unemployed, walked into a grocery store in Fort Myers, Florida, a few weeks ago, tore open a package of sweet rolls and began eating one.

According to a witness, William Corbitt, 40, a truck driver, Shanks told the store personnel who were watching him: "I'm hungry and don't have the money to pay for this."

The storekeepers reacted with a certain amount of restraint: They did not beat him to death.

They did grab him, pin his hands behind him, bend him forward, and push him into a back room.

The sweet rolls cost $1.09.

Shanks did not even get to enjoy the full fruits of his crime.

"He did not get the whole thing ate because the manager took the last little bit from him," Corbitt told the *Fort Myers News-Press*. "The man offered no resistance visible to me. His arms were excessively bent. It seemed to be creating a fair amount of pain."

Perhaps remembering the story of the Good Samaritan, Corbitt twice offered to pay the $1.09 for the man. But, he said, the store management twice refused.

"I don't understand why I couldn't have paid for it," Corbitt said. "The man was hungry."

The police were called and Jimmy Lee Shanks was arrested and charged with retail theft.

At the jailhouse, Shanks was asked if he had money for bail. Since he did not have money even for a sweet roll, he replied in the negative.

So he had to spend the night in jail. Some people might consider a night in jail a little stiff for $1.09, but the best was yet to come.

The next morning, Shanks came before Lee County Judge William McIver. No witnesses appeared against Shanks and he did not have a lawyer. A lawyer would have been provided for him, but Shanks would have had to wait in jail for a public defender to be assigned and the case to come to trial.

Instead, Shanks pleaded guilty. Judge McIver sentenced him to three days in jail.

I could not find out precisely how much it costs to keep a man in jail for three days in Lee County, but I'll bet it is considerably more than $1.09.

Criminal justice, however, does not have to make sense. It just has to be just.

Consider for a moment that Shanks did not gobble up the store's pâté de fois gras or its smoked salmon. He did not slip a filet mignon into his pants or break into a six-pack and start guzzling.

What he did, in plain view of the storekeepers, was to partially eat a sweet roll, claiming hunger.

Corbitt, the man who tried to help him, said, "We should have compassion for people who are hungry enough to break open a package of food in the store and start eating it."

But, upon reflection, perhaps he misses the implication of Shank's crime. What if every poor person in America went into a grocery store and snarfed down a sweet roll?

I called the Census Bureau in Washington, D.C., and asked them how many poor people we have at the moment. They told me that according to the latest figures we have 34,398,000 poor people in this country.

So you can see what kind of chaos would ensue if all of them did what Shanks did.

At the very least it would lead to a serious shortage of sweet rolls.

I spoke to Judge McIver yesterday. He is 38 and has been a judge for seven years. I asked him what the public reaction to his sentence had been.

"I got about 25 phone calls and six letters condemning me," he said. "I don't know what people wanted me to do. Did they want me to give him $5 and pat him on his heinie?"

Well, I said, you could have sentenced him to that night he had already served in jail and then let him go, couldn't you?

"Yes," the judge admitted. "But, you know, I had no idea someone had offered to pay that $1.09. It wasn't on the report."

Did Shanks look genuinely poor to you? I asked.

"Well, he wasn't in a Brooks Brothers suit," the judge said. "But there is a Salvation Army center just down the block from that food store and he could have gotten a meal there."

Did you ask him if he knew about that center before you sentenced him? I asked.

"No," the judge said. "Maybe I should have. Look, I had to handle 30 people in the space of an hour, an hour and a half. Maybe I was a little insensitive.

"But, at the time, I was wondering if I wasn't being too lenient. I mean for only three days in jail, maybe other people might try something like this."

Which could lead to that dreaded sweet roll shortage, of course.

Granted that this guy broke the law, did his punishment really fit the crime? I asked.

"Look," Judge McIver said, "it's the system. Unfortunately if you're poor, you end up spending time in jail when better-off people can just pay a fine. But that's the way our system is."

Makes you proud to be an American, doesn't it?

January 12, 1984

Salute to Nation's Glorious Failures

Every now and then, columnists feel called upon to say something profound.

This is almost always a mistake.

But it was July 4, 1976, and I felt I had to say something—*especially because I would not be around for America's* tri*centennial.*

I have done some pretty awful things in the name of American journalism. I have rushed up to interview mothers who have lost children, husbands who have lost wives, families shattered by a variety of emotional and physical calamities.

All reporters do these things. They wear a protective cloak of professional indifference while they write the names and ages and addresses in their notebooks. The deed is done quickly and quickly forgotten.

But I am going to have a hard time forgetting a long, cinder-block corridor in a small Wisconsin town that led to a bare, large room where eight girls sat on folding chairs facing a television set.

No accident had befallen these girls. No one had died or gone to jail or been shot. What had happened to them, instead, is just about the worst thing that can happen to a person in this country. And this is why it was so tough for me to face them.

What had happened to these girls is that they had failed. They had wanted to be Miss America and now they never would be.

I had spent three days in Oshkosh, Wisconsin, talking to the girls entered in the Miss Wisconsin Pageant, the final step before Atlantic City, where the winner would meet fame, fortune, and Bert Parks.

I had come to do a magazine article on the American Dream and I had really come half expecting to make fun of the kind of girl who would engage in anything as ridiculous as a beauty pageant.

For three days I saw them go through endless hours of walking up and down a stage wearing evening gowns and bathing suits, trying not to wobble on high heels while the same thoughts ran through their heads: "What if I trip? What if I faint? What if I throw up?"

They lived in isolation in a nearby dormitory that was guarded by uniformed police day and night. They were not allowed to see or telephone any members of their families or any of their friends.

Their workdays were 18 hours long as they practiced their dancing and baton twirling and singing. One girl would sit down and play an imaginary piano keyboard wherever she went, at a picnic table or on the bus, mentally pounding the notes into her head.

I interviewed each contestant about her hopes and dreams and found each shockingly bright, articulate, and candid.

But on the last night, the smiling stopped. The names of the finalists were read and the eight losers ran offstage and were lead to a room where they could watch the victor on television.

I couldn't make myself go into the room. I knew them too well by then.

I walked past the door three or four times and turned away. And then, I just did it, and plunged through the doorway as they swiveled on their chairs to look at me.

They still wore their evening gowns, some in red, others in white, others in blue. I had gotten to know them by the names of the Wisconsin towns they represented, and that is the way I think of them still.

Miss Watertown—Mary Elizabeth Noon—who had the brightest smile and the cheeriest outlook during the contest, spoke one of the two thoughts that were dominating each of their minds.

"I just feel bad for my town," she said, fiddling with the hem of her gown. "I feel I let them down. I feel I let all the people down."

Miss Sheboygan—Janice Kay Sadler—the girl I secretly had been rooting for, spoke the second thought. "I don't know how I will face the people who came here to see me," she said. "I'm dreading the moment."

I wish I could have told them then what I feel now. That they, at a very tender age, had branded themselves as failures in a nation whose national religion is success. They were true dreamers of the American Dream and now they were paying for it. And it is ironic, considering our nation's history, that this should be true.

America was a country founded by failures who could not get along in the Old World and who came to a wilderness because there was simply no place else to go.

America was a country settled by failures—pioneers who could not adjust to the crowded life of the Eastern Seaboard and who went West because there was no place else for them.

America was a country built by failures—men and women who never attained the dream of owning their own business and being their own boss. Men and women whose lives were ruled by the alarm clock in the morning and the factory whistle in the evening.

Years and years of history books have taught us that America was shaped by the great deeds of great men. It was not. America was shaped by the great deeds of ordinary men.

On the Fourth of July, 1969, at the height of the Vietnam War, I refused to stand up for the playing of the national anthem.

I didn't know then what I have learned since. That America—thank God—always has been better than its government, that its people have always been more decent than their presidents, and that the strength and greatness of this nation lies in them, the men and women who are not great and who never will be.

So on this Fourth of July—for Miss Watertown and Miss Sheboygan and for all the other glorious failures who have made and sustained this country—on this day, I stand for them.

July 4, 1976

Where There's a Will, There's a Shill

I have always enjoyed reading syndicated columnist George Will. He is a fine writer; he is witty and he uses *Bartlett's Familiar Quotations* better than anyone I know.

I don't always agree with him. In fact, I rarely agree with him. He is a conservative and a patrician and believes deep down, I think, that God just doesn't like poor people. And that's why He gave them bad table manners.

But I like to read Will, anyway. Even when he is wrong, which is continually, he is elegant about it.

I guess I knew that Will likes to wine and dine with Ronald Reagan.

This is no crime. I personally don't believe in this kind of thing, but then again Ron has never gotten on the phone to ask me over.

The job of the journalist is to reveal, not conceal. And politicians almost never want you to reveal what goes on at their private little dinner parties.

Will has criticized Reagan, but rarely. He likes Reagan. Again, this is no crime. But where is the line drawn between George Will, journalist, and George Will, friend of the president? As far as I can tell, the line isn't drawn at all.

You may have read recently about how the Reagan campaign came up with documents apparently pilfered from President Jimmy Carter before the presidential debate in 1980.

But did you know George Will was shown some of those documents back in 1980 and kept silent about them? And did you know he was shown those documents so he could help Reagan prepare for the debate?

Will went to Reagan, who was in Wexford, Virginia, just before the debate so he could pose sample questions to Reagan. Before that, David Stockman had shown Will the Carter documents. But, Will now says, he didn't write about the documents because "their origin was unknown and their importance was nil."

New York *Daily News* columnist Jimmy Breslin tore Will's hide off in a column last week, saying: "Will's position on the 'pilfered' documents is familiar. He didn't know the car was stolen. He was only a passenger. He didn't ask the driver where he got the car from."

But Will did something worse.

After the presidential debate, Will went on ABC's "Nightline" and masqueraded as a journalist rating Reagan's performance. He decided—surprise, surprise—that Reagan had done well.

But Will didn't tell anyone he had helped Reagan prepare for that performance. Will now says it was known to everyone that he was "at Wexford" with Reagan.

But he was more than "at" Wexford. He was part of Reagan's team.

And Breslin quotes Will's own words on "Nightline": "I had a chance to see a bit of the preparation for the debate as an observer," Will told the TV audience.

Observer? Baloney. Will was no observer. Breslin calls Will a "shill" for the president and he is exactly right.

Will now says he asked Reagan a tough sample question at Wexford and "the candidate did not distinguish himself."

Thanks, George. You waited nearly three years to tell us that. How come you didn't tell us that before the election?

Will has fallen victim to the most common disease of journalists: stargazing.

He cannot stand to be a "mere" observer with his nose pressed up against the bakery window. So when Ronald Reagan invites him inside to fondle the goodies, Will is not going to blow his chance for another invitation by informing the public what goes on.

Newspapermen should try to get the inside story. But when they get it, they should print it, not conceal it as Will did.

In a column printed Sunday in his own defense—a column more notable for its length than its candor—Will could not resist such name-dropping as: "Last winter I attended a small dinner with Reagan, who enjoyed himself enormously—which is easy to do when Lee Iacocca is present and feeling feisty."

Wow . . . George Will not only eats in the same room as the leader of the free world, but with Lee Iacocca, too! What next? Water skiing with Burt Reynolds? Jogging with Victoria Principal?

I thought George Will was smarter than this. I thought he was smart enough to know one of the principal rules of journalism: If you sleep with the elephants, you can't cover the circus.

But, as it turns out, Ronald Reagan is the smart one. He got exactly what he wanted from George Will: praise and protection.

And now that the news of Will's role has come out, it is not Reagan who looks bad. Reagan looks like a canny politician who knows how to manipulate a newsman.

Because Will likes quotations, I leave him with this:

There's one born every minute, Georgie.

July 12, 1983

Snow-Wimps Head for Cover

WASHINGTON, D.C.

Having lived all my life in the Snow Belt, I never realized how snow panics whole regions of America.

An inch of snow in Chicago is nothing. In New York, it is a minor inconvenience. In Denver, it is good weather.

In Washington, D.C., it is instant paralysis. Heck, the president canceled the inaugural parade because of *cold* when it wasn't even snowing.

Do you think the Russkies cancel parades because of cold? You bet they don't. They just hand everybody a bottle of Stolichnaya and say, "Drink up and march."

But out here, people look on snow as a personal attack. They believe each flake has their name written on it.

They are, I hate to say it, snow-wimps.

It is easy to recognize a city of snow-wimps. Next time you're watching a national blizzard roundup on TV, watch for those cities where people are walking through the snow with their umbrellas up.

The first time I saw it, I couldn't believe it. I thought there was a "Mary Poppins" revival in town.

Umbrellas, I keep telling people, are for rain. That's the wet, liquid stuff that splashes. Hats, hoods, and earmuffs are for snow, which is the soft, flaky stuff that piles up.

As a rule of thumb, if you can make a man out of it, it's snow. If you can mix it with scotch, it's rain.

In a recent snowfall, I approached a woman who was walking down the street with her umbrella up.

"Why are you doing that?" I asked her.

"To protect my hair," she said.

"But don't you realize that snow could collect on top, build up to massive depths, and then collapse the umbrella, crushing your head like an overripe grape?"

"Yarrrghhh!!" she yelled, throwing her umbrella into the air and running down the street.

I felt good the rest of the day.

I also find that in snow-wimp cities—Atlanta and Dallas are two other good examples—TV goes out of its way to panic people.

I was in Atlanta a few weeks ago, and I listened to a TV weatherman urge people not to go to grocery stores and hoard food if it snowed that night.

Hoard food? Do some people confuse snow with nuclear war? Do they assume their neighbors are going to resort to cannibalism when the first flakes start falling?

Last Sunday, I made plans to meet somebody for brunch in Baltimore, where there had been a brief flurry of snow that morning.

I drove through the deserted streets of downtown—the fact that nobody else was out except a doctor delivering a baby and a Red Cross bloodmobile should have tipped me off—and I immediately ran into trouble on the first hill.

My car, a car that had never failed me in Chicago, slipped and slid and could not get enough traction to make it to the top.

That's because not a sprinkle of salt had been laid down on the street, even though the snow had stopped hours earlier.

I later asked somebody why the city was so stingy with salt. "Well, they've only got so much," he said. "And if they use it up early in the season, they might not have enough at the end."

To me, this is like a coach not playing to win. I say: Go for it. If you've got the salt and the streets need salting, what the heck, throw caution to the wind and spread a little.

Because what happens if the city saves its salt and by the end of the year it still has a mountain of it? What is the city going to do with it? Make a 200-ton corned beef?

Such logic, however, is hopeless in the face of the utter panic that grips people in snow-wimp cities.

It was a few days ago at noontime. It had snowed earlier in the day, but now it was clear.

I got up from my desk and asked a few colleagues if they wanted to go out for lunch.

They looked at me as if I had asked them out onto the surface of the moon in a meteor shower.

"Out there?" they said. "In *this*?"

This, I pointed out, was bright sunshine.

"But it was snowing," they said. "Who knows what the streets are like. Better to stay inside."

I said I had boots and a ski cap [note: *not* an umbrella] and I was going to go out anyway.

One grabbed my arm. "Look," he whispered, "don't tell anybody, but I've been hoarding some food. I'll share my Ding-Dong with you if you want."

Another took the ribbon out of his typewriter and tied one end around me.

"If you get lost or snow-blinded," he said, "just follow the ribbon back here."

Another handed me a flare gun. "If you get trapped in a drift," she said, "send one up."

"And you'll come get me?" I asked.

"No," she said. "But we'll look for the body in the spring."

January 28, 1985

Walk on the Wild Side with an Old Pal

A lot of reporters would like to be cops. The cops can't figure out why.

Both professions seem romantic to the outsider and considerably less so to those involved.

I saw Ken Wallace at our 10-year high school reunion and he soon learned one essential of the newpaper business: Everything is a story.

I wrote these columns about him and he had to take the ribbing of his fellow cops. Afterwards, he took me to the cop bars and I took him to newspaper bars. We shared each other's worlds for a while, but just for a while.

We both learned they are two professions that bump up against each other, but do not quite mesh.

Kenny turned around in the front seat. "Remember Linda?" he asked, naming a girl I had danced six dances with at the eighth-grade prom.

"Sure," I said. "Of course. What's she doing now?"

"She's a hooker," he said. "She's turning tricks on Wells Street."

"Baloney," I said with a jolt. "You're crazy." I hoped he was kidding.

When old friends meet, this is the kind of thing they talk about. What the other old friends are doing, who made it, who didn't, who died in Vietnam, who has three kids. I hadn't seen Kenny Wallace for 10 years, not since high school, and when we met again I asked him what he did.

He told me and invited me to spend a night with him, watching him do it. "I can't believe it," I said. "Not you. Anybody but you."

"Hey," he said as we drove down La Salle Street. "You know That Steak Joynt? The restaurant? I love that place. I like to—" He stopped talking and listened to the murmur of the radio.

"862 Sedgwick," he said. "Man with a shotgun."

The guy driving the car stamped the brakes and jerked the car into a vicious U-turn. I went skidding across the back seat and came up hard against the door.

Cars fled from in front of us as we picked up speed. We took squealing turns with the noise from our tires louder than the siren. We came up to the Cabrini-Green public housing project and stopped with a jolt.

Kenny took a .45 automatic pistol from under his jacket and flicked off the safety with his thumb. Just before he got out of the car, he looked back at me. "You wanted to know what I did," he said.

Not until I saw the gun in his hand could I really picture Kenny Wallace as a cop. Other people become cops. Not your friends from high school.

Kenny and his partner walked quickly into the building, elbowing their way through a group of about 20 kids who stood sullenly in front, hands in pockets, refusing to move.

The staircase was on the outside of the building and Kenny took the concrete steps two at a time. He was always a big kid, a swimmer, and I remembered as I watched him leaping up the stairs into the darkness how he used to work out every day on a chin-up bar bolted to the doorway of his bedroom.

At each landing, Kenny flattened himself against the cold cinder blocks, scraping gently against the wall as he eased around the corners. He held the pistol down at his side and slightly in front of his body, the hammer pulled back.

Earlier in the evening I asked him whether he had ever pulled his gun on a guy. He looked at me strangely. "You watch me tonight," he said. "I pull it every time I make a stop. It's too late to pull it when you're sitting on the curb, coughing your guts out with a bullet in your chest.

"I go to a party and people ask me what I do. I tell them I'm a cop and they say, 'Do you have a gun? Is it loaded?' "

He made a disgusted noise. "No, I tell them. I tell them that I keep pebbles in my pockets to throw at the bad guys."

Kenny moved up another flight. Other policemen glided past. The only lights came from the curtained windows of the apartments and the blue-white lights of the ball fields far below. On each landing the cooking smells mixed with the sharp smell of marijuana and the sticky, sweet odor of disinfectant. There were only a few floors left until the top.

"Roger?" Kenny said softly.

I stepped up behind him. "Uh, stay somewhere close to me," he said. I tried to say something but couldn't. All I could think of was the last thing Kenny had done before leaving the East Chicago Avenue police station that night.

He had left the meeting of his tactical unit and signed out for a radio and checked to see whether he had an extra clip of ammunition for his gun. "Got to call Mom," he said, walking toward a telephone. "I tell her what my beat number is every night so she can listen for it. She's got a police radio at home and she keeps track of me. She doesn't miss a night. And if I forget to call, I really get it."

Kenny stepped out into a small pool of light. From out of the shadows stepped a man dressed in a black jacket. In his hands he carried a pump-action shotgun. He had one hand on the barrel and one hand on the trigger.

Kenny and the man stared at each other for a second. "You be careful," the man with the shotgun told Kenny. "Bullets sting." Kenny smiled at the man, recognizing him as another policeman. "I will certainly keep that in mind," he said. "I certainly will."

On the top floor all they found was a kid smoking dope with his girlfriend. As they searched his pockets for a gun, his head and his arms hung down limply. They let him go and we all walked down the steps.

We walked back to the car and someone screamed behind us, "Hey, white boys!" I turned around and looked at the person who screamed. "Rat-tat-tat," the person yelled, stitching imaginary machine gun bullets through our bodies. He was about seven.

"It's the greatest job in the world," Kenny said. "I couldn't do anything else. I'm serious. The guys who leave the force always come back to it. They have to.

"It's the thrill. The chase. The pinch. The wild exhilaration. Getting on the scene! Doing it!"

A call came through on the radio. There was a robbery in progress in Old Town. Kenny stamped on the accelerator.

"Besides," he said, yelling over the siren, "I love to go through red lights!"

September 9, 1976

Cop Sees Beauty

Kenny sized up the door like a prizefighter measuring an opponent. He tugged his blue jacket more tightly around his shoulders and counted off eight steps. He ran forward, smashing his right shoulder into the faded wood.

There was a splintering sound and a sharp crack. The door exploded inward. The hinges flew off into the darkness, flashing once under a streetlight.

Kenny stumbled through the doorway and recovered quickly. He stood there with a flashlight in his hand. Inside the abandoned building, a woman stood in the beam from his light with her hands held over her head.

"My god, I'm a whore!" she wailed. "I'm just a whore, don't shoot me, I'm a whore!"

"Nobody is going to shoot you," Kenny said politely. "Especially not with a flashlight."

The woman squinted into the light. "Oh, mercy," she said, putting her hand over her heart in relief. "It's Kenny."

When I knew Kenny in high school, he didn't want to be a cop. He wanted to be an electrical engineer. I wanted to pass high school chemistry. We both succeeded. I got a C and he went on to get a bachelor of science degree from one of the best engineering schools in the country. And then he gave it up. And now he is a cop.

"What do you see?" he asked me. "What do you see out there?"

We were riding in an unmarked police car. It was a beat-up '74 Dodge.

I looked out the window. I saw a bunch of factories and some empty lots covered with weeds. Every few blocks there was an abandoned building with broken windows staring out onto the street like the face on a jack-o-lantern.

"What I see is beauty," Kenny said. "This is a beautiful area. Vice— we got it. Beyond belief." He started ticking off items on his fingers. "Prostitution. Narcotics. You name it. We've got an affluent area by the lake and we've got the housing projects at Cabrini-Green. It's not like a ghetto district where all you've got is poor people robbing poor people."

Kenny is part of the tactical unit of the East Chicago Avenue police district. The tactical units are the elite corps of the department. The members dress in plain clothes, have great freedom of action and believe in aggressive police work. They do not like to wait around for crimes to happen.

"I love this job," Kenny said. "You can be as intelligent or aggressive as you want. Or you can stand around and be the big, dumb cop that everyone expects."

The tactical units do not stand around. "We roust people," Kenny said. "We go in after the bad guys. We go in after the good bust. We move. I have a partner and he's great. His name is Tommy and we've never had a fight.

"It sounds like a cliché, but it's like being married. Other cops, they'll go into the park with their partners and they'll just beat the crap out of each other. Literally. With fists. It happens."

The members of Kenny's unit all have nicknames. Hillbilly. Prince. Squire. Bobby Darin. Cockroach. Called the Gerber Baby because of his baby face and blond hair, Kenny is 6'2" and 222 pounds.

We drove through Lincoln Park. The lights of the car were off, and we drove on the sidewalks and over the grass. Every now and then we would come upon a startled couple, who sat up quickly as we passed.

"It's a shame the places you can't go in this city," Kenny said. "The parks. A lot of people are afraid to go into the parks. I'm obviously not. I carry a cannon, right?" He slapped the gun that sat on his hip under his jacket.

"I have this metal detector. It's a hobby. On my days off, I take it around the parks looking for coins. Just to relax, to unwind.

"Well, one day, I'm on the South Side in Jackson Park. Remember?" Kenny and I grew up a few blocks from Jackson Park. "I'm standing there, bending down over what I think is a coin and I look up to see that I have company."

About eight guys were standing around him in a circle. They were smiling. "What do you got there?" the biggest said.

Kenny told them it was a metal detector.

"Yeah, well, I think I want that thing." the guy said, holding out his hand.

"I think you probably don't," Kenny told him.

"Man, you better gimme that and you better gimme that fast," the guy said. The circle closed tighter.

In a movement that was almost too fast to follow, Kenny's gun was in his hand. He stuck it in the big guy's face.

"Well, just go ahead and take it," Kenny said very softly. "Just go right ahead." The eight guys ran away.

Kenny laughed remembering it. "What did I do then?" he said. "What do you think?

"I got the hell out of there. Before somebody called a cop."

September 12, 1976

A Split Second Makes the Difference

The kid came out of Walgreens much too fast. He kept looking back over his shoulder as he half ran, half stumbled out into the bright sunlight. He wore a thin, light shirt and a dark pair of pants. His shirt seemed to bulge around the middle.

Kenny Wallace watched him from the car. "Oh, is he wrong," Kenny said. "This kid is definitely dirty. What do you suppose he's got under there, huh?"

The kid ran into a cul-de-sac and disappeared for a second. Kenny was already out of the car. "Freeze!'" he shouted, coming up on the kid quickly. "This is the police." Kenny's gun was in his hand. "Police!" Kenny yelled again. "Put your hands up!"

The kid looked at him, his eyes wide with fear. His right hand darted to his belt. Out came something bright and metallic.

Kenny was already in his combat stance. Two hands on his gun, legs crouched, he centered the front sight of the pistol on the middle button of the kid's shirt. And then he did what he always did before he shot. He closed one eye. And he started to tighten on the trigger.

"You dream about it," he had told me earlier. "You know it is going to happen sooner or later. You know that somebody, someday is going to pull a gun on you. And you wonder. Will I be able to fire in time? Can I get to my gun? Can I get him before he gets me?"

He had put the gun in my hand. It was a .45-caliber, steel-frame Colt Commander. It was heavy and huge, overflowing the palm I cradled it in. Its blue-steel barrel glowed dully in the light. He told me it was the finest combat weapon in the world. I had never held a gun before.

I held it out, elbow locked, with one hand and I steadied its base with the other. When I closed one eye, the target leaped into place. Pulling the trigger was like drawing a knife through soft cheese.

I was not ready for the huge, flat thud, the orange flash, and the blue-white cloud of gas. The gun kicked a few inches in my hand like something alive and the hammer came back automatically. I pulled the trigger and the target jumped this time. I fired again.

Kenny reached over and took the gun away. "Now you know," he said. "You wanted to know and now you do."

I knew. There was no feeling like it. The soft, smooth easy pull of the trigger followed by the violent release of the bullet. It was power in its rawest form. The form that a policeman carries strapped to his hip.

Kenny held the gun on the kid. It takes only a few pounds of pressure to pull the trigger of his gun. Less pressure than it takes to open the door of a refrigerator.

By law, by Chicago Police Department rules, and by training, Kenny should have sent a lead ball crashing into the kid's chest at about 800 feet a second. He hesitated.

"Drop it!" Kenny screamed instead. "Drop it!" The kid dropped it. And then in a scene so senseless and unbelievable, a scene that seemed to happen in slow motion, the kid began to reach down for the object he dropped. He would have it in a second.

Kenny swore and covered the distance in two long steps. His gun was in his hand sideways and he brought it up against the kid's head in a short, hard arc.

The kid went tumbling backward. Kenny held the gun on him while he groped on the ground for what the kid had. He came up with a pair of sunglasses. One of the 14 pairs the kid had just stolen.

"Jesus," Kenny said.

He took the kid to Henrotin Hospital to get four stitches put in his head. Kenny sat in a chair. It was about an hour before he felt good enough to go back on the street.

"That would have been great," he said. "I would have killed a kid. For unlawful use of sunglasses. I had every right to draw my gun. I probably had every right to shoot him.

"But I would have been up before the state's attorney. Maybe court. And they would have had days to decide whether I was right or wrong. Maybe weeks. What did I have? One second? A tenth of a second?"

We were standing in the Slammer Inn at Western and Belmont, a police bar crowded with off-duty cops. On the walls were blown-up pictures of the 1968 Democratic National Convention. They showed lines of cops with riot helmets and clubs standing on the Michigan Avenue bridge. We were playing a game called Gun Fight. Two electronic men duck out from behind barriers on a street and shoot at each other. When one gets hit, he falls to the ground dead.

"You know it's funny," Kenny said, moving his man quickly down the street. "I went hunting once. Birds. I couldn't pull the trigger." He fired once—high, over my head. I ducked behind a barrier.

"I can't understand how anyone could kill an animal," he said. "I was supposed to shoot a dog once. It had been crippled. But I couldn't do it." I poked my head around the barrier and Kenny fired again. He missed.

"You'll come in here sometimes and they'll be up because a cop shot a guy and saved a life. I don't know what I'd feel exactly. I wouldn't feel happy, but I wouldn't feel sad. It's my duty. I'm prepared to do my duty." He looked up at me, making sure I understood. I moved quickly from behind the barrier and drilled him. He flopped to the ground.

"You win," he said. "You can tell everyone you shot a cop."

We went to a booth in the back and I tried to remember what he was like in high school, the last time I had seen him. Back when everyone dreamed about becoming doctors and lawyers and nobody dreamed about becoming a cop.

"I'll spend my life in the department," he said. "I've found what I want to do. The only hard part will be leaving the street. When you get promotions, eventually you have to move to a desk job. That will be hard. It will be hard to leave this." And if a man did stay outside on the street, I asked, how long could he last? Kenny shrugged: "Until you burn out, I guess." We played with our beers a while.

"Sometimes I ask people if I have changed," he said. "If I have hardened. I asked my mother once. She said that I walked differently, that I come into a room differently. But that deep down, when I dropped my guard, I was still the same.

"What the hell," he grinned. "Maybe there's hope."

September 16, 1976

Simon Keeps on Saying It

Admit it. All fish tastes pretty much the same.

◆

There is nothing worse than being on a plane with a drunk.

◆

Why do people bother to order their steaks well done? Why don't they just eat their shoes?

◆

People who wear lapel pins should be beaten with sticks.

◆

Stay away from men who wear navy blue shirts.

◆

Anyone who could actually pick a lobster out of one of those restaurant tanks and then eat it should consider therapy.

◆

I'm getting pretty tired of those signs on the backs of trucks telling us how much road taxes they pay. Why don't they tell us how many roads they destroy?

◆

Why do people who call you on wrong numbers always act like it's your fault?

◆

Is it my imagination or are drivers getting worse?

Just once I'd like to ask for something in a store and not be told that "everything we have is on display."

◆

Are Dom DeLuise and James Coco *really* two different people?

◆

You aren't being honest if you say you never filched something off a maid's cart in a hotel corridor.

◆

How come people don't drink iced coffee anymore?

◆

I never believe it when an entertainer tells me I'm the best audience he has ever had.

◆

Cab drivers should ask you before they turn on their radios.

◆

The more conventions a hotel has, the lousier a place it is to stay.

◆

People who have four-wheel-drive cars seem to have real trouble in two-wheel-drive traffic.

◆

Only a real nerd would stick pens in his shirt pocket.

How come gas stations have those huge American flags? What's so patriotic about gasoline?

◆

When is the last time the United Nations did something right?

◆

Don't you love to spot the name of your street in another city?

◆

Peanut shells don't taste as good as they used to.

◆

There is something terribly sad about old train stations.

◆

Are kids still nervous before their first kiss?

◆

"Coke is it" ranks right up there with the most meaningless advertising slogans in history.

◆

Think of it: If Edison hadn't invented the light bulb, we'd have to watch TV in the dark.

◆

About the only thing I don't have in my glove compartment is gloves.

◆

Guys who drink with both elbows on the bar are good guys to avoid.

I always thought FALN was a kind of custard.

◆

Bath people should not marry shower people.

◆

People who ride elevators for only one floor drive me crazy.

◆

Besides A.J. Foyt, who actually uses his tachometer?

◆

A restaurant that does not ban pipe and cigar smoking is not worthy of your patronage.

◆

William Holden is the father we never had.

◆

Men, if you own anything velour, feel free to start the barbecue with it.

◆

I resent the whole concept of "turkey franks."

◆

People who wear their college rings are the biggest jerks I know.

◆

Men who wear garters have a lot of explaining to do.

◆

The trouble with fancy hotels is that they don't have soft drink machines at the end of the hall.

New tipping rules for the eighties: 20 percent if the food arrives well prepared, 15 percent if the food arrives on the plate, 10 percent if the food arrives.

◆

When is the last time you saw anyone use a pencil?

◆

Confidential to "Bewildered in Bensenville": Yes, Hawaiian Punch can be served with Beef Wellington. The rule is: red meat, red punch. White meat, 7-Up.

◆

Why did we ever think Jill Clayburgh could act?

◆

Admit it. Whenever you go up to a bookstore cash register, you always put the least embarrassing book on top.

◆

The trouble with designer chocolates is that they melt five minutes after you put them on.

◆

How come when guys get old they start wearing pastel colors?

◆

You can never go wrong with candlelight.

◆

Admit it. When you heard Princess Diana was pregnant for the first time, you counted backwards on your fingers.

You've got to admire people who still own waterbeds. Imagine how people must laugh at them.

◆

I have never found a salad bar worth the walk.

◆

Life is unfair and Ronald Reagan intends to keep it that way.

◆

America's rejection of the metric system may go down in history as one of our proudest moments.

◆

One of the worst things a restaurant can do is put the tables too close together.

◆

You can tell a lot about a person by whether he likes his peanut butter smooth or chunky.

◆

In small doses, there is something almost appealing about the smell of a skunk.

◆

Talking Coke machines are one sign of progress I could live without.

◆

Most people are ashamed of their feet.

◆

You know you're an adult when you stop eating sloppy joes.

'Tell How the Smoke Came Out of His Head'

Tell 'em about the smoke," she said. "Tell 'em how the smoke came out of his head."

Mary Carr, the foster mother of Steven Judy, sat on the plastic couch in Howard Johnson's in Michigan City, Indiana. She sat forward, hunched over, balancing an ashtray on her knees.

Her husband, who had just witnessed Steven's execution a few minutes before, stared at the tops of his black work shoes before he answered.

"We seen the smoke come up from the cap," he said. "They put this metal cap on his head. He reared up. His fingers clutched. His hands gripped the chair.

"Then it was over. I don't think he felt anything."

The first surge of electricity is 2,300 volts and is called the "mercy shot." It is supposed to knock out the nervous system, so the condemned man feels no pain from the next shot. Actually, doctors do not really know if it prevents pain.

But no one has ever complained.

And to answer the question that almost everyone outside the prison asked when it was all over, no, the lights did not dim. It just doesn't take that much juice to kill a man.

Steven Judy raped and killed a young woman, a motorist in distress, for no apparent reason. Then he drowned her three children. It was not a crime of gain or passion. It was just a crime. "It just happened," Judy said.

Just after midnight yesterday, it just happened to him.

Two guards led him from his special cell at the Indiana State Prison into the death chamber. He could not see. A black, cloth mask, attached around his head with elastic, covered him from his eyebrows down.

He stumbled along docilely with the guards. Earlier that afternoon they had asked him if he wanted a tranquilizer shot and to their surprise, he said yes.

It was the first sign that his facade of cockiness, his bragging, his laughing in the face of death, was wearing thin. As the time grew near, he realized what was facing him.

The guards led him over to the black-painted wooden chair. In a poetic gesture that Judy would have appreciated, it was made out of the old Indiana gallows, torn down in 1913.

The law states that executions must take place between midnight and dawn, as if to hide the deed from the light, as if to hide it from the world of decent people.

Robert Carr, his foster father, stood behind a glass barrier at Judy's request. Judy could have had 10 people there. He came up with only two. Carr and his lawyer.

He was supposed to wave to Carr at the last moment and give him a little sign that he was all right. But he did not. Perhaps it was the drugs, perhaps he forgot, perhaps he was too afraid.

The guards sat him in the chair and pinned his arms and legs with iron, u-shaped rods. Then they strapped him in around the chest, the arms, and the legs.

There was no minister present. Judy had refused one.

They put the metal cap on his shaved head. A guard called to the room where the switch was to be pulled. A hot line to the governor of Indiana was in that room. But there was no last-minute call. The switch was pulled.

The "mercy shot" lasted 10 seconds. Judy's body arched and slammed against the restraints. His lips pulled back from his teeth in a grimace of death. The smoke came from directly underneath the cap. There was a second, 500-volt shot for 20 seconds.

The doctors waited 4½ minutes before approaching the body and pronouncing him dead.

"He never flinched or nothing," Carr said. "He just . . . well, he just really did it."

"He wrote us a note," his foster mother said. "He said that he knew he hurt us. He was sorry. He wished he could take the hurt away. He was sorry he never made clear how much he loved us."

"It wasn't near as bad as I expected," Carr said. "But I hated it. My heart speeded up watching it. But I wanted to be there. I wanted to comfort him. I'm sure he had to be thinking about it."

He thought about it a lot. He planned his funeral service down to the flowers. He even discussed whether it would be an open casket. "You better check and see how I look after it's over," he told his foster mother. "Then decide."

"He cried, you know," she said with some anger. "He cried on his last day. He hugged me and cried. No matter what you've heard, Steven Judy does cry."

She listened to what she had said and stabbed out her cigarette in the ashtray. "Did cry," she said. "Did. I should speak in the past tense now."

He could have stopped it, but that would have spoiled what to him was his finest moment. Steven Judy died yesterday morning only because he wanted to. He had a hot line to the governor, too, and all he had to do was pick it up and say he wanted to appeal.

But if he had, he would have been just another con like the 732 other men in America condemned to die.

To Steven Judy, death would make him what life had not: a person who was noticed, a person who was talked about, a star.

"I talked to him all day," Mrs. Carr said, "until they made me leave. I told him not to let pride stand in the way of saving himself. I told him to call it off. He said: 'You know me better than that.' "

On his last day, he received 20 telegrams, all from religious groups, asking him in the name of God to halt his own death. "He read them," Carr said. "Then he kind of laughed."

Outside the prison, people lit candles and sang. The religious people did not want a child of God to die. The civil libertarians did not want the state to kill. Even the governor called the task "unpleasant."

But Steven Judy knew what he wanted.

"These people don't want to do this," he told his foster mother. "And that's why I'm going to make them do it."

The condemned man was granted his last request.

March 10, 1981

The Night the Lights Went Out

Ten-thirty at night in Brooklyn. The streets, the stores are dark. Down the block come the sounds of breaking glass and muffled shouts.

Joel Benenson sits in front of his store. It is hot, even with the sun down. He is wearing cutoff blue jeans and a gray T-shirt with the name Adidas on it.

The sweat trickles out from under his beard, down his arms and onto the 12-gauge shotgun on his lap. He has never held a gun before.

But he holds one now. Because it is the night that the lights have gone out.

It is a Remington pump-action shotgun. It has a long, blue-steel barrel and a walnut stock. He grips it with both hands, holding it tight across his stomach. He sits in the dark in a lounge chair out in front of his store.

"The first shell is solid lead," he says. "The next are double-ought buckshot."

A solid lead shotgun shell will blow a hole through a man that you can drive a truck through. Double-ought buckshot can knock an elk off its feet.

"The first one is for anyone coming at me with a weapon," Joel says. "The next are to disperse the crowd."

Where are these words coming from? From whose mouth? I have known Joel almost 10 years. He is a big, laughing, curly-haired man of 25. First came college and now he has an acting and directing career. A few months ago he received his first review in the *New York Times*. The critic liked his play very much.

And now he sits with sweating palms holding a 12-gauge shotgun and speaking of whom and how he will shoot. All because the lights went out.

A few years ago, in order to hedge against the uncertain life of the theater, Joel bought one-third interest in a Brooklyn beer distributorship. It is this place of business that he now sits in front of, protecting

15,000 cases of Schlitz and Budweiser and Rheingold from the looters who roam the streets in packs.

"My first thought when the lights went out was that the burglar alarms were not going to work," he says. "I headed for the store. I knew they would empty the place. It was very unreal. Who was I to hold a shotgun? I got one from a friend. I wasn't going to let anyone ruin me in a night just because the power had failed."

Joel grew up in Queens, in a middle-class neighborhood. He was a born mimic, a natural actor, a man who loved to read and discuss Heinrich Böll and Thomas Pynchon. Growing up in the sixties and seventies he was very much like others his age. He was opposed to the war, abhorred violence and bloodshed, was sympathetic to the civil rights movement.

And now he was sitting in a lawn chair, with five shells in a shotgun, drawing the line.

"Having that gun in my hands is security," he says. "I feel more powerful than anyone out there." You can see the bands of kids roaming the streets with broken bottles in their hands. The looting has been enormous. Whole stores on both sides have been wiped out. What they cannot carry, they destroy. If a couch was too heavy to carry, they got out their knives and cut it apart.

Police arrested 3,500 looters on the night and days that followed the New York blackout. The mayor of New York called it "a night of terror." Eighty policemen were injured. Every borough of New York except Staten Island was looted.

None of the looters carried picket signs. This was no protest. No police harassment had preceded it. No grievances had been rejected. The lights had gone out. That was all.

After it was over, Joel and I talked again. Throughout the night, police had passed him and seen him sitting there with a shotgun on his lap. He gave them Cokes from his cooler and they went on their way.

"It was a sickening night," Joel said. "And scary. You realize how uncontrollable a city is. A small percent of rioters can outnumber a police force 5 to 1."

Joel had always loved New York, had bragged about it. It was not only that he had grown up there. But he had the New Yorker's pride of being not only able to survive in the city, but to conquer it. To take all that was unlivable about it and live there anyway. To not only survive, but to prevail.

And then the lights went out.

"I am in no position to pack up and move from the city," he said. "Can you honestly tell me it would have been any different anyplace else?"

I told him that I could not say, I did not know.

"I drove around and looked at the looted stores, the burned buildings," he said. "Some people have their whole lives tied up in these stores. Look, I was against the war in Vietnam. I have been against violence, but I found myself sitting there, ready to shoot. Yes, I would have shot.

"You realize how close a city is to savagery," he said. "I felt like some kind of pioneer out there. Just me against them."

Twelve years ago during the last New York power failure, there was no looting and no rioting in the city. You can blame the difference between then and now on a lot of things. The urban riots of the late sixties. Vietnam. Watergate.

I guess that sociologists and columnists will think it all over and come up with something that sounds nice. But whatever we were back then, we are not now.

And whatever it is below the surface of our cities and ourselves, it takes very little to bring it out.

Sometimes, all that has to happen is for the lights to go out.

July 17, 1977

Where the American Dream Is Safe

The first thing you feel is safe. And you notice that things are quieter than they should be. And people walk more slowly than they usually do.

The urban scurry, the over-the-shoulder glancing, the keep-your-purse-under-your-arm walk of the city dweller is absent.

You are in Walt Disney World in Orlando, Florida, the most calculated interpretation of the American dream ever created.

It is an American city where people walk without fear. It is a place where people stroll hand in hand and don't worry about much.

For the price of admission, for the *high* price of admission, peace can be yours.

Walt Disney guessed correctly many years ago that someday our greatest wish would be: "Please don't hurt me."

Nothing bad is allowed to happen to you here. Maybe that is why the best known part is called the Magic Kingdom.

You could, I suppose, leap in front of a horse-drawn trolley. But the horses probably get training every week in stepping over people.

Every detail is taken care of. Need a washroom? There are more than even the weakest kidneys could require. There are first aid stations and places to get a cash advance on your credit card and centers where you can nurse your baby.

There are no newspapers. Disney was smart enough to see to that. But his real genius was to realize that people want an America that never existed.

That is why the entrance to the Magic Kingdom is an idealized American Main Street, the kind of Main Street we all dream about.

The streets are always clean on this Main Street. The water is pure. The bugs have been removed from the air.

There is no graffiti. Nobody asks you for spare change. The trains run on time.

Even the unexpected is carefully calculated.

On the nearby race car ride, the smallest child is allowed to drive just as long as his feet can reach the accelerator.

The cars are guided by rails and it is impossible to swing over into the next lane and have an accident. No matter which way you twist the steering wheel, you will always go safely forward.

As you go around the first corner on the racetrack, hidden speakers emit the horrible squeals of tortured rubber, as if you were taking the curve at terrifying speeds.

But not to worry. The cars go only a few miles per hour. It is the perfect Disney thrill: minimum terror with maximum safety.

A monorail takes you from the Magic Kingdom to Epcot, Disney's monument to corporate America.

There, I went on the ride sponsored by General Electric. The rides in Epcot are essentially the same no matter whether they are sponsored by GE or Exxon or General Motors.

They all show you a future shaped by the benevolence of giant corporations, a squeaky-clean future where there are no unsafe products, no poisoned air, no risk of nuclear accident.

There is no hunger. There is no want. Big business has seen to that.

But the GE ride makes a major miscalculation. It is the only mistake I found in Disney World.

The people in each little car get to choose their own ending to the ride. Everyone gets to punch a button and vote.

The votes are totaled by computer and the majority rules.

The ending is then projected on a screen and it is either a space journey or a trip under the ocean or something like that.

But the other couple in my car froze when the time came to vote. You choose, they said. You do it.

They had not come to Disney World to make decisions. Choice is very un-Disney. His is a world free from the burden of choice.

The rides pick you up and drop you off and show you things. All you have to do is observe.

It is comforting. It is almost narcotizing. And again, it is a pretty good analysis of what we have become.

We have become a nation of watchers. TV, movies, video recorders. You name it and we'll watch it.

Epcot stands for Experimental Prototype Community of Tomorrow, even though it is none of those things. The best part of it is something called "World Showcase."

Around a man-made lake (crystal clear, of course) stand replicas of cities from around the world. There are small but nicely done versions of the Eiffel Tower and Chinese temples and Mexican pyramids.

Each country creates its own idealized version of how it would like to be thought of. You can walk through seven countries and dine in local restaurants and buy local goods.

And everywhere you go, you hear people saying the same thing: "I guess we don't have to go to Europe now. We've *been* there."

They say it as a joke. But they are only half kidding.

Disney's goal was to make it possible to see the world without ever having to leave America.

It is a world that speaks English and takes dollars. It is a world where everyone loves us.

It is a safe world.

And, like everything else here, it is a fantasy.

But it sure is nice while it lasts.

April 18, 1984

Ethics a Press(ing) Issue

The reporters at the Republican National Convention were standing in line for their free shrimp and talking about Geraldine Ferraro's ethics.

They were talking about her "performance" on TV and whether she could "survive" her terrible sins.

We were told we could take as many platters of shrimp as we wanted—there was some real good crabmeat salad, too—and some of us took two or three platefuls.

Then we headed over to the beer coolers. There were hundreds of cold ones stacked up, all glistening with dew and waiting to be popped open.

We could, of course, take all we wanted. We were the press.

One reporter was so loaded down that he turned to one of the many people provided to wait upon us and said: "Hey, you got a box for this stuff?"

A box was instantly and cheerfully provided by a member of the Dallas Welcoming Committee. And the reporter stuffed a few more seafood platters and beers into it and walked off.

I couldn't hear whether he said thank you. That's because the reporter behind me was saying very loudly what a "sleazebag" Ferraro was.

He was balancing two plates of shrimp on two cold beers while he said it.

I admit I am having some trouble following the ins and outs of Ferraro's sins. I guess she took a loan from her husband and failed to report some stuff.

And so she had to go on live TV and be grilled for 90 minutes by hundreds of reporters. It must have been an intensely unpleasant experience.

But she chose her profession and it would be wrong to feel any compassion for her.

I don't know if any reporters are going to be grilled when they get back from Dallas about all the stuff they are taking, but, let me tell you, we are living like kings out here.

There are free and lavish parties sponsored by everyone from politicians to huge corporations to the Teamsters.

The biggies in the press are taken in limousines or even helicopters. But even the non-biggies, who don't get invited to many parties, still make out OK.

When every reporter arrived at the convention hall in Dallas (where work space is provided rent-free) he was handed a nice canvas carrying bag, courtesy of Dr Pepper and a bunch of local media.

Federal Express, which is located where every reporter must pass, just inside the glass doors of the huge press arena, does not put its freebies on display.

But the word is out. And one can see a steady stream of newspeople going up and asking for stuff.

"Can I have a 'Don't Panic' button?" the reporter will ask.

"Sure," the Federal Express guy says, taking one out of a drawer.

"Uh, and how about a whistle?" the reporter asks.

"Sure," the guy says, taking one out.

The game goes on and on, each new trinket taken out and handed over.

You can hardly blame Federal Express. If the press is going to beg for plastic whistles, why not provide them?

A lot of the gifts and parties are provided by the press for the press. There were huge parties by *Time* and *Newsweek* and *The New York Times* to name just a few.

And both the print and the electronic media are giving away book bags, hats, T-shirts, golf shirts, sweatshirts and windbreakers.

Gerry Ferraro's husband can't give even a loan to her, but the press can give gifts to each other. And even though the media cover the media—the larger papers and the networks have full-time reporters who cover the media as a beat—this is not considered payola.

The gifts are much sought after. I got a nifty *Dallas Morning News* pen that is attached to a string and hangs round my neck. And I also got a swell CBS News baseball hat that I only had to whine for two or three times.

Needless to say, I cannot be bought. But I do think both those news organizations are among the finest in the world.

Can I have my windbreaker now?

Ray Hunt, youngest of the billionaire Hunt brothers and president of Hunt Oil, sent a little gift pack to the reporters in the Hyatt Regency, the main press hotel.

THE BEST OF ROGER SIMON

It contained beer, wine, guacamole, and two beer mugs shaped like cowboy boots.

If anybody was outraged by an oil exec sending them goodies, I didn't hear any complaints. Except from me. Because I didn't get mine. (If Hunt would like to send it to me at home, I suggest he use Federal Express. I hear they're very good.)

And there is the famed Railroad Lounge, which is always at these conventions providing weary journalists with food, beer, a place to sit, and a television for watching.

Sponsored by "America's Freight Railroads," the place is admission-free and is always packed.

And you wonder why the railroads are in trouble.

I am not suggesting that any of my colleagues or I can be bought for a book bag or a pen or a party or 10 or 20 free meals or anything like that.

And I should point out that the media will spend millions of dollars in Dallas and some would say that being offered a free meal in return is just a gesture of gratitude.

But I also know that none of us would like to fill out lengthy ethics forms, listing everything we get and every person or organization we get it from.

And I'm sure none of us would like to face an ethics panel or a press conference for 90 minutes and explain how none of this affects what we do or say.

Politicians have to do that, because they are politicians.

We don't have to, because we are the press.

What could be more fair than that?

August 23, 1984

I Got a Gun
Past O'Hare Security

Undercover reporting has become controversial. Some newspapers won't condone it, saying it is neither seemly nor necessary. I believe that it can be both.

In the summer of 1979, after an airplane hijacking, an airport security guard told me about mismanagement of security at the nation's busiest airport, O'Hare. I printed that story and, while the Chicago City Council promised it would investigate, little to nothing was done.

But when I, and reporting intern Diane Balk, went undercover at O'Hare and reported our findings in a series of stories—that created a real stir. Scores of others came forward to confirm our findings and the results were turned over to the Federal Aviation Administration for corrections to the system.

Going undercover should not be a first resort. This is the only time I have ever done it. But as a last resort, it is a powerful reporting tool.

It was easy. I wanted to hijack a plane at O'Hare Airport and I found out it was a breeze.

I avoided all the security apparatus. And I did it with a gun in my pocket. It was simple. Too simple. Dangerously simple. I did it without even trying very hard. I walked past the security guards and the fancy X-ray machines right up to the gate where the plane was waiting. I carried a heavy, blue-steel starter's gun—not a real weapon, but very realistic—and walked up to the boarding gate.

Nobody stopped me. If anybody gave me a first glance, he didn't bother giving me a second one.

Earlier in the day, I had put a knife and simulated bomb in my luggage and got it through various metal detectors without ever being caught. Next, I wanted to see if I could avoid the detectors altogether.

I was checking security at O'Hare because of what had happened in June. On June 20, a hijacker, who had boarded a plane in New York, held it on the ground at O'Hare for hours as he negotiated with the police and FBI for the release of the passengers. Eventually, the hijacker took the plane to Ireland, where he gave up.

But an O'Hare security guard had told me a terrifying story of incompetence and mismanagement of security at O'Hare. She said security was so bad that anyone could get a bomb or a gun on board a plane. Other security guards also called me and told similar stories. After I wrote a column quoting the security guard, the Chicago City Council announced that it, too, would take a look at procedures at O'Hare.

In the weeks following, I had spent some lazy afternoons just walking around O'Hare, looking at how security worked. I saw, as any hijacker would instantly see, that pilots and stewardesses and maintenance people almost never went through the security gates. They didn't have their luggage X-rayed, nor did they walk under those little archways called magnetometers. They were not checked for weapons.

Instead, they walked past the security machines and up to the corridors that lead directly to the planes. Because the corridors are intended for exiting passengers only, security guards were always placed there to keep people from entering. But the guards always allowed airline personnel to go in.

The airline pilots and stewardesses and maintenance men were supposed to have ID cards clipped to their uniforms. Some did, and some didn't. But even when they did, the guards hardly ever looked twice. They just looked at the uniforms and allowed the pilots to enter.

I decided this would be the easiest way to hijack a plane. Why bother trying to sneak a bomb through the X-ray machine? Why not avoid the machines altogether?

I didn't do anything elaborate. I didn't even go to a costume store to rent a pilot's uniform. I just went home and put on a dark blue suit and a light blue shirt and a dark blue tie. On one breast pocket I pinned an Illinois driver's license, figuring that it looked somewhat like an official ID. Any security guard who took a good look would immediately catch me, but would they take a good look?

On the other side of my suit jacket, I pinned a pair of toy Delta Air Lines wings, the plastic kind that stewardesses hand out to children. Trying to penetrate the Delta Air Lines would be the easiest since I had Delta wings, but I wanted to give the security people every break I could. So I picked TWA, instead.

At the airport, I saw two security people guarding the TWA corridor. It was their job to make sure that people like me did not get

past them. This should have been one of the tightest security points in
the whole system, because anyone who walked past them was not
checked for weapons.

I put on a pair of sunglasses and walked toward them. My palms
were sweaty. I looked, and was, nervous. But I figured a hijacker
would be, too. I didn't really look that much like a pilot. My suit was
not cut like a uniform nor made out of uniform material. My hair was
too long, and I had no fancy stripes on my sleeve or other insignia.
Most of all, I had no uniform cap, which just about every pilot was
wearing. And the corridor was not busy; I could not hide among a
group of real pilots. I walked up to the two guards.

One of the guards, who was young and cheerful, took a step toward
me. She glanced at my Delta wings and then at the driver's license
pinned to my pocket. I'll never make it, I thought.

"Hi, how are you?" she asked with a smile.

"Have a nice day," I said.

And that was it. The other guard didn't even look at me. I was past
the guards and into the gate area with the airplanes. I could have
been carrying anything in my pockets: grenades, dynamite, anything.
I had beaten the elaborate security system of the world's busiest
airport by wearing a blue suit.

The planes were mine for the taking. I passed TWA jets bound for
New York and Harrisburg, Pennsylvania, and then saw the one I
wanted. Flight 146 to Philadelphia. The City of Brotherly Love. What
could be more perfect? My hand went into my pocket and tightened
on the starter's gun. I walked up to the boarding gate, where
passengers were entering the plane. . . .

For a month, we had taken an undercover look at the O'Hare
Airport security system, a system that is supposed to protect the lives
and safety of 50 million passengers a year.

Reporting intern Diane Balk had gone undercover to get jobs at two
security firms that provided the guards for most of the major airlines
at O'Hare.

And even though the guards, many of whom are teenagers, are the
only thing that stands between a terrorist and a plane, getting hired
was shockingly easy. One firm hired Balk the same day she applied;
neither checked her references.

At an airport as large and important as O'Hare we expected no less
than the best in security. Instead, we found that the O'Hare security
system is riddled with flaws. Some of the flaws were so obvious that
even a bad hijacker would have a chance for success.

We found that:

- Some of the X-ray machines do not work well enough to detect weapons. They produce hazy images in which bombs, guns, and knives are extremely difficult, if not impossible, to detect.
- Some magnetometers (the machines that passengers walk through) are erratic. Some did not sound warning signals even when large metal objects passed through them. Others beeped randomly even when nothing went through.
- A hand-held metal scanner had been broken at one airline for four months. When Balk said that she could not properly check passengers, she was told to "fake it."
- Chicago policemen, who are supposed to work with the security guards at the highly vulnerable exit gates, are often absent or not within hailing distance.
- Some veteran security workers had received no formal instruction on how to use the security equipment, but were allowed to do so anyway. Of those who received training, many said they still were not sure what dangerous weapons would look like on an X-ray screen.

  Said one security guard, who had been working for three months: "I don't know what I'm doing. I wouldn't know a bomb if I saw it."
- Some security guards were simply so bored with their jobs that they did not even bother to look at the X-ray screens as luggage passed through or do anything if the magnetometer gave a warning signal.
- Restricted areas at the boarding gates are often unguarded and unlocked. Balk was able to gain easy access to such areas, including the airfield itself.

Perhaps all the problems—equipment that does not work, poor screening and training of security personnel, bad security procedures—were best summed up by a veteran security guard named John. "If the FAA [Federal Aviation Administration] ever came down and saw what was going on, we'd be gone," he said. "If [we] don't straighten up, something's going to happen. *Then* they'll tighten up."

We want O'Hare Airport to tighten up *before* something happens. That is our purpose in exposing the flaws in the system. We are not providing a handbook for hijackers. Certain information we discovered, such as specific methods of passing weapons through the X-ray machines, we will not print, but will pass on to the proper authorities.

But the important and even shocking thing to keep in mind is that we found all these things *after* I wrote that column in June saying that security was "terrible" at O'Hare. Further, the City Council's intention to investigate O'Hare had been widely publicized.

We expected, therefore, that security would be much improved. But, in fact, we found that O'Hare Airport is an accident waiting to happen. The FAA is proud that, of the 25 hijackings that have taken place in this country in the last six years, none involved a real firearm or explosive. What the FAA should say is that none has involved one *yet*. The potential for such a hijacking is tremendous.

Balk found that many if not most of the security people she dealt with were hardworking and dedicated and took their jobs seriously. But the security system at O'Hare is without backup. If an untrained operator, or a bored operator, or an operator working with bad equipment, allows a suitcase or passenger with a knife or gun or bomb to go through the system, there is nothing to prevent that passenger from bringing the weapon aboard the plane.

It is the classic example of a chain being as strong as its weakest link. Too many of the links at O'Hare are too weak. The chain is too easily shattered.

And it doesn't take elaborate plans or devices to do it. Sometimes all it takes is a blue suit, a driver's license, and a set of plastic wings. . . .

I had gotten past the security system and was ready to hijack my plane. I walked up to the boarding gate of Flight 146, bound for Philadelphia. I looked out at the sleek, white Boeing 707, its metal skin shimmering in the summer sun. I wanted it. And it was mine for the taking. I had my fake pistol in my pocket, and nobody could stop me. All I had to do was jab it in the ribs of the flight attendant and walk down the ramp and be off.

The passengers began to board. As I stood staring at my plane, I was blocking the way of one of them. "Excuse me," an exasperated lady said. "Are you taking this plane?"

"No," I said. "Just looking."

July 29, 1979

Elevator Episode
a Four-Story Saga

ashomon, one of the most famous movies ever made, deals with a moment of violence viewed by four persons.

In the movie, each person recounts the moment from his own perspective. And though each person saw the same thing, all four accounts are dramatically different.

The movie tells us something about myth and reality and how close together they sometimes are.

This week, I felt like one of the people in *Rashomon*.

I had picked up a Chicago newspaper and had come across a column that hit me like a slap in the face by a wet mackerel.

The columnist had written about an event in which we were both involved. In order to mask his identity, I will identify the columnist merely as Bob Greene of the *Chicago Tribune*.

Greene wrote about a day a number of years ago during which a group of journalists paid a surprise birthday visit to a friend.

We had all gathered together in the elevator of the friend's building. Greene then related how the elevator got stuck.

"It was about 100 degrees in that elevator," he wrote. "We were belly-to-back; there was not an inch to turn around.

"One of the other guests—he is a calm, intelligent, dignified columnist for another paper—began scratching and tearing at the elevator door like a strongman trying to open a can of sardines with his bare fingers. For a few seconds, it had no effect; it was like a gerbil trying to get footing on a sheet of greased metal. But, amazingly, it worked. He yanked the door open, and we were almost level with the host's floor and we climbed out."

As I'm sure you guessed from the description, I was that columnist.

Yet I recall the episode very differently. So, in order to arrive at the truth, I interviewed some of the people on the elevator and in the building that day. I begin with myself.

Roger Simon, columnist:
It was raining. Mist hung from the lamp posts like a bad memory.

Out on the lake, a gull sounded its lonely cry and was silent.

Either that or it was sunny. One of the two.

We were all packed onto this elevator. It began to rise. Then it stopped. It began to fall.

I shouted: "Save yourselves! Climb on top of me. I die so that journalism might live."

Greene shouted: "Mommy!"

The other passengers were too stunned to react. I knew it was up to me.

I calmly reached over and grabbed the steel doors. I pried them open, saving us all.

A cheer went up from the other passengers.

Greene tried to kiss my hand, but I brushed him off.

"Your strength is as the strength of 10," he said. "I owe you everything."

I shrugged. "I'm a newspaperman," I said with my cruel half-smile. "I cheat death every day."

Brian Kelly, author:
Both of you were pathetic. We were stuck in the elevator for about 12 seconds and you both fell apart.

I remember turning around and seeing great streams of sweat pouring off Greene's face. He was whimpering something over and over. Maybe he was praying.

You were clawing at the door like a maniac. Nobody could figure out why. We were in that elevator with six pizzas, two birthday cakes, and 12 six-packs of beer.

We could have lived there for a week.

I remember Pat Wingert turning to me and saying; "Are those two wimps with you?"

Pat Wingert, reporter:
What elevator? I would never get on an elevator with you and Greene.

Paul Galloway, feature writer and birthday boy:
I had just gotten off the phone with the president, who was calling to wish me a happy birthday.

I heard strange noises like muffled screams. I ran into the hall and realized the noises were coming from the elevator.

Through the closed door, I asked what was happening.

A strong, firm voice called back: "We are trapped in here with two madmen. Please call the animal control office and ask them for a dart gun."

I went back to my apartment. I wasn't worried.

I knew no matter what happened, both you turkeys would get a column out of it someday.

August 12, 1982

Dickie's Dream:
A Home for Momma

He was short and heavy and slow. He could not read. He could barely sign his name.

He was the kind of kid who'd stand on the sidewalk while you washed your car and say, "Hey, mister, what're you doing?"

You'd look at him and say, "I'm washing my car, dummy, whattya think I'm doing?"

He'd look hurt and so you'd go over to him and he'd offer to wash the car for you and you'd give him a few bucks.

Once when that happened, he ran to the corner grocery afterward and spent nearly all the money on chicken wings for his family.

"Why'd you do that, Dickie?" his mother asked him. "Why'd you spend all you had on those wings?"

"Cause I want to help," he said. "You need help, don't you, Momma?"

He was 24 when they killed him.

The police said it was an argument over a bottle of wine. His mother says no; her son was no wino. Two men were charged with the crime. I wrote about the case a few months ago.

Now, a judge has found the two men not guilty. So it is all over.

Except that Nellie Garrett still must walk out of her building every day and see the spot where her son crawled to her bleeding to death from his stab wounds and said: "Don't let me die."

"My son was retarded," she said. " 'Funny' I used to call it. He was . . . not right. He tried to go to school, but he couldn't do it. He'd come home and cry and say, 'They laughin' at me, Momma. I can't read and they laughin' at me.'

"I'd say: 'We're gonna read together. You and me.' And we'd try, but he couldn't. I couldn't blame him. He was like Big Moose in the Archie comic books, you understand? And the kids would laugh at him and he said to me: 'Not going back. I'm not going back to school.' "

He would walk the streets on the West Side of Chicago where he lived. His name was William, but his family called him Dickie; they can't remember why. He was good with his hands and liked to work around cars, but he never could find much of a job. He would help a person here or there and they'd give him a dollar or two.

"He would be on the street, you know, with the others," his mother said, "and he'd say: 'I'm gonna buy my momma a home.' Bragging like. And the others would laugh and say, 'How you gonna do that? You don't even have a high school degree.'

"And he'd come home and he'd say, 'Momma, don't you worry. I'm gonna get you off this street. I'm gonna.' "

To be in a gang is almost a way of life on the West Side, and the morgue pictures of Dickie, introduced at the trial, show a gang tattoo on his arm.

"But he was no gang-banger," his mother insists. "He got that tattoo when he was 14 and our pastor said to him one day, 'Remove that off you' and he was gonna do it. But that takes money and he never had that.

"And listen, you know how these gang members dress? Well, my son when he was killed had a pair of three-dollar pants from Amvets up on 26th St. and a lumberman shirt from Amvets and a pair of black shoes my sister give him. That's no gang member.

"And at his funeral—I went to a gang funeral once and there were hundreds there—but Dickie's funeral it was very small, very small. And there were no punks there. There were no punks at my son's funeral."

He tried to get off the street. He tried again and again to pass the test to get into the Army, but he couldn't do that.

"He couldn't even really read the test," his mother said. "And then his brother, Sherman, well, him and Dickie took the Job Corps test and Sherman passed and Dickie didn't and Dickie went into the bedroom and cried.

"A 24-year-old man crying. But you got to be humble to cry. And I went in there and he was making these crying sounds and I put my arm around him. He was my son, you understand?"

I asked her what she had in mind for him, what she wanted for him.

"I thought maybe a janitor's job," she began. "Just sweeping up. He could do that.

"And I always wanted a wife for him. I wanted somebody to love him like I did. He clung to me because he didn't have nobody else.

"He'd be out on the street and they'd yell, 'When you going to leave home, fat boy?' And he'd run home and he'd start talking those dreams to me, how he was going to buy me a house, and it would make me feel so bad when he started talking those big dreams.

"See, I knew he was never going to be an Einstein. He wasn't going to be president or mayor or even on a basketball team. He wasn't going to be big. But he was my son. And he had those big dreams. He had those dreams for me. And now he's gone."

She didn't say anything for a while and it seemed like I ought to.

I think he would have bought you that house, I said. I think if he could have, he would have.

"Oh, yes," she said. "Oh, yes."

May 12, 1983

CAMPAIGN '80

Once upon a time, in a place called America, running for president was fairly simple.

You took a stand, you saddled a horse, and you went out to address the multitudes.

Today, an entire industry exists to sell the candidate to the people. There are media experts and speaking coaches and—as Richard Nixon found out—makeup men.

And while the candidate and the message reach a heretofore undreamed of number of people, something else gets obscured: what these candidates are really like.

I was in the back of the press bus at the end of another burnt out day, not trying to figure out what town we were in—that, I knew, was hopeless—but at least trying to figure out what time zone we were in.

I began a conversation with a reporter crammed into the seat next to me and asked him: "What do you think these guys are like, deep down?"

He thought for a moment. "I'm not sure that deep down they have a deep down," he said.

Debatable Issues:
Hair Dye, Makeup

MANCHESTER, New Hampshire

The hired guns sat in the high school auditorium joking easily with one another.

They were the professionals, the top aides, the men and women who made the campaigns work. They were here to hammer out the ground rules for tonight's League of Women Voters debate.

It will be televised nationally both on CBS and PBS and will mark the first time all seven Republican presidential candidates are on the same stage.

Technically called a forum, although everyone is calling it a debate, it is arguably the single most important event of the New Hampshire primary.

Up in the rows of seats, the TV technicians were setting up their cameras on a huge scaffolding and snaking out foot after foot of thick, black cable.

Carpenters were sawing sections of raw, unfinished plywood. Very serious women were walking around carrying very serious clipboards.

"Will the audience be allowed to cheer and clap?" the Philip Crane aide asked.

The conservative candidates did not want cheering and clapping from the audience. They figured most of the audience would be members of the league and they figured most of the league would not be cheering and clapping for conservatives.

"Yeah, what about yelling?" asked the John Connally aide. "We going to allow yelling?"

"How about laughing?" the John Anderson aide said, laughing herself.

"And sighing," said the Bob Dole aide.

"And crying," said the Ronald Reagan aide.

Lee Hanna, the league director for the debates, who is running things with good humor and cool efficiency, calmed everyone down.

No laughing, no sighing, no crying, he told them. The audience would be told not to react to anything.

Hanna then ran through the schedule, outlining when each candidate would be brought in for makeup.

"We'd like to start alphabetically with John Anderson," he said, turning to the Anderson woman.

"No," she said firmly. "Let's draw lots for who gets made up first."

"Well, our man never uses makeup," the Reagan man said.

Everyone burst out laughing.

"And we don't use hair dye," the Crane man hooted.

The Dole woman spoke up. "We want 15 minutes beforehand just to let the candidates stumble around the stage," she said. "You know, let them look at the door they have to walk through, let them sit in the chair, let them see the microphone."

The others agreed strenuously. They knew that taking a presidential candidate into a strange place was like taking a kindergartner to school on the first day.

"We gotta find out where all the cans are," one aide said to another.

I was the only reporter present and had been tipped off to the meeting by a campaign worker who felt it would be a show not to be missed.

"What does everyone want?" I asked one of the hired guns. "To be first in the seating order on stage?"

"That and something else," he said. "But you didn't hear it from me."

I promised.

"It's Dole," he said. "Nobody wants to sit next to Dole. He's got such a sharp tongue that the s.o.b. might turn it on whoever is sitting next to him."

"Are notes permitted?" the Reagan man asked.

Hanna said the league had no objection to notes.

"What about interruptions?" the Connally man asked. "Can the candidates interrupt each other?"

Hanna said, no, that didn't seem like a good idea.

"Let's black out the audience," an aide suggested. "I want them sitting in the dark."

"Wait a second," said the Crane man, "that's going a little far."

If the audience were blacked out, the TV cameras could not take pictures of the audience reacting to what the candidates said.

Hanna stepped in. "We can't control that," he said firmly. "This is a news event and we can't control what television does, we can't control reaction shots. The federal election law forbids us from doing that."

"Will the candidates remain seated throughout?" the Reagan man asked.

To the aides and to the candidates, this was serious stuff. These debates could make or break a candidacy and nobody was taking any chances.

It was agreed that all the candidates would remain seated throughout.

An NBC producer and director were brought in to answer questions. NBC was the "pool" network, meaning it provided the coverage for everyone.

The aides were extremely worried about camera placement, wanting to know exactly what angle their candidates would be shot from.

"Will each camera have a red light when it is on?" the Connally man asked.

"All except the minicam, which will be roving," he was told. "Otherwise each candidate will know when the camera is on him."

"If my candidate is on stage left, where will he be looking?" one aide asked.

"Will there be cameras in the wings?" another asked.

"Can my candidate practice speaking into the microphone?" another asked.

The aides asked again about reaction shots, knowing that if the audience looked bored or angry or laughed while their man was talking, it could be devastating.

"We're covering an event," the NBC director said. "This is news. There will be reaction shots."

"Look, we consider ourselves a fourth entity, separate from NBC when we are doing something like this," the producer said. "We will be scrupulously fair about cutting away from the candidates."

"Did you hear that?" the Reagan man whispered to the Crane man. "He said he had to be separate from NBC to be scrupulously fair."

Hanna decided it was time to pick the stage positions, which would also determine speaking order.

A league worker brought out a Styrofoam coffee cup with seven folded pieces of paper inside.

"Let's pick alphabetically," Hanna said. The Anderson woman stood up to pick.

"Hold it," said the Reagan man. "That means I go last. I get what everyone leaves over. Why does she go first?"

Hanna asked what method he would prefer.

"Let's pick to pick," he said. "We pick a number to determine what order we pick the numbers in."

Everyone groaned. "Look," the Anderson woman said. "You want to pick for me?"

"I want to pick for *me*," he said.

"OK, OK, you pick first," she said and sat down. "We'll go in reverse."

He picked. He slowly unfolded his number. It was 7. Dead last.

Everyone shouted with glee. The others picked in reverse order until there was only one slip left for the Anderson woman.

She picked No. 1.

The laughter fell upon the Reagan man like a thunderstorm. Not only was Reagan last and Anderson first, but Reagan would have to sit next to Bob Dole.

The Reagan man tried to take it in stride. He looked up at the stage and ran down the seating order in his mind.

"Oh, well," he said with a shrug, "at least we're on the extreme right."

February 20, 1980

Guns, Butter: That's Rich, Ron

BELLEVILLE, Illinois

The girls lean forward on their knees, looking up at the stage. They are wearing white blouses and blue slacks and bright red ribbons that say REAGAN in white letters. Their home-permed curls are crushed beneath straw hats that repeat his name in blue letters. In each hand, they hold a pom-pom.

Their incredibly young faces—uncreased by care, unmarked by woe—follow the candidate's every word with unblinking devotion.

Ronald Reagan stands above them, flanked by an American flag and a local politician. He is wearing a blue-black houndstooth jacket reminiscent of a forties dance band or a fifties bar mitzvah. On his right lapel he wears a white rose surrounded by baby's breath. His dark hair glistens under the shopping center lights.

It is one of those shopping centers that has destroyed 10 acres of countryside greenery to re-create 10 acres of countryside greenery. There are trees and plants, walkways of fake brick, and lighting that conveys a faint Main Street, good-old-days air.

Reagan is concluding his speech. "I just hope," he says, pointing down to the crouching girls in front of him, "that these children will know the freedom we once knew."

The applause is warm. Members of the crowd hold up signs saying, "Thank You For Opposing ERA." A four-year-old girl, sitting petitely on a chair, waves a sign saying, "We Love Ronnie," back and forth over her head with two hands.

The Collinsville High School Band strikes up "When the Saints Go Marching In." People cheer. They press close to the restraining ropes to shake his hand. He works the crowd slowly, enjoying the crush.

We are in southern Illinois, where Republicans are Republicans and Democrats are Democrats. In others words, the Republicans are for Reagan and the Democrats aren't going to cross over and vote for John Anderson.

That is a good feeling to Reagan. He likes it down here and it shows. Although he left Illinois more than 45 years ago, in a sense he is home. His speech works, the laughs work, the lines work, the theme works.

And the theme these days is good times for all.

Let the Democrats whine and moan and tell you to conserve. Let John Anderson tell you to sacrifice. Let George Bush try and tell you anything.

Not Ron Reagan. "How many times has Jimmy Carter come before us and acted as if this economy were our fault," he says. "As if it were some kind of plague that came out of the air because you and I are spending too much, we're buying too many things, we're living too well.

"Carter says we've got to get used to *austerity* and *sharing* and *scarcity* and give up *luxury*," he says, pausing professionally for two beats.

"Well I don't believe that! I think we should cover our children's ears when they hear that kind of talk!"

And who could be a more perfect candidate to sell this?

Look at the guy. Can you look at this guy and think *you've* got troubles? You say you're tired and defeated? You say when you come home at the end of the day your feet hurt?

My God, when Ron Reagan comes home at the end of the day, his *face* hurts. And is he crying? Is he worried? You bet he's not. This guy is happy.

Let others show you how the glass is half empty. Ronald Reagan will show you how it is half full, and will promise to fill it up until it slops over on your shoes.

He says he wants to slash the budget and the applause is tremendous.

He says he wants to increase military spending and the crowd goes wild.

He says he wants to stop inflation and he brings down the house.

He says he wants more luxury and everyone cheers.

What the hell. Why *not* guns and butter? And not only guns, but the biggest guns, the best guns. And butter? We're talking the high-priced spread, prosperity like you've never seen.

Why not? Let others promise you less; Ronald Reagan promises you more.

"The president is trying to tell you we're energy poor!" he shouts. "He's trying to tell you to give up driving or drive less or dial down your thermostat or turn it off or wear blankets!"

The audience is laughing with him now at that crazy ol' Jimmy Carter. What an old lady that guy is.

"We're not energy poor," Reagan tells them. "We're rich. Rich!"

What, us worry? Not us. Not America. We've got so much, why, if big government would just get out of our way, the goodies would flow from the cornucopia like milk and honey.

And it goes over. Here anyway. I do not know if Ronald Reagan will carry the state or if he will carry the country. I do know he will carry this shopping center.

He shakes hand after hand, the press trailing along behind. And when we go back to the bus, there, next to the driver is a plastic garbage pail filled with ice and studded with glorious cans of Stag and Budweiser. Cans so glistening and cold that the beads of water on them look like dew on a mountain flower.

And on each of our seats, a box lunch of fried chicken! With cole slaw and potato salad and a shiny red apple. And do we tear into it! Fifty reporters ripping into that old chicken, sippin' down the suds, and lookin' and noddin' at each other with big greasy smiles.

And then it strikes me. We have found the metaphor for the Reagan campaign:

Ronald Reagan holding out a frosty one to America and saying with that little boy grin: "Here's to good friends."

Ronald Reagan—for the good life.

March 16, 1980

◆

Jerry Brown Rides in on a Doombeam

CONCORD, New Hampshire

It is the politics of apocalypse.

Gone is the talk of Spaceship Earth and small is beautiful. Gone is Jerry Brown as the guru of goofiness.

The theme these days is simple: Vote for Jerry Brown—or die.

"The prospects are bleak. We are looking down the road to depression and world war.

"The chickens are coming home to roost. We are an island of affluence, sinking in a rising sea of despair."

Wha? Huh? Who is this guy, Martha? Do I need this at nine in the morning? I haven't got enough troubles?

About 75 employees of the Sears store in the Mall of New Hampshire have gathered together before opening time to hear the candidate.

They expected a little politics, a few jokes, some nice talk about a better America and a little coffee and danish. But this? What is this?

"Draft registration is just a way of getting kids to die to make oil companies richer," Jerry Brown is telling them, and you can see the shock on their faces, a visible recoil as he plunges on.

"Nuclear power is grossly immoral. All it gives you is a legacy of bankruptcy and cancer. They are lying to you about nuclear power.

"It can destroy our gene pool, irradiate our food chain, and the people making the decisions don't care. They just want to get re-elected and collect their pensions.

"Have you got your iodine for your thyroid cancer yet?"

He stands there, gray-suited and lean, much leaner than he appears on TV, one hand in his pocket, his digital watch still set to California time, and lobs these . . . hand grenades.

"We're being pushed to a war to divert attention from the fact that America is declining as an industrial power.

"There is a deterioration of human, technological, and environmental assets.

"We face increasing social tension, the unraveling of our social fabric, and perhaps a change in our democratic form of government."

He stands there in the middle of Sears, amid the contempo towels and the superplush bath mats, amid the swivel rockers and the queen-size sleepers, amid the seven-piece dinette sets and the 30-inch electric ranges, and lowers the boom.

"Our economy is out of control and Carter and Kennedy know it's out of control. So they hope they can distract you with grain embargos, Olympic boycotts, and the draft arguments," he says.

While there is considerable applause, not all the Sears employees are falling over each other to climb on the Brown bandwagon this morning.

"Hey, what about the Russians?" an Auto Center worker, dressed in green coveralls and a baseball cap, asks. "They want to take over everything. What you gonna do about them?"

"Who says they want to take over everything?" Brown snaps back, jaw thrust out. "You want to go to war over Pakistan? You want to prop up a dictator who burned our embassy?

"OK, go ahead. But do you know what that will mean? That will mean nuclear war. And do you know what that means? Do you?"

The guy shakes his head, taking an involuntary halfstep back.

"It means, " the governor of California tells him, coming down on each word like a drummer hitting the bass pedal, "it means you . . . will . . . be . . . vaporized!"

Jerry Brown is eating nails and spitting out tacks these days. Let other candidates tell you about a better future, Jerry Brown is telling you that unless you sacrifice—right now!—there won't be any future at all.

Up in Maine a few weeks ago, he got about 14 percent of the vote and even though he is virtually without money, he feels that his campaign will catch fire. He would like to get from 10 to 20 percent in the New Hampshire primary.

After the Sears store, his informal motorcade, made up of five or six reporters each driving his own car, blasts down to the Budweiser plant in Merrimack.

Inside the plant he delivers his cheery little pitch, ending with his theme song:

"Let us look at all we have not as something we inherit from our parents, but rather as something we borrow from our children."

After that, he speeds through the plant, shaking hands, refusing a beer (he is on the Pritikin diet and is a scotch drinker, besides) and then plunges on to an energy conference in Concord.

In 1976, Brown came in first in five primaries and for a few weeks there he looked like a real contender.

He was hoping to do better this time around and believes that his call for a balanced budget and gasoline rationing will win support after foreign policy stops dominating the campaign. Ted Kennedy, he believes, just ain't got it.

"Look, I can stay in this thing longer than Kennedy," he says. "I am spending less money. Once it's just Carter and me, there is my real chance.

"I'll fire the staff if I have to. I'll hitchhike, I'll beg food. I'm lean and frugal and low to the ground.

"I am broke and in trouble," he says, and then, almost as an afterthought, he grins. "And that is why I am just like America."

February 19, 1980

The Cheer Kennedy Loves to Hate

NEW YORK

H e must hate them. Just a little.

Even as they cheer him, he must hate them.

Teddy Kennedy must hate the ones who came to him when the polls were so sweet and begged him to run. He must hate the ones who said they would stand up for him but faded away when the time came.

How many of them could he see out there last night? As his tired eyes scanned back and forth over the delegates at the Democratic National Convention, did he count how many had betrayed him?

They cheered him, of course. They cheered like madmen, like fanatics. Their faces grew red, and their voices grew hoarse and raw as they yelled his name over and over.

They always love you when you are through. They cheer your name and shout for you when you are all washed up.

The press praises you. They call you gutsy and gracious. They say you weren't such a bad guy after all.

They always praise you when it no longer counts.

Ted Kennedy's candidacy lasted 279 days. Bobby Kennedy's candidacy lasted 82. John Kennedy's presidency lasted just over a thousand.

There is something about the Kennedys that makes you measure them in days.

It would be nice to say that it ended in a 12-room suite in the Waldorf-Astoria Hotel, as Ted Kennedy, shoes off, tie unknotted, watched three TV sets carry the message of his doom from the convention floor.

In fact, it ended long ago. Somewhere in Illinois in March, perhaps, or maybe much earlier. The votes simply were not there.

Self-doubt is a luxury candidates seldom engage in. The rest of the country kept asking, "Why do you keep running?"

Kennedy kept answering, "What else is there to do?"

It would have been harder to stop than to continue. These men live to run. Running is to a politician what action is to a gambler. You never get enough. And, if you play long enough, you usually lose.

They say that Ted Kennedy is unaccustomed to losing, but that is not true. He had lost continually for years. Every year he is not president, he loses.

If high ambition is the trademark of the Kennedys, it is also their curse.

For months, we said it was Chappaquiddick that did him in, that made him unelectable. But Chappaquiddick was just an excuse.

In fact, we just disliked him. He had too much. It seemed too easy for him. He had looks and wealth and power and could get any woman he wanted. We were not about to forgive that.

We wanted him to suffer a little. We wanted him to know that he was not the equal of his brothers. We wanted him to feel pain.

It did not matter to us that he had two brothers who were murdered, a troubled wife, and a kid with cancer. That was not enough. We wanted to bring him low.

And for all the fine words he delivered in such striking cadence last night, he had been brought low. He had just been told by the Secret Service that his agents would soon be removed.

The body of Ted Kennedy was no longer of official interest to the Republic.

He had announced for the presidency on a spectacular fall day in Boston. Standing in stately Fanueil Hall, he carefully read his speech under a somber picture of Daniel Webster. He rarely looked up.

It took him 16 minutes to say he wanted to be president.

It took him less than two the other night to say he wasn't going to be.

Kennedy's fatal flaw this year was not his character. If anything, he had too much character. He refused to twist and turn in the prevailing winds. Instead, as he liked to say, his brother John had taught him to sail against the wind.

No matter what you might think of him, the record will show he was the only candidate who spoke for the poor and meant it.

No matter how you feel about him, he was the only candidate who spoke for the minorities and believed it.

No matter how much you hate him, he was the only man who looked at those with little and felt they should have more.

Perhaps he will try it one more time, perhaps not.

But something will remain.

"The dream," he said, "shall never die."

August 13, 1980

Simon Can't Stop Saying It

I don't know anyone who has as much fun as those people on the beer commercials.

◆

Now that you're grown up, aren't you sorry you read the Cliffs Notes instead of the book?

◆

I suppose we'll all be wearing them in a few months, but I'm not sure I'm ready for gravity boots.

◆

I get inexpressably sad every time I hear "Auld Lang Syne."

◆

There is something about pony-tails that drives me crazy.

◆

Don't you panic when those little cracks appear in your credit card and you know it will split before you get a new one?

◆

Taken together, *The Godfather* and *The Godfather Part II* were the best movie ever made.

◆

People will eat things on airplanes that they would never eat anywhere else.

◆

I don't know what roughage is, but it sounds good.

People who insist on asking bank tellers if they have any free samples today should be hit with a roll of quarters.

◆

Why does it take just over two minutes to run the Kentucky Derby but 90 minutes for TV to talk about it?

◆

Instead of executing criminals, why don't we just make them watch public TV on pledge nights?

◆

People who use the word party as a verb, as in "Let's party," should be beaten with sticks.

◆

I don't care what those commercials show, I've never been able to get a flashlight to go on without whacking it two or three times.

◆

I can't help it, I'm in love with those Grolsch beer bottles.

◆

There is nothing more nerve-wracking than trying to parallel park with a stranger in the car.

◆

You know you're growing up when you prefer dark chocolate to milk chocolate.

Somehow, miniskirts just aren't as exciting the second time around.

◆

People in theaters who put their feet up on the seat in front of them should have their legs cut off at the ankle.

◆

I still haven't made up my mind about cole slaw.

◆

You know you're in love when you share a Chapstick.

◆

I'd like steak tartare better if it weren't so rare.

◆

If God had meant baseball to be played indoors, he would have given the players plastic feet.

◆

What's the excuse for Leroy Nieman?

◆

Does any woman still brush her hair 100 times every night?

◆

When people see something they think is a tuba, it's usually a sousaphone.

◆

Weathermen who assume personal responsibility for the weather really irritate me.

◆

I have yet to see a pitcher who could compare with Sandy Koufax.

Don't you wish you were young enough to use a swing set again?

◆

There will never be another James Dean.

◆

Why is it supposed to be manly to drink your coffee black?

◆

Aren't you sorry that your mother saved your baby pictures?

◆

Why do I always break out in a sweat when I have to use a coupon in a grocery store?

◆

You can tell a lot about a person by where he likes to sit in a movie theater.

◆

The process of dry cleaning is one of life's great mysteries to me.

◆

Whatever happened to painting-by-numbers?

◆

Don't trust anyone who puts ketchup on his steak.

◆

How come they can't make stamps that don't tear in half when you try to get them out of those little books?

◆

People who pronounce almond without the "l" drive me crazy.

The real test of a car wash is not just how well they wash the car, but how well they dry it.

◆

People who have trays on their desk that are actually labeled "In" and "Out" are the kind of people I try to avoid.

◆

I'll bet there are as many coffee cans with pennies in them as with coffee.

◆

I think Bud Collins has been hit in the head by too many topspin forehands.

◆

Check your cupboard right now. If you save grocery bags, I'll bet you'll find enough there for three lifetimes.

◆

I wonder about people who get in an elevator and face the rear.

◆

If we can land a man on the moon, why can't we invent a quiet motorcycle?

◆

I worry that there will never be another Charles Kuralt.

◆

If people with dogs have to carry pooper-scoopers, what do mounted policemen have to carry?

◆

Do Jacques Cousteau's fingers ever prune up?

You know you are rich when you can order a shrimp cocktail without checking your wallet first.

◆

True confessions:
- I borrow pens and don't return them.
- I look in other people's medicine chests.
- If I spill something on a friend's rug, I cover it with my foot.
- I always agree with cab drivers, even when I think they are wrong.
- I watch "Family Feud" whenever I can.

◆

The decline of America began when paper napkins replaced cloth ones.

◆

Wearing clip-on sunglasses and understanding the metric system are two sure signs of nerdhood.

◆

I bet you don't know your own blood type.

◆

I don't like trains, but I sure would like to ride in a caboose.

◆

Can't you sometimes tell nobody is home just by the way the phone rings?

◆

Is there anything more embarrassing than being caught singing along to your car radio?

Now They Are
Only Two Numbers

*I don't know exactly why I called the morgue when I heard they
were pulling bodies of young men from beneath the floorboards of
John Wayne Gacy's home.*

*I have no excuse for the press's fascination with the horrible. Or for
the public's.*

I just knew it was a story and so I went.

*Later, I would get the only newspaper interview with Gacy, America's number one mass murderer, now on Death Row at the Menard
Correctional Center in Chester, Illinois. Gacy was given 12 separate
death sentences and 21 sentences of natural life in prison with no
hope of parole for the 33 lives he took.*

*First scheduled to die on July 2, 1980, he is appealing his
convictions.*

*"Most people are looking for a raging maniac, an animal," Gacy told
me. "I am just the opposite. I am quiet and kind."*

*In fact, he is a vicious killer who strangled some of his victims very
slowly so he could watch them suffer. Yet he gets many "fan" letters,
90 percent, he said, from women.*

*As for the occasional hate letter, Gacy has an explanation: "There are
sick, sick people out there. Our society is made up of a bunch of sick
people."*

*He does not think he is one of them, however. Nor does he think he
will ever be executed. He says he sleeps just fine.*

It was cold in the room, and through the harsh chemical smell
came the faint jungle odor of decay. The tiles were green and the
floor was bare.

Douglas Childress wheeled in the steel cadaver cart and stopped it
under the lights.

The Cook County medical examiner, Dr. Robert Stein, tugged the
white, plastic bag into position.

"They are perfect skeletons," he said. "No dismemberment. No damage to the skulls. Three had cords around their necks. It reminded me of clothesline. And knots, tight knots."

In black ink on the body bag was scrawled: Body 14. That is who this man is to the police. Also on the bag was a tag that said: Case 1329. That is who he is to Dr. Stein.

Somewhere he has a name and parents and maybe brothers and sisters. Somewhere, Body 14 has a past. Here, in what is known informally as the Cook County morgue, here lies his only future.

All we know for certain is that he and nearly a score of others were taken from the home of John Gacy, remodeling contractor, children's clown, Democratic precinct captain, and now a murder suspect.

Even as these words are written, the death toll in the Gacy home rises. Fifteen of the bodies are here in the morgue, neatly labeled, waiting for someone to find out who they are.

During their wait they are kept in a room just down the hall from this one. It is called Crypt 1. It is a large room with horizontal racks along the wall. A refrigeration unit pumps near-freezing air into the crypt. Outside in the hall, the regular collection of bodies lies on carts in different degrees of agony. Some lie in peaceful repose, and others lie twisted, arms locked in the memory of their final moments of life.

But the bodies in Crypt 1 are special. "We put a lock on these," Childress said, twisting a key in the heavy metal padlock. He pulled open the door to reveal the 15 young men, the 15 white plastic body bags, called pouches, stacked on the metal trays that fit onto the walls.

"There was a tremendous health hazard in getting the bodies out of the house," Stein said. "We found one under concrete in the garage, one under a concrete slab in the crawl space under the house, and 13 just under dirt in the crawl space.

"When we first dug up the body from the garage, we all got woozy. It was the methane gas from the body decomposition. I ordered a stop for a while.

"Look, we are literally working in a grave down there. We've torn up the floors, and we are working in the raw earth and mud. I'm just worried about the walls of the house collapsing on us.

"The men are digging with their fingers—their fingers! Sure we've got heavy gloves, but even a scratch on the hand could be dangerous.

"We go in there in firemen's boots, with disposable coveralls," Stein said. "We have gloves. No, no face masks. The skeletons lift very nicely, very nicely. You put your hands underneath and take a little dirt with them. Sometimes they break, but that's OK.

"At first, the whole area resembled trench warfare. Next, I thought of a horror movie, where you see the decomposed bodies.

"Now, it's a maze down there. A maze. But the things in the maze are not marbles or checkers. They are bodies. The bodies of young men."

Stein is a compact, dapper man. His graying hair, his neat mustache, his three-piece suits and conservative ties make him look like a Norman Rockwell drawing of the friendly family doctor.

"What I am wondering," Stein continued, "is how in hell he got away with all this unnoticed. Here is a man socially acceptable, politically acceptable, children love him as a clown, good at his business, the neighbors swear by him.

"People are now wondering, looking. You go have a beer at a tavern, and you look down the bar, and you see some ordinary guy. And you wonder how many bodies does he have buried?

"I don't know. The psychiatrists will have fancy words for this. The toughest part for me will be the identification of the bodies. The teeth are in good shape. They have characteristic markings, fillings, caps, the like. When we get dental charts, we will be in business. But so far we have received no charts. We need those charts.

"The bodies are really just skeletons. We will do some toxicology tests, but all the meat is gone.

"I can't say we will ever identify everyone. We may never identify some. I talked to the medical examiner in Houston [where 27 bodies were found in 1973]. He's still got a whole bunch that have never been identified."

Once more, Stein snapped back from thoughts of the dead to the living. "You know," he said. "He must have been sitting in his living room, sitting there at the built-in bar, watching TV or listening to his stereo and knowing that there were 15 or 20 or who knows how many bodies underneath him."

He shook his head in silence.

We knew the time had come. Stein pulled on the surgical gloves and then looked up for a moment before he began. "No photographs of what's in the bag," he said. "I won't allow that."

He unzipped the body bag from the feet up to the head. On top of the mud-caked skeleton, a shoe rested in the liquid earth and bone.

"Every piece of dirt is important," Stein said. "Every sliver of bone. Everything. It is all important. It is what we do."

And if you ask why, the answer lies upstairs from here. Upstairs, away from the harsh light and smells, in Stein's book-lined office.

On the wall is a motto, in Latin and English, of his childhood hero, the medical examiner of New York. It says:

Let the conversation cease.
Let laughter flee.
This is the place where death delights to help the living.

December 29, 1978

Janna (Almost 15)
Is a Classic Adviser

I have decided to form a National Advisory Board that will keep me informed on important issues.

Presidential candidates do this and all of them look like geniuses—don't they?

The first person I am naming to my board is Janna Beckerman of Cleveland Heights, Ohio.

Not long ago, she read one of my columns in the Cleveland Plain Dealer in which I said I neither knew nor cared about the difference between Punk and New Wave music.

Janna knows and cares. She wrote a very serious letter about it. One line in her letter really captivated me.

Establishing her credentials, she wrote: "I am (almost) 15."

I liked that line because it made me think of how young 14 sounded when you were 14, and how mature 15 sounded by comparison.

Janna then told me all about Punk and New Wave. How the music was the "dark" side of life, like Edgar Allan Poe's poetry. Most people avoid the dark side because it is ugly, she said. "But inside all ugly there is beauty. Morbid beauty, yet beauty nonetheless."

Janna is a New Waver. I know this because I called and asked her.

"Punkers are very, very angry people," she said. "Some think killing people is a good way of showing aggression. Other say no. I say no."

Janna said some people misunderstand those who like modern music.

"I don't use drugs or terrorize the city—it's hard to do when you're only 4 feet 11—and I'm not into S&M," she said. "I happen to be trying to convert to vegetarianism because I can't stand the thought of eating a cow, chicken, pig, or turkey.

"When I get older, I hope to go to Yale or Princeton and get a career in the biomedical field."

Janna said she will be entering the ninth grade at Monticello Junior High in the fall, so I asked her if kids were still divided into groups like when I was in school.

"Oh, sure," she said. "The division that is too bad is how the white kids stay together and the black kids stay together.

"Kids are also divided into groups like the preppies. They're everywhere. I'm surprised the preppies haven't taken over the world.

"And of course there are the burnouts. There are always the burnouts."

I asked her what things upset her.

"When they let Down's syndrome babies die at birth," she said. "I think that's terrible. I know Down's syndrome teenagers that are a lot nicer than some other teenagers."

I asked her what she did for fun.

"I'll go to friends' or to the movies. Not many kids date," she said. "It's group things mostly."

I know this is stupid, I said, but do girls still have slumber parties?

"How old *are* you?" she asked.

I admitted I had just hit 35 like a brick wall.

"Well, of course, we have slumber parties," she said. "I had a wild one until four in the morning. John, my friend, had his friends over, too, at his place and we set up tents and we ran back and forth with the music *blasting*."

I asked her if she was interested in politics. I soon learned that my time in high school, the mid-sixties, was not exactly an admired era anymore.

"Well, I'm not political like in the Hippie Era," she said. "In the Hippie Era, people said they were against violence, so they had all these 'nonviolent' demonstrations and people ended up *killing* each other."

We talked a little more about music and how she is going to buy a pair of black tennis shoes and then I hit her with a high, hard question.

And it was her answer to it that assured her a seat as Youth Consultant on my National Advisory Board. She doesn't get the seat merely because she is young and bright.

No, she gets this dubious honor because she possesses the finest quality of youth: unquenchable optimism. Which is, of course, the only reason to be young.

In your opinion, I had asked her, what will last forever?

"Well, Bowie," she said with a laugh. "David Bowie."

I laughed, too.

"But, I mean, seriously, some things last forever," she said. "I mean like John Kennedy."

You couldn't remember Kennedy, I said. He died five years before you were born.

"I don't *remember* him," she said. "But I read about him. And, you know, I really liked him. And I wish he were alive. And I mean, well,

Kennedy is a *classic*. And some things do last forever. Don't they?"

Ahh, Janna, (almost) 15, grow older if you must, but stay the way you are.

Believe in the classics. And in dreams that never die.

And you will be young forever.

July 28, 1983

Don't Fix It, Forget It

My friend asked me where he should go to get his watch repaired.

Nowhere, I told him. Forget it. Throw it away.

He looked shocked, so I told him my little tale:

I used to have a pretty nice watch. Not real nice, not carved out of an antique gold piece or one of those Rolexes that I'd be afraid to wear out of the house, but a pretty nice watch.

It ran fine for years. But one day it stopped running fine and I went searching for a repair shop where a little hunched-over man with thinning hair, an eye-loupe, and a European accent would fix it while I waited.

Ho. Ho. Ho. I found that these guys rarely exist anymore. What exists are jewelry stores where they will take your watch with the greatest reluctance and return it three weeks later with a big bill and a lot of brand new scratches.

I ended up taking my watch to one of these fancy jewelry stores. Three, four weeks later, I got my watch back and paid a pretty high bill. The next day, the watch stopped running.

Back to the jewelry store. Three, four weeks later, I got the watch back. Now it runs. If the humidity isn't too high and I don't do anything too active with it like taking a walk or eating lunch.

So I went to a department store and bought one of those plastic $30 Swiss watches. It doesn't look as nice as my old watch. In fact, it looks pretty much like a plastic $30 watch.

But I bought it because it can never be repaired.

That's right, never. Its casing is permanently sealed and when (notice I don't say if) it breaks you go and get a new one.

I like this because it recognizes what I have long felt about one aspect of American life:

It is not just that nothing works anymore. It is that we no longer expect things to work.

Last weekend, the fan belt broke in my car. Lucky for me, it broke near a gas station, and luckier still, there was a mechanic on duty.

Some luck. The guy in the gas station worked and worked on the car. He told me stories while he worked and was a good talker.

But as I listened to him and watched him, I realized that he didn't really know what he was doing.

After an hour, he pronounced himself finished. I paid him. And I drove off listening to the loose bolt he had left rattling around in the engine.

I eventually limped to an auto dealer where they had to repair his repair.

What surprised me is that I was not surprised.

I realized I no longer expected a guy who is a full-time mechanic for a living to be able to make a simple repair.

Some mechanics can. They can even do difficult stuff like tune your car and—gasp—fix your clutch. And when I find such a person, I treasure him like a rare gem. I whisper his name to others I know, but only to those who can keep a secret.

I am delighted when I find anything that really works. No, I am not delighted, I am stunned.

For some weeks now, I have been boring my friends to tears on the subject of self-starting charcoal. This is charcoal that does not need lighter fluid but simply a match to ignite.

"Why are you droning on about this?" a friend asked. "I live in a condo. I don't have a balcony. I don't have a barbecue. I am not even sure if my windows open. Why do I want to know about charcoal?"

Charcoal is not the point, I told him. The point is that I had found something that actually worked as well as advertised.

He looked at me blankly. "Things work," he said. "Most things work." Then he paused and thought. "Don't they?"

We began a list of things we owned that didn't work very well. The list grew too long. We started with small things (cigarette lighters, fountain pens, cheap telephones) and moved up to the big-ticket items.

I had a six-year-old television that had never given me a bit of trouble right up until the day it broke. Unrepairable, the repairman said. Not worth fixing. Buy a new one.

So I did. What else could I do? It isn't like major surgery. You don't feel right telling someone you want a second opinion.

I asked the TV salesman how long I could expect my new set to last. "Not as long as your old one," he said, shaking his head. "They just don't make them like they used to."

In my former apartment building almost nothing really worked. When, during the few bitterly cold days of last winter, many people complained about an absence of heat, the management told us we had heat pumps and could not expect too much.

As a heating company employee later explained: "You can't really expect warm heat."

Ever since, I have been grappling with the concept of unwarm heat.

It reminds me of when Jerry Brown, the former governor of California, ran for president. He ran on a platform of lowered expectations.

In the future, Americans would have to accept less, he said. Raw materials were expensive and energy exorbitant and pride in workmanship had disappeared and we no longer could expect to live as well as our parents had lived.

He lost the campaign. But I wonder if we haven't grown to accept his theory. I wonder if we haven't already lowered our expectations for ourselves and our children.

In the trunk of my car, I carry an aerosal can of gook to fix flat tires. This is because I am not sure I could ever get the strange-looking, high-tech, low-quality jack in the trunk to operate.

But the advertisements for the spray gook say all you have to do is spritz it into the flat tire and drive off. I carry it to make me feel better.

And I would feel better. If I really believed it would work.

Which I don't.

July 14, 1985

Never a Lieutenant, Always a Man

I n the very early morning, with the sky just beginning to turn all pink and rose above the highland foothills, Martin Masterson would leave his home and go down to the mines.

He may have wondered as he labored in the damp blackness just how his life would turn out. At age 14, even in a Scottish coal mine, all things are possible.

People have been thinking about the life of Martin Masterson recently. People do that when you die. To some, his life is a sad irony. To some, it is the story of a man who died just before he achieved a lifelong goal. To some, his story is a tragedy.

They are wrong. Upon examination, the life of Martin Masterson is one of triumph and success, greater even than what that 14-year-old boy could have possibly imagined.

Martin Masterson was a Chicago cop for 25 years. He walked the streets of this city in the days when cops still did that. He made sergeant and got letters of commendation and praise. If his name ever made the newspapers, there is no record of it.

He studied. He studied night after night, week after week, month after month. He studied to take the lieutenant's exam. He studied until late at night and early in the morning.

For a poor boy who was born in Ireland and moved to Scotland without being able to pick up much formal education along the way, becoming a lieutenant was something.

One day, the studying was done and he took the test. Out of nearly a thousand men, he scored 69th. That was very good. The first 68 men became lieutenants and Martin Masterson waited his turn. He waited for nearly two years. His name was the next on the list.

Everyone in the department had heard the rumors. The next men on the list would become lieutenants by Christmas of 1980. But as Christmas approached, a slight delay was announced.

"Well, I've waited this long," he told a friend. "I can wait for a few weeks more."

He could not. He died on Christmas Day. Had he been gunned down in an alley by some crazed felon, his death would have been front page news. But he died in bed of a heart attack at age 53 and only those who loved him learned of it.

There were a lot of them. It is not merely a journalistic phrase to say they lined the streets. A thousand people came to his wake, some standing outside in the winter chill for hours.

"Did you know there were nine priests on the altar at the funeral?" Deputy Chief George McMahon said. "Nine. Martin and I were sworn in on the same day. He had the last real Irish brogue in the Chicago Police Department. The thickest anyway.

"I'll tell you: He was one good copper. One good copper."

Years and years ago, Martin Masterson had stopped a speeder. The man's little boy was in the car with him.

"I'm not giving you a ticket in front of your kid," Masterson had told him. "I don't want him to think bad of his father. But I'm telling you: If you don't care about your own life, at least drive like you care about your kid's!"

That man showed up at his funeral and told that story. Martin Masterson was a man people remembered.

He was born in County Mayo, Ireland, the fourth of 12 children. His family moved to Bannockburn, Scotland, where his father worked in the coal mines. Soon, Martin followed him down.

Times were terribly hard and Martin came to America, where he promptly went off to fight in the Korean War. He fought at Pork Chop Hill and made corporal and got some medals. In his joking way, he would always blame Korea for his bad teeth.

"It was the water over there," he told his kids. "That's how I lost them."

"Daddy was just kidding, I think," Mary Jo, his eldest daughter, said. "We always told our boyfriends: 'You'll know when Daddy likes you when he goes around without his teeth in.' "

Back from Korea, Masterson met Ann Halloran at an Irish dance. She was 20 and working in Chicago to send money back to her parents in Ireland. They married. They would have eight children: Mary Jo, Kathleen, Eileen, Martin, Theresa, Margaret, Michael, and Bernadette.

It was an Irish household. The church was important. A family rosary was said every night. "Our faith is our own," Martin would tell the children. "You don't have to be ashamed of it."

Every day when he left for work, no matter what the shift, one of the kids would sing out, "Daddy's going!" and they all would line up and kiss him goodbye. Then they would stand at the window and watch him go. They did it when they were three and when they were twenty-three.

One would iron his shirt and one would polish his shoes and one would shine the visor on his cap. "Martin," his friends would say, "what would you do without those kids?"

"I remember when we were little he would always sit us down at the kitchen table and talk to us," Mary Jo said. She is 25 now, a delicate beauty with a face like fine Irish china.

"No matter what age we were, he would talk to us. About everything. He would tell us: 'Respect yourself and others will respect you.' "

He was always saying things like that. Happiness is a frame of mind, he would say. If wishes were horses, beggars would ride. If you can't say anything good about someone, don't say anything at all. Your family is the most important thing you have. You'll always have each other.

He not only said those things, he meant them. When he first joined the police force, Ann was in labor for 11 days with Mary Jo. He told the department he'd quit rather than leave her side. He never came close to quitting again.

He brought his brother, Hugh, over from Scotland. "I came out with nothing and he gave me everything," Hugh said. "Now I'm burying him with my sons as the altar boys."

At Easter time when Mary Jo was seven or eight, she remembers her father coming home and assembling the children. "I have been talking to the Easter Bunny," he said, "and he says you have been very good. But he also says that some poor children have been very good. He'd like to give them your Easter baskets if it's all right with you." The kids decided it would be all right with them.

Martin was a saver. He had to be. At Christmastime, the same ritual was always carried out.

"Don't buy presents; save your money," he would tell the kids. "It makes me sick to see money spent like this. Wait until after Christmas for the sales."

They never did. They would always get him underwear, socks, and a box of Fannie May chocolates, the only gifts he would accept.

On Christmas Eve, the family would go to midnight mass. They would come home to a huge Irish breakfast of sausage and black pudding and bacon. Then they would call Scotland and talk to the relatives.

With six pretty daughters, there were always boyfriends around and Martin loved to have them in the house. He was famous in the neighborhood for his barbecues. He was a big handsome man who loved to sing and insisted that everyone sing with him. He enjoyed a beer or two at Exton's, a neighborhood bar whose owners were like family.

"He would go down there when we were little and sometimes Momma would be mad and we'd beg her not to be mad," Mary Jo said. "Then Daddy would come home and he would put one of us on his shoes and wrap one of us around his stomach and put one on his back and one on his shoulders and dance around and around and around with us."

Everyone worked. Everyone helped. Mary Jo was the first Masterson to get a college degree, an event Martin was enormously proud of. Two more children followed her through college. Three are in college now. Two more are in high school.

"I don't want to make us sound like goody-two shoes," Mary Jo said. "We had our fights and all, but . . . we were a family. None of us ever got in trouble. I swear that to you on my father's grave.

"My father would tell us daughters: 'Always be like your mother and you can't go wrong. If you're half as good as your mother, you'll be all right.' "

He never brought his work home. The kids knew he was a policeman, but they never really knew what that meant. Mary Jo found out only once, by accident, when her father did not know she was listening to him repeat the story.

He was in a squad car when he heard screams and saw a woman being raped. He burst out of his car and drew his gun. But the rapist was a big, athletic kid who rushed him and knocked the gun from his hand.

Martin grappled with him and wrestled him to ground until bystanders called for help.

"It was the toughest fight I ever had," he said.

It should have been. He was 53 at the time. It was the last year of his life.

"We thought he was invincible," Mary Jo said. "I am 25, educated, but I never realized until I heard that story that he could have been killed. 'Never be afraid to meet your maker,' he would tell us."

Just a few weeks ago, on Christmas Eve, the family went to midnight mass. Martin was happy. He had his family with him, a few weeks earlier he had seen his first grandson, and in a few weeks he would be a lieutenant.

Later, on Christmas Day, he went over to his brother Hugh's and had a few beers. When he left, he hugged Hugh on the doorstep. He went down the path a few steps, but then went back and kissed his brother goodbye. He never explained why.

He went home, had two pieces of pumpkin pie, and went to bed. It was family tradition that one of his children always tucked him in.

That night it was Theresa's turn. She tucked in the blankets and said, "I love you, Daddy."

He could not sleep, though. He went back to the kitchen to smoke a cigarette. He smoked three packs of Camels a day and was always trying to quit. He was not feeling well. He rubbed his left arm and shoulder and put a cold towel on his forehead. He went back to bed.

When his wife joined him later, his body was cold, his face perfectly restful. While a fireman friend from next door pumped on his heart and while both an ambulance and a priest were rushing to him, Mary Jo found a cross and put it in his hand.

Thirty-four days later, the Chicago police department swore in the next group of lieutenants. It would have been Martin Masterson's group. It no longer was.

"He wanted to make lieutenant for the kids," a family friend said. "He said: 'When I make it, I think I'll take life a little easier.' "

"He didn't live his life to make lieutenant," Mary Jo said. "He lived it to be a good father and a good policeman. But we all wish he could have made it. We wish they made him an honorary lieutenant after he died. It would have been nice."

It would have been. But Martin Masterson had something better. And he surely knew it.

He had a wife who loved him and eight kids who adored him and a life to be proud of.

And what is being a lieutenant compared to that?

February 4, 1981

History Rewritten in LBJ Museum

AUSTIN, Texas

Great men have great egos.

In the beginning, this helps them. In the end, it consumes them.

In the beginning, they worry what other men will say of them. In the end, they worry only what history will say.

Lyndon Baines Johnson was a great man. Whether he was a good man is an entirely different matter.

But, as he neared the end, he decided that what he could not attain in life—the love and respect of all his countrymen—he would attain in death.

To do this was a simple matter. All he had to do was rewrite history.

There is no way to be in Texas and not hear Lyndon Johnson stories.

Like how he used to land his helicopter down by the Austin Municipal Auditorium and have his car take him to the local newspaper.

He would walk into the newsroom and say, "Hi, I'm Lyndon Johnson. Who can I buy a cup of coffee?"

That is how he wanted to be remembered. The good old boy. The smart—not crafty, he hated to be called crafty—politician. The dispenser of favors, the architect of the Great Society, the man of goodness.

That was the image. But history was more cruel. History remembers Vietnam and riots in the streets.

And that would never do.

So LBJ and his friends built an extraordinary monument to him. They built a library and put 31 million documents inside it. Scholars could go through it and do what scholars do.

Scholars never worried Lyndon. He figured the people who listened to scholars were not his kind of people, anyway.

But the library would be inside a museum. Not a dull and dusty museum, but the kind of museum where Walt Disney would feel at home.

And here, long after he was gone, Lyndon Johnson would reach out to the people.

Here, history would be dusted off and cleaned up and packaged. Here would be the Truth According to Lyndon.

And here, Lyndon Johnson would be loved. Forever.

As I approached the building, a dirty gray rain was sweeping across the eight stories of nearly windowless marble.

It is a monstrous thing that sits on a grassy knoll and looks like nothing so much as a mausoleum.

Inside, there are flashing TV screens and slide shows and movies and rotating display cases. Inside, there is a fine blend of the historic and the ludicrous.

Right next to the original copy of the speech LBJ wrote on the plane carrying John Kennedy's body home from Dallas is the frumpy red dress with the fun-fur collar that Lady Bird wore at Lyndon's inaugural.

The place is an audiovisual wonderland. TV screens beg you: "Press the Button and See the Humor of Lyndon Johnson. Six minutes, 55 seconds."

A sign tells you that LBJ was a lot funnier than the media led you to believe.

"LBJ was a masterful storyteller," the sign says, "a fact not widely known to the American people because he rarely used humor on television."

So you press the button and hear LBJ tell the story of the man who is losing his hearing because he drinks a pint of whiskey every day.

The doctor tells him to stop drinking and his hearing will return. After a month, the man bumps into the doctor and the doctor asks if he gave up the booze.

"I did for a while, but now I'm drinking again," the man says.

Why? the doctor asks.

"Because," the man says, "I liked what I drank so much better than what I heard."

There were a lot of things that Lyndon Johnson heard that he, too, did not like.

So they do not exist here.

The masterpiece of the museum is a multiscreen, carefully edited, superbly produced slide show of LBJ's life. And there is no unpleasant news in it.

The years of humiliation when LBJ was vice-president? Gone. The black riots that he could neither control nor understand? They do not exist.

And Vietnam? Well, LBJ ended the war in Vietnam if you believe the slide show.

That's right. His advisers egged him on into that bad war, but LBJ set the gears in motion to get our boys back home.

When the building was dedicated in 1971, a few years before he died, Lyndon said that he hoped "the young people who come here will get a clearer comprehension of what this nation tried to do in an eventful period of its history."

At the museum's gift shop, you can buy everything from a $25 bust of Johnson to Texas Blue Bonnet flower seeds.

You can buy any one of a number of biographies. But you cannot buy historian Robert Caro's devastating portrait of a mean, driven unscrupulous LBJ whose sheer lust for power overshadowed every other emotion he possessed.

No, you will not find that here. What you will find, as I found, are classes of schoolchildren walking around in awe and wonder.

Bill Mortimer, a volunteer guide, took 150 second-graders around the museum this day.

"They don't know anything about him," he said. "So, really, when you think about it, they are learning history as they walk through here. What they know of LBJ, they will get here."

And you can bet that wherever he is, Lyndon Johnson is having his last laugh.

May 2, 1984

Moooving Tour Down on the Illinois Farm

CARBONDALE, Illinois

W e are in a large green station wagon belting through the American heartland on a two-lane blacktop that is dancing and shimmering in the summer heat.

Inside the car are two members of the newest cultural exchange program in America. Stephen Solarz is a Democratic congressman from Brooklyn, New York. He has decided to come to the great, solid middle of America to see the natives, pick an ear of corn, and pet a pig.

"Wrong," a press aide replies. "There has been a change. The congressman will not be petting a pig. The congressman's district is 67 percent Jewish and he is going nowhere near a pig. Instead the congressman will pet a cow."

Solarz's host in southern Illinois and the other member of the exchange is Democratic Representative Paul Simon (no relation). In the fall, Simon will travel to Brooklyn to ride the subway, go to Coney Island, and eat a blintz.

But first, we have a small problem. "I used to have a little difficulty distinguishing horses from cows," Solarz, who has seen few of either, admits.

Simon points to a squat, solid animal grazing by the roadside. "What's that?" he asks.

Solarz scrutinizes the white-faced beast. "Cow?" he replies.

The congressman is one for one. "What are those?" Solarz asks, pointing to tall, round buildings standing next to a large, red barn.

"Those are si-los," Simon says as if he is talking to a Martian.

"And what do they keep in the si-los?" Solarz asks.

"Corn, things like that," Simon replies. He points to green, leafy things that are growing row upon row in the fields. "Guess what that is," he says.

"Uh, cabbage," Solarz answers. The southern Illinoisans in the car begin to laugh. "Cole slaw?" Solarz tries.

"Wrong, wrong, wrong," Simon says. Solarz soon learns that whenever a middle-American asks an Easterner to guess what something is, the answer is usually "soybeans."

Even when your host is clearly pointing to a chicken or a tractor, it is always better to shout "Soybeans?" at the top of your lungs. For some reason, Midwesterners find soybeans hysterical.

Solarz cannot be blamed for not recognizing them. Unlike trees, soybeans do not grow in Brooklyn. There are certain other differences between Simon's 24th Illinois District and Solarz's 13th New York District.

"How many Jews you got?" Solarz asks.

"About 300," Simon replies.

"You mean 300 in one apartment building?" Solarz asks.

"No, 300 in the whole district," Simon says.

By law, the two men's districts must contain about the same number of people—about 400,060. But Solarz's district is 18 square miles, contains more than 300 Jewish synagogues, and can be driven through in 15 minutes if you catch all the lights.

Simon's district is 9,600 square miles, contains only one synagogue but more than 375 towns, and takes four hours to drive through. You don't have to worry about the lights, though. There aren't many.

"I could swear this was a Jewish neighborhood," Solarz says. "I saw a Chinese restaurant."

One could ask why these two men are spending their own money to do this. Solarz's concerns are ethnic and urban; Simon's are agricultural, minerological, and rural. Solarz worries about the many elderly people who have been murdered this year in his district. In Simon's district, few people lock their doors at night.

"I think we both recognize that aside from representing districts we also have national concerns and must vote intelligently on national issues," Solarz says. "Besides, I've seen so much cow manure on the floor of the House, I wanted to see the real thing."

He will get his wish. But first, he will get a whirlwind tour of our great national heartland, passing through corn that is high as an elephant's eye and stopping off to visit a coal mine. Solarz never stops asking questions.

"How many dead people vote in your district?" he asks. "Can you buy a *New York Times*? What does that sign mean: Auto Demolition Derby?"

It is explained to him that dead country dwellers vote much less than dead city dwellers, that the *New York Times* is rare but obtainable, and that an auto demolition derby is a southern Illinois cultural event.

Because of his visit to a coal mine and a cattle farm, Solarz has dressed down for the occasion. He has shown up in a bright red Lacoste shirt, the kind with the little alligator on the front; prefaded bell-bottom Levis; and brushed-pigskin jogging shoes. "Is there much indoor tennis down here?" he asks.

Aside from both men having a lot of fun and joking about each other's district, both are developing serious data that may someday be used who knows where. Both were first elected in 1974 and are among the bright, liberal New Breed from which bigger things have been predicted. Some day, an Illinois vote or a Brooklyn vote may come in handy. In politics, one never knows.

Solarz finally arrives at a farm. He sits on a tractor. He chases cows, which run away from him in terror. He peels an ear of corn off a stalk. Then, to the horror of the assembled farmers, he bites into it. "Say," he says, "these things taste better cooked."

At the end of the day, Solarz pronounces himself well satisfied and ready to return the favor. "We are going to show Representative Simon Brooklyn's biggest industry when he comes," he announces with a huge grin. "We are going to show him the biggest money-maker in New York.

"We are going to get him mugged."

July 10, 1977

Paul Simon went on to be elected to the U.S. Senate in 1984.
Stephen Solarz is currently serving his sixth term in Congress where he is on the Budget and the Foreign Affairs committees. He still has no idea what a soybean looks like.

Beach Cleanup Job
Is No Bummer

W e would go out on the beach just before dawn when it was still cool enough to work. The sharp smell of the lake would be strong then and there would be no sound except for the lapping of the waves.

We dressed disreputably. Ripped sneakers, blue jeans, sweat shirts with the sleeves torn off. We carried 3-foot sticks that were tipped with sharpened nails. Over our shoulders were canvas sacks, stained an indeterminate color by years of garbage.

As the sun struggled up through the purple haze of steel mill smoke that lay on the horizon, the beach's banquet of trash would be revealed to us. It spread for nearly a mile along Rainbow Beach, from 75th Street up to the mills themselves on the South Side of Chicago.

We were hired to impale garbage on the end of our sticks and place it in our bags. Except for my current one, it was the best job I ever had.

I once referred to the job in front of my foreman as unskilled labor. I meant no insult. I had completed my freshman year of college and, therefore, knew everything. For me this was a summer job to earn enough money for my sophomore year.

My foreman was insulted by my characterization. He led me over to the low concrete wall that separated the beach from the park.

At that hour of the morning, you could just hear the snoring of the bums who were sleeping off the previous night's wine binge under a grove of trees.

He pointed in their direction. "That," he said, "is unskilled labor. You are semiskilled."

Four or five of us would spread out along the beach in a line and march forward, picking up the trash as we went. There was a wide variety. Not just food and paper and bottles, but every possible article of clothing. I never did figure out how people could possibly walk home lacking some of the things they had left behind.

Beer cans we liked. They were still made of steel then and they would yield to our nailed sticks with a satisfying crunch. We had contests to see from how far away we could spear them.

It was a point of pride to pick up everything on the beach. The great sin was to kick sand over a piece of garbage that was too difficult or too disgusting to handle. Hot dog buns, soaked by the morning dew, fell into that category.

The lifeguards, clean-shaven, muscled, athletic, were the heroes of the beach. But we were the antiheroes. Sweating, filthy, wearing our work gloves as a badge of honor, we scowled professionally whenever our friends waved to us as we rode by on the tractor that dragged the wire trash baskets up the beach for collection.

I came from a family where physical labor was neither romanticized nor degraded. My father was a truck driver. And I remember the mornings when the beach was particularly filthy—the fifth of July was always the worst—and halfway through the job, looking back and seeing only the bare golden sand where before there had been a half-ton of garbage.

I learned that summer the palpable satisfaction of doing a job well, even if that job is picking up garbage.

I got the job the way you get a Park District job: through clout. I didn't have any, but the father of a friend got me a letter from Marshall Korshak, then city treasurer and a Democratic ward committeeman.

I brought the letter to Park District headquarters and waited in a long line of job applicants. A passing clerk saw the envelope in my hand and took me by the sleeve to the head of the line and into an office.

"Why dincha say something?" he asked, writing out my job assignment. "You had a letter. You don't have to wait if you have a letter."

And so I began learning about Chicago.

Years later, when I was not only reformed but a reformer, I interviewed Korshak when he retired as a committeeman. He did not, of course, remember the letter he had written for me. But I reminded him of it.

"I controlled maybe 100 to 200 jobs a year," he said with pride. "Over the years, I placed thousands of people. Thousands."

But it wasn't really fair, was it? I asked. Giving out jobs that way?

"Tell me something," he said with a weary smile. "You did the job? You picked up the garbage?"

Sure, I said. I did the job. I did a good job.

"So what wasn't fair?" he said. "As long as the job got done, what wasn't fair?"

I am recalling all this because the complaints have been coming in for weeks now about how the beaches are dirty and the garbage isn't getting picked up.

"It's politics," one caller said. "That's why the beaches are filthy."

Maybe. But maybe it is something a little more basic. Maybe it is what my foreman was trying to tell me that morning:

That the difference between doing a job and not doing it is the difference between a worker and a bum.

July 22, 1982

Death Rides
a Newspaper Truck

A newspaperman died yesterday.
His name was Walter Lipke and he drove a truck and he was 52. No one ever asked for his autograph. No one ever recognized his name. No headwaiter ever got him a good table.

And no one ever called him a newspaperman. Not until he was shot in the back of the head and died on the floor of his delivery truck, his bright red blood soaking deep into the stacks of papers.

When I got there, the blood was still fresh and making small puddles on the rough sheet metal that lined the truck. It had flowed and dripped on the day's editions so that all you could read was the headline on the bottom of the page: "Sox lose 9–8; Cubs win."

The police sergeant handed me the orange change apron that the deliverymen wear. It was stained now and said *Sun-Times* in the old-fashioned type we don't use anymore.

I wouldn't take it. "C'mon," the sergeant said. "He's from your paper." He's from my paper. I looked through the little pockets in the front. There was a black comb, there were nineteen quarters and a penny.

The two thugs who put a .32-caliber bullet into the back of his head left those. They also missed the $57 in his pocket. But they got his wallet. It contained about a hundred dollars. Almost all the rest was in a truck safe, where the drivers always put it.

Two men were arrested shortly after Lipke's body was found in his truck at 85th and Calumet. The police say a bloody .32-caliber revolver and Lipke's bloody wallet were found on them.

They are John Washington, 21, and Lawrence McMillan, 18.

In case they are wondering about the man they are charged with killing, here is something:

Walter Lipke left the garage at 222 S. Racine in the predawn darkness, just like every morning. Like always he was wearing his tan yachting cap at a jaunty angle and he was already chewing on the cheap cigars he liked. He pulled out at 3 A.M., the captain of his ship.

He guided his green and red truck through the streets on the South

Side of the city. It was a run he made three days a week and it was a run he worried over but never complained about.

Like all men who work alone in the late night and early morning, paper truck drivers are good crime victims. Not because they carry so much money, but because they are so vulnerable sitting high up on their driver's seat, the wide door next to them usually open so they can hop in and out.

"Look," a driver told me. "I carry a gun. Some other guys do, too. Lipke asked me for my gun, he was worried about that area. But I needed it."

Delivery truck drivers have become used to trouble. A few weeks ago a *Sun-Times* truck was shot at, a bullet piercing the windshield and grazing the arm of the driver. Reports of beatings and attempted robberies are not unusual. It is part of making the rounds.

Lipke made his rounds yesterday morning. He was Route 304, Truck 102D. A route and a truck and a day like any other.

Oscar Langford was probably the last man besides Lipke's killers to see him alive.

"I have a delivery route for the *Chicago Defender*," Langford said. "I meet Lipke all the time. He was a good guy, a happy guy.

"We talked about what drivers always talk about. Who pays their bills, who doesn't. Stuff like that. I saw him driving one way down Ingleside while I was driving down the other. He waved to me. I waved to him."

Lipke had already finished delivering most of his papers. That part of his job came early in the shift. The back of the truck would be loaded down with stacks of papers, tied with white twine.

Lipke would put on a pair of heavy, rubber work gloves and swing the heavy stacks off the rear. George Espinoza, 19, sometimes worked with him. Yesterday he didn't.

"It was good working with him," Espinoza said. "He'd have the names up front and I would swing the papers in the back. He had a whole system. He made it real easy. He always wore that hat and smoked on that cigar. After work sometimes he would go over to Sonny's Inn and have a drink. What a great guy."

At the end of delivering the papers, Lipke would double back on the route, picking up the money from the vendors and checking to see who needed more papers. It's the part of the shift the drivers call the recovery.

The last stand he recovered from was at 83rd and Ellis. The next one was to be at 87th and King Drive.

"See," the police sergeant said, pointing to a route ticket half-floating, half-submerged in a pool of blood. "It says 87th and King."

That was the last stop Lipke would ever make. According to police, his two killers were waiting for him. The police say that one of the men arrested, McMillan, is the brother of the man who runs the stand.

At 87th near King, while Lipke paused to fill out the ticket, two men jumped into the truck. One drove while the other held the gun on Lipke. They took his wallet and made him lie face down on the papers in back.

A few minutes later, the first shot was fired.

We have become so accustomed to crime, it is so much a part of our lives, that we sometimes believe that the victims share in the guilt of the crime. "He must have struggled," a man said outside the emergency room of Jackson Park Hospital, where Lipke's body was taken.

A policeman whirled around. "Struggled!" he said, spitting out the word. "You don't get shot in the back of the head for struggling."

The bullet entered directly under Lipke's right ear. "Death must have been instantaneous," the emergency room supervisor said. "He didn't know what hit him."

Tom Micaletti drives the same route as Lipke on different days. They have talked about the trouble that can happen to a driver. "He always said that if he got held up that he would give them the money," Micaletti said. "He said that he wouldn't give anybody any trouble over the money."

According to police, money did not cause the death of Walter Lipke. The killers were just removing him as a witness. Police Investigator Edward Leracz said that McMillan drove the truck while Washington held the gun on Lipke.

Washington told police he asked McMillan: "Do I have to kill him; why can't we just tie him up?"

Washington said McMillan responded: "He knows my face. He's been delivering here for two years."

Then, police say, Washington fired a shot at close range into the back of Lipke's head. His hat was found a few feet away near the stack of papers upon which Lipke's head lay.

The police are calling it an execution. The state's attorney's office is calling it a possible electric-chair offense.

About 9:30 A.M., a woman living near 85th and Calumet heard a truck drive up. "I was expecting a Marshall Field's delivery," she said, "so I looked out the window. I saw a newspaper truck and two young men coming out of it. One was trying to break the lock on a strongbox in there.

"They must have gotten scared, because they took off running through Nat King Cole Park. I called the police."

Officer Dale Gatliff arrived, and peeked through the window of the truck. He saw the body. "I knew he was dead, but I'm no doctor," he said. "So I called an ambulance."

He also got a description of the two men from the woman who had seen them. He put it on the radio and the men were picked up in minutes.

"What a rotten thing, what a dirty rotten thing," a policeman said. "They killed him for what? For quarters? For a few dollars? Is that for what?"

At the hospital, Lipke's daughter, Darlene Cortopassi, 18, had no answers. She sat in a tiny room that was filled with oxygen tanks and hospital equipment. She sat by a window.

"He said once that it could be bad," she said. "He said guys could get killed, but who ever expected this? He had worked for your paper for about three years and at the *Chicago American* and *Chicago Today* before that.

"He liked driving a newspaper truck, I guess."

I guess. I don't know anything more about Walter Lipke. All I know is that he worked for this paper and I never saw his face and I never knew his name and never would have.

All I know is that he spent the last hours of his life bringing stories like this to people like you and that is the death of a newspaperman.

August 4, 1977

John Washington and Lawrence McMillan were convicted of murder and armed robbery. On April 14, 1978, they were sentenced to serve 75 to 150 years in prison on the murder charge and 10 to 20 years for the armed robbery, the sentences to run concurrently.

CAMPAIGN '76

I didn't realize how quickly America changes until I began covering presidential campaigns.

In 1976, with the memories of Watergate and Vietnam still fresh in our minds, Jimmy Carter was able to get from a peanut farm to the White House by selling American "goodness" instead of American greatness.

Just four years later, Ronald Reagan would beat him by calling for a great America, a strong America, an America unafraid to flex its muscles.

Some say these campaigns are too long, too costly, too wearying and too dull.

Me, I think they're the best show in town.

Prodigal Press Welcomed Back to the Fold

LOS ANGELES

There were only five reporters covering the guy and we were so bored that we were trying to guess what he would say next.

The candidate began his speech. "I want you to be . . ."

"Proud of me," the New York reporter said.

"I appreciate your . . ."

"Friendship," the Los Angeles reporter said.

"I'll never do anything to make you . . ."

"Ashamed," the Boston reporter said.

"I want a nation that is filled with . . ."

"Luhhh-ve," we all shouted and collapsed into giggles.

The month was January, the place was Iowa, and we were there to catch the first look at the men who wanted to be president.

Because there were only the five of us, the candidate and two staff members, we rode on two tiny planes. The planes were so small that there was room for only one reporter at a time on the candidate's plane. The rest stayed on the press plane, where we drank beer and talked dirty.

It was in Ottumwa that I got my chance. It was the first time I had talked to a man who actually admitted he wanted to be the leader of the Free World and I had a high hard one waiting just for him.

"Uhm. So you want to be president, huh?"

Candidates, like football coaches, have trained themselves to believe that every question from a reporter, no matter how blatantly stupid, deserves a serious answer.

"Good question," the candidate said. "I'm glad you asked me that. The narrowing of the field begins here. And the one who will stick it out, the one who has the determination to be there in Madison Square Garden when they count the convention votes, well, he's going to be a peanut farmer from Georgia."

And just for a moment, the sun caught his grin, and the glint filled the cabin.

After about 45 minutes, the plane landed in the town of Reston, and I thanked the man. "Oh, no," he said, gripping me by hand and elbow, "I should thank you."

After the Reston speech, the reporter from New York hatched the plot that later came to be known as The Great Escape.

"I cannot stand it," he said. "I cannot take one more of these speeches. We've heard everything we're going to hear. Let's charter a plane and fly back to Des Moines by ourselves."

Someone expressed the fear that the candidate might be assassinated or have a plane crash while we were gone.

"Look," the guy from New York said, "if this guy is as tight with the Lord as he says we've got nothing to worry about."

So we decided to leave. The only bad part was telling the candidate that the entire press corps was leaving and that he would have to go on alone.

"Don't you worry about it," Jimmy Carter said. "You all will be back."

He was right. We came back. When I walked onto the plane in California, his last primary, it was a chartered 727 and there were 44 reporters bouncing red, white, and blue balloons back and forth between the seats. Something else was a little different, too.

"Stewardess," a reporter called, holding up a glass, "I said Cutty Sark and this is Johnny Walker."

At breakfast we were served sweet rolls and champagne. For lunch it was filet mignon and burgundy. For dinner we had an amusing little Pinot Noir that traveled well. The beer was always Coors, the cheesecake always came with strawberries, and nobody walked out on the man who rode up front these days.

I had decided in March that our next president was going to be a peanut farmer from Georgia and I didn't want to take any chances.

High above the San Andreas fault, I cornered one of the staff people who was with us that time in Iowa. "Remember that crazy day we all just sort of ran out on Carter," I said. "Pretty funny, huh?"

"Now, you just tell the boys not to fret," he said, understanding perfectly. "There'll always be seats for you on Air Force One."

June 13, 1976

◆

Southie Rises Again for Wallace

BOSTON

They wheel him in backwards, his head straining to see the people who cheer and yell behind him. Pieces of confetti, thrown by little girls in straw hats, catch in his swept-back hair. He twists in the wheelchair and waves.

We are in Southie, that part of Boston that is both a location and a battle cry. Just a few nights ago, police and antibusing protesters clashed once more. Forty police officers and 20 protesters went to the hospital.

The police have announced a get-tough policy. They will not retreat another inch, they say.

And in Southie, people walk the streets with armbands that say "Resist!" and buttons that say "Never."

Now, George C. Wallace has come to speak. He is seeking votes in Massachusetts' March 2 presidential primary. He is a long way from Alabama, but do not think that he is not home.

In the corner, Joe Falzone turns on an earsplitting tape of the "Beer Barrel Polka" and follows along on his drums as Wallace is wheeled across the stage.

There is always music at Wallace rallies. Half-a-dozen members of the Grand Ole Opry in Nashville have volunteered their services. But no matter what they play, the audience stands in place chanting the same refrain: "Here we go Southie! Here we go Southie! Here we go Southie!" They seem never to tire of it.

Wallace is lifted into his special bullet-proof podium. It is three-sided, about five feet high and edged on top by about five inches of thick glass.

"It is good to be in South Boston," he says, and even this gets cheers. "It is good to be with the great majority of America—the people of the working class.

"I am aware that I have been the object of a tremendous amount of propaganda from the media, but I am here to put first things first and last things last."

He leans forward in his wheelchair, his eyes narrow in a hawk-like gaze and he grips both sides of the podium with his large hands.

"You will be the kings and queens of American politics! You. The working men and women will be the kings and queens instead of the ultraliberal left that has been getting everything all the time.

"Paul Revere rode to say the British were coming. I will ride to say, 'The People are coming.' "

Applause now, almost continuously.

"The People of America are coming!"

Now the shouts come.

"The People of South Boston are coming!"

The audience is on its feet and there is wild cheering. Joe Falzone plugs in the "Beer Barrel Polka" again and turns it up full blast. There is nothing in the room but sound, continuous waves of it. Sound and George Wallace smiling from the stage.

"I warned them," he says. "I warned them 12 years ago. I said someday the federal government will take over every aspect of your life. They will tell you where to go to school, when to go, and who will teach there.

"I told the Democrats in 1972—from my sickbed in Maryland—that if they endorsed busing they would go down to the worst defeat in American history!"

Even Wallace must stop now. There is no one left to listen. No one left who is not cheering and clapping.

This used to be the territory of Kennedy—any Kennedy. This and working-class areas around the state launched those magic and tragic careers. But then a federal judge ordered the people of all-white South Boston to bus their children to black Roxbury. And the black Roxbury students would come to Southie.

It is one of the most divisive issues in American life since the Vietnam War. Even those who defend busing don't like it. And Teddy Kennedy—the last Kennedy, the darling of Southie—split with the voters over it. Now, when he dares to enter, he is verbally abused and, once, spat on. There are new heroes now.

"Busing is the most asinine program ever thought up by the thick heads in this country," Wallace says. "These pointy-headed bureaucrats who never worked a day in their life get out of some college of repute and go into government and make guidelines about your children and your life!"

For those who say Wallace has slowed down, for those who say he has mellowed—let them come to Southie. Carefully pacing himself at rallies around the state, he speaks in hour-long chunks. Tonight, after addressing 500 people, he will go downstairs, where 300 more wait patiently. His voice does not grow weary. He seems to feed upon the crowds.

He is careful to advocate only peaceful protest and peaceful means and his speech even contains jokes. But he includes one ominous joke about power in America. His power. Southie power.

"There were two men in a bar," he says. "Big guy and a little guy. The big guy hits the little guy with one big hand and says, 'That's karate. I got it from Korea.'

"Then the big guy picks up the little guy and throws him all around. He says to the little guy, 'That's judo. I got it from Japan.'

"So the little guy leaves the bar. He comes back 10 minutes later and—the big guy is on the floor out cold.

"The little guy turns to the bartender. 'That was a tire iron,' he says. 'I got it from Sears, Roebuck.' "

George Wallace did not invent Southie. He did not create it. In the crowd here, there are no monsters, no beasts.

They are people, Americans. But they are Americans near the edge.

They fear, they hate, they lash out. And there is always someone willing to lead them.

"My strategy?" Wallace said that night. "I put down the hay where the goats can get it."

Ask not to whom George Wallace speaks. He speaks to thee.

February 23, 1976

◆

Pat Boone Goes Shining On

Eliza Sprinkle, 80, of Virginia was another holdout. She refused to divulge her vote until roll call, but said later she had been persuaded to vote for Ronald Reagan by Pat Boone.

—UPI news item

KANSAS CITY, Missouri

Pat Boone and I had gone about as far as we could go. We had climbed flight after flight of stairs and finally sat down in the seats of the Guam alternate delegates at the Republican National Convention. I figured nobody would think of looking for Pat Boone in Guam.

As we looked down at the people on the convention floor, who were swirling around like confetti in a windstorm, I assembled some questions in my mind. It is important to keep the proper perspective when interviewing people involved in politics. One must be impartial and dispassionate in presenting them to the public.

I think I am ready. Pat Boone is the best human being in the history of the world. He is everything good and decent and true about America. He is the boy next door and Mom and her apple pie and baseball and football. He is moonlit drives on soft, summer nights and holding hands after the prom. He is the last day of school and roasting hot dogs on the beach and singing songs at summer camp. So I asked him how he could have supported a zany madcap like Ronald Reagan.

"We need strong moral leaders," he said. "Someone with the proper stands on ethical and spiritual matters. Most politicians think they can't get elected without immorality and perversion. We had one president who wore his religion on his lapel but when he got to the backroom we saw his immorality.

"I tried to get Richard Nixon on the phone during Watergate. I wanted to have him call for a day of national humiliation, of fasting and prayer. I wanted him to go on television and get down on his knees in front of the American people and beg their forgiveness.

"He wouldn't come to the phone. So I talked to an aide."

I suggested that anyone who wouldn't come to the phone to talk to Pat Boone deserved whatever he got.

"I thought Reagan would have given us strong moral leadership, but I like Ford," Boone said. "The first thing that Ford did when he took office was to ask the American people to pray for him. His voice broke and his chin quavered.

"I am grateful to Jimmy Carter for bringing religion into politics. It is proper that we know what motivates a man. If a man speaks strongly about his faith, it tells us something about him.

"The trouble is that I think Carter is a Christian George McGovern."

I have to admit that there are a few things about Pat Boone that I find slightly weird. He was kicked out of his church in California for his belief in glossolalia, which is not as bad as it sounds. Glossolalia is the belief in "tongues," when people, supposedly in the grip of God, babble in strange languages.

There was also an odd incident a few years ago when Boone, who is not a minister, baptized 17 people, including a trapeze artist, in the swimming pool of his home.

But then people are always quick to attack greatness. I called a colleague in Chicago to ask him to check the clippings on Boone.

"I've got some great stuff," he said when he returned to the phone. "Did you know that Boone wears a hairpiece?"

I told him he was scum and hung up.

I didn't have the heart to tell Boone that we really didn't much agree on politics or that my own religious beliefs made me a born-again Druid compared with him.

I just wrote down his answers in my notebook and when the interview was over and he got up to go, I stopped him.

"There's something I've got to say to you," I said and he turned.

"*Bernadine* was one of the greatest movies of all time," I said. "You should have got the Oscar."

"Well, gee whiz," he said. "That's nice of you to say that."

Some people will leave this convention with memories of Gerald Ford and Ronald Reagan. Some will leave with recollections of long speeches and cheering crowds. But I will leave with only one thing on my mind: the single impression of a pair of shining white bucks walking slowly, slowly through Guam.

August 22, 1976

Simon Says It and Says It

People who stand when there are empty seats on the bus make me nervous.

◆

Never trust a Chinese restaurant that has non-Chinese waiters.

◆

I panic every time I have to open one of those envelopes that say "Hold here and snap."

◆

Does anybody really use the second level of a three-way lightbulb?

◆

Why do camera stores always have the rudest salespeople?

◆

Swiss cheese wouldn't taste as good without the holes.

◆

There is something about lighthouses I really like.

◆

I know why it's done, but it drives me crazy that all the phone numbers you hear on TV shows begin with 555.

◆

Wouldn't zucchini bread taste a whole lot better without the zucchini in it?

Every time I think the toothpaste tube is empty, I always manage to bash two more weeks out of it.

◆

I don't care what the weathermen say: Nobody can tell the difference between partly cloudy and partly sunny.

◆

There should be a law against putting advertising fliers under windshield wipers.

◆

I don't feel so bad going to lousy movies when I go early and waste only $2.

◆

People who leave their ski tickets on their parkas don't impress me as much as they think they do.

◆

They may not be the most efficient, but out-of-work actors can be the friendliest waiters.

◆

Admit it, you get embarrassed every time you order the surf and turf.

◆

I don't care how fashionable it is, terry cloth belongs in the bathroom.

What's all this talk about multiple personalities? A lot of people I know have trouble coming up with even one.

◆

There is nothing worse than reruns of "60 Minutes."

◆

How many people do you know who turn their dinner plates around until the meat is in just the right place?

◆

I'll reduce my speed to 55 m.p.h. when the truckers reduce theirs to 75.

◆

I've never been on one of those flights that offered a choice of dinners that didn't run out of what everybody wanted.

◆

A good suntan is like a good love affair: nice while it lasts and quick to fade.

◆

Have you hugged your bus driver today?

◆

It is the rare woman who can paint her toenails and not look like a chippy.

◆

If American Express cards get any more expensive, people will be forced to use cash.

I can never remember if Diego Garcia is a country or a cigar.

◆

I'd rather eat pâté than know how it's made.

◆

People who name their cats "Cat" and their dogs "Dog" have my sympathy.

◆

The whole concept of roll-on deodorants is disgusting.

◆

How come the playbill never tells you anything about the play?

◆

Eating lobster is more trouble than it's worth.

◆

Never marry a man who wears his sunglasses on his forehead.

◆

There are only two kinds of people in this word—those who throw away the dust jackets of books and those who want to beat the hell out of those who do.

◆

Are there still women who wear white gloves?

◆

Never wait more than 15 minutes for a dinner reservation, 20 minutes for an appointment, or 25 minutes for a spouse.

You know you're getting old if you can remember:
- when the movies had newsreels.
- when gas stations washed windshields.
- when telephone numbers started with letters.
- when AM radio was all anybody listened to.
- when McDonald's didn't have Big Macs.
- when a man with a beard was a member of a religious group or a lumberjack.

◆

I can never remember which one is Manhattan Clam Chowder and which one is New England.

◆

Does anyone still iron sheets?

◆

People who wear beepers are usually jerks.

◆

I've never met a shoe salesman who liked his job.

◆

Just once, I'd like to see someone fix up an apartment building *before* it goes condo.

◆

You can always tell a really rich person by how badly he dresses.

◆

Does anyone eat the tomatoes in the sweet and sour pork?

People who talk during the overture should be beaten with sticks.

◆

What *really* goes into Velveeta cheese?

◆

Why do salad bars have protective glass over them? To keep you from drooling on the pickled beets?

◆

How come the people who always whistle are the ones who can't?

◆

Have you ever wondered about those people who prefer the front row seats in movies?

◆

Do dentists' tools really have to look that painful?

◆

At what age does it become unacceptable to stoop down to pick up a penny?

◆

I try to avoid movie theaters where my feet stick to the floor.

◆

Cars that take up two parking spaces should be towed away.

◆

If you look around, you'll see I'm right: We're in between fads.

Myth America, an American Dream

O
ne year ago this week, I was in Atlantic City, New Jersey, judging the Miss America pageant.

I never talked about it much. Mainly because whenever I did, my friends would say things like, "How *could* you?"

Well, I could. And I did. And I liked it. I met some nice people. The contestants were, for better or worse, interesting. I got to stand up on national TV in a rented tuxedo in front of 70 million people and wave.

When I was done waving and the camera had moved on, Gavin MacLeod, the captain of the Love Boat and a fellow judge, leaned over and kissed me on the forehead. "You were magnificent," he said. "A star is born."

We giggled the rest of the night.

The judges were treated very nicely, although spending a week in Atlantic City in late summer is a lot like spending a week inside a very ripe cheese.

Wherever we went as a group, a person from NBC's Broadcast Standards Department went with us. She told us that accepting a bribe or not reporting a bribe attempt was a violation of federal law. As far as I know, nobody was offered one.

And to answer the question going through your filthy minds, no, no contestant called us up late at night to say that she would do anything, just *anything*, to become Miss America.

First, they wouldn't. Second, we wouldn't. Third, they are very well-guarded. Their chaperones even sleep in the same rooms with them. I am told.

This is not to protect them from predatory judges, but from the creeps who stalk the pageant.

"Every year someone breaks into the girls' rooms and steals shoes," Mildred Brick, the chief hostess, told me. "Shoes! I think that is sick!"

Some people think the whole pageant is sick, of course. In past years, it has been picketed by feminists and blacks, but those protests have stopped. Largely, I think, because protesters no longer view the pageant as very meaningful.

And in the largest sense, it isn't. It is as meaningless as the World Series or the Super Bowl. All are contrived contests that do not change the course of history, yet are hard fought and important not only to the contestants but also to millions of others.

When I expressed that view in a press conference in Atlantic City, I thought I was being candid. The story was moved by the wire services and ran in one newspaper under the headline: "Miss America Judge Slams Pageant."

These reporters, they never get anything right.

To many, the pageant is a celebration of American values, real or imagined. And contrary to what many people think, it is popular not only in southern hamlets, but also in northern cities. At least that is what the TV ratings show.

Many myths surround the pageant. Even some of the judges were surprised to find out it is perfectly legal for the contestants to pad their swimsuits. And, no, they don't have to be virgins. The rules state they must never have been married, divorced, or had a marriage annulled.

In the old days, the organizers figured that took care of virginity. Times change.

The biggest myth is that the winners lead lives of tragedy. The only thing America likes more than a good love story is a good sob story. Actually, the winners do about as well or poorly as anyone to whom notoriety and money come young. The divorce rate of Miss Americas is almost exactly the national average.

When people ask me why I agreed to be a judge and why I would do it again, I have to say that Miss America is part of the American experience and the American dream and I am fascinated by both.

I know there are those who believe it exploits women. But most of the contestants I talked to knew the score exactly. There was money and fame to be had. And the price to pay seemed small.

I once interviewed Rebecca King Dreman on what it was like to be Miss America 1974.

"It paid for law school," she said. "I used it and it used me."

There is an air of hypocrisy surrounding the pageant, though. Sex is the underlying theme, yet it is never spoken of.

The organizers, many of the contestants, and nearly every judge I talked to would like to do away with the swimsuit competition. It is anachronistic and too much like a display of prime beef on the hoof.

But the TV people will not allow it. They know why men watch the pageant.

Still, the pageant is almost holy to many.

I was waiting for an elevator in my hotel one night last year, wearing the large purple judge's badge we were required to wear.

I discovered that I was standing next to a true American legend, a man whose fame was once so great he became a symbol for an entire era. And out of the corner of my eye, I saw a young man approach him, clearly to ask him for an autograph.

He turned to give it, only to see the young man walk past him and stop in front of me.

"Hey, you're one of the judges," the young man said. "Whaddya think of Miss New Jersey? She gotta chance?"

The elevator came while I was babbling some neutral answer. And as the doors closed on him, Joe DiMaggio smiled a knowing smile.

September 3, 1980

A Just Judge to Care for the 'Little Cases'

I had not thought about him in years until the letter reminded me: He was the only judge I ever knew who shot craps on the bench.

I could see him standing there, a stocky, powerful little guy, his frayed black robes billowing out around him.

A 70-year-old man had come before him charged with stealing $150. The guy said he had taken the money from a man who had won it with loaded dice.

"Let's see the dice," the judge said.

The guy gave him the dice. And the judge stood up in front of a shocked court and started rolling them bones.

"First I throw an eight," the judge told me. "Then a 10. Then an eight. Then a 10. That proved it. They were loaded. Case dismissed!"

Just another day for Judge Joseph Mioduski, the judge nobody knows.

Or likely ever will. He has been a judge for 14 years and has never had a big case. He is not supposed to. He is an associate judge. He gets the misdemeanors. The little cases.

I met him that day in Bum Court. That is not its official name, but that is what everyone called it.

The bums were scooped up off the street at night and thrown into the tank. And in the morning, they were brought yawning and blinking and scratching before Judge Mioduski.

It was one of those murderous early winter days in Chicago when the rain falls in gray sheets and splatters up from the pavement in clouds. The court, just off Skid Row, was as gloomy and damp as the bums themselves.

They were charged with disorderly conduct, but that was just a legal fiction to get them off the streets. The arresting officers never showed up to testify against them. Technically, the judge should have just dismissed the cases without a word. And at first, Judge Mioduski did that. But then a terrible thing happened: He began to care.

And so he began questioning the men and berating them and even humiliating them. He told them to take showers, and clean themselves up. He found them shoes, and a meal, and a TB test.

He kept a big book with every name. "I've got you right down here," he said to one man. "It says October 26—needs a bath. Well, you still need a bath. I can smell you from here. Get cleaned up, get a job. I won't let you throw your life away."

Day after day they stumbled before him bleary-eyed and greasy-jawed and wooly-mouthed. They nodded at his commandments and took the little cards he gave out showing them where they could get a free meal.

Outside the court, the cards floated in the pools of oil slick water where the bums threw them. But every card that was not thrown away, that was a victory for Joe Mioduski. That was his "big" case.

That was eight years ago. And since then he has bounced around from traffic court to housing court to child support court.

I got the letter the other day. It was the rarest kind of letter. A citizen was praising a judge. He had worked hard, the citizen said, right through lunch. His name was Mioduski.

I called him. "God, how long has it been?" he said. "I see the column, you know, your column. I see it and I tell people: 'See this guy, I knew him when he was a cub.' A cub!" He laughed at the memory.

We chatted. At the end, I tried to put it diplomatically: Does it bother you, I asked, to still be getting the little cases?

"But, gee," he said. "They're not little to the people in them."

A good line. Too good, I might normally have said. Except for one thing. One thing that happened those years ago when a cub reporter went to Bum Court.

It was the end of the day and the last case was a blind man, a boy really, who had been arrested for selling pencils without a license.

He had not been in court when the case was first called and a warrant had been issued for his arrest. But at the very last moment, he hurried into the court, his dripping hair plastered against his forehead.

"I'm sorry," he said in a too-loud voice. "I was hurrying to get here and I broke my cane and I had to go back home to get another. I took a cab. I'm sorry."

Judge Mioduski very gently explained that a license was required to sell pencils. The law was the law.

"But I have a license," he said. "Will somebody look at it please?" He held out his wallet.

The prosecutor took the wallet. And found the license inside.

"Oh, God," Mioduski said, dropping his head to his chest. "Oh, God, I'm sorry. We're all sorry."

He dismissed the case and the blind boy sat down in the front row of the court. Everyone gathered up his books and papers and headed for the exits. The maintenance man came in and turned off the lights. Soon, all you could hear in the court was the steady beat of the rain outside.

I had gone into a small waiting room to get my coat and as I came out, I saw Judge Mioduski begin to walk out of the courtroom. He did not see me.

And I saw him turn back from the door and walk up to where the blind boy was still sitting, staring forward, his white cane clasped between his knees.

"Do you have a way of getting home?" Mioduski asked.

"I'm OK, don't worry, I can get home," the blind boy said, again too loud, his words echoing in the empty room.

"Sure," said Mioduski. "Sure you can. But come on anyway. I'll give you a ride home."

And Mioduski took his arm and they walked out together into the rain.

A year later, two legal groups rated Judge Mioduski unqualified for office. His temperament was not sufficiently judicial.

He was reappointed to another term, anyway.

Sometimes, you see, even judges get justice.

June 30, 1982

Here's Looking at Newspapers, Kid

So you want to be a reporter, eh, kid?
Even after hearing about all the terrible things they've done?
The stories they've made up? The lives they've ruined?

OK, kid, pull up a stool and we'll talk about it.

I guess you've seen that newspaper movie, *Absence of Malice*? Well, don't believe it. It's about Sally Field and Paul Newman, not newspapers.

Sally Field plays a beautiful investigative reporter who sleeps with the people she writes about. But that's OK, the movie says, because she's warm and caring.

Kid, it ain't OK. Not for reporters.

There are a lot of other things wrong with the movie. Anytime you see a newspaper movie where the reporters are careful and conservative and the editors are aggressive and crazy, you know things are a little mixed up.

There has been only one movie that told the truth about newspapers. And nobody in it looked beautiful or handsome, not even Humphrey Bogart.

He looks old and tired in it. The men reporters in the movie are losing their hair. The women reporters are dried up and bitter. They all drink too much.

The movie is called *Deadline U.S.A.* and you can still see it about once a year on the Late Show. In it, the newspaper is called the *Day* and Bogart is the managing editor. The newspaper's motto is: All the News—Every Day. It's a good paper, maybe even a great paper, but it's dying.

It is about to be bought by its sleazy competition, the *Standard.* The *Standard* has twice its circulation and three times its advertising.

What's that, kid? If the *Day* is so good and the *Standard* is so bad, how come the *Day* is dying and the *Standard* is doing great? Because it's a realistic movie, kid, that's how come.

Bogart answers the question himself. His staff has gotten the word that their paper is about to be bought. They go down to a bar called

O'Brien's. Bogart picks up a copy of the competition and sees a photo of a seminude woman under a sleazy headline.

His lips curl in disgust. "It's not enough anymore to give them just the news," he says. "They want comics, contests, puzzles. They want to know how to bake a cake, win friends, and influence the future. Ergo: horoscopes, tips on the horses, interpretation of dreams so they can win on the numbers lotteries. And if they accidentally stumble on the first page—news."

Well, they all drink up and go out to get the last story, a story that might save the *Day*. They are trying to get the goods on the crime syndicate boss who runs the city. They know a great story like that might keep the paper alive.

And Bogart fights in court to stop the sale of the paper. "The *Day* is more than a building," he tells the judge. "It's people. Men and women whose skill and brains and experience make a great newspaper possible. We don't own a stick of furniture in this company, but we, along with the people who read this paper, have a vital interest in whether it lives or dies."

The movie gets really dramatic. People get thrown into printing presses, reporters get beaten up. But nothing stops the paper from going after the story.

And finally, the big break comes. An elderly immigrant woman appears at Bogart's office with the missing piece of evidence. She has read the *Day* ever since coming to America. She learned to speak English by reading it.

Bogart asks her if she knows what she is risking by coming forward.

"You are not afraid," she says. "Your paper is not afraid. So I am not afraid."

Kid, that is the truest part of the movie. Stuff like this *happens*. People do grow up with newspapers. They believe and trust them. Even those rare times when newspapers go wrong, the people care about them and gain courage from them. They learn from them and love them. They love them like they'll never love a TV set, kid.

And in the movie, a kid just like you comes into the newsroom. He's green as grass and he wants a job.

Bogart tells him there are no jobs. The newspaper is dying. But the kid will not give up. He must be a newspaperman.

So Bogart hires him. And the *Day* breaks the big story on the crime boss. And the next day, the paper is sold to the competition and shut down. And everyone is out of work.

But, kid, they have all done their jobs. They have gotten the last story.

Most reporters don't lie and cheat and make things up. They go out and get as much of the truth as they can and write it the fairest way they can. Sometimes great things happen because of it. Sometimes they don't.

"Here's some advice," Bogart tells the kid who loves journalism. "Don't ever change. It may not be the oldest profession. But it's the best."

Aww, hell, kid. Don't be embarrassed. I always cry at the end, too.

December 2, 1981

You Bet Your Life in Las Vegas

LAS VEGAS

The slot machines had melted down to slag. The once plush carpets were waterlogged and charred.

The ceiling, above which steely-eyed men in handmade suits had once watched the movement of every nickel, was gaptoothed and gutted.

The ones who had died here, here in the casino of the MGM Grand, had died quickly at least. For a brief moment, perhaps only for a minute, firefighters believe, there was a hurricane of flame.

The people died where they stood. At slot machines, at crap tables, at the registration desk. One newsman wrote that he saw three bodies slumped over the bar.

Everyone who read that had the same thought: How do you meet your Maker at 7 A.M. with a scotch and water in your hand?

Upstairs, death was more subtle. Upstairs there was now only the faint smell of smoke, like the not-unpleasant burning of leaves on a fall day.

Upstairs, as the survivors went back to their rooms to get their belongings, the golden drapes billowed through the open windows on the gentle desert breezes. Invariably, the people fell silent as they went through their rooms.

Death had come so quietly here, so hushed, so insidiously on the creeping smoke.

Across the street, in the John Wayne Room of the Barbary Coast Hotel, the Clark County fire chief met with reporters.

"The hotel provided these drinks," he said with a grin, "not me."

Everyone laughed. You could get any drink you wanted while the dead were being counted.

The chief looked at all the lights and cameras. "You know," he said, with a little twinkle, "this room is electrically overloaded."

The laughs were a little weaker this time.

"Don't worry," he said, "this room has sprinklers."

Lucky us.

The press conference began and things got a little nasty. Yes, the chief said, the fire could have been prevented by smoke detectors and sprinklers.

No, the MGM was not required to have them, he said. No, he had never gone to the MGM and asked it to voluntarily put them in.

Why? The chief mumbled something about the courts not backing him up, but everyone in the room knew the real answer. You don't buck a hundred million dollars, not in Vegas, not anywhere.

A casino can sell topless showgirls to the public, and big-time singers. It can sell champagne brunches and double odds on the crap tables. It cannot sell safety. So why bother with it? Why spend the dough?

"Look," the chief, Roy Parrish, said, "I'm very sorry for the 83 people who died and their families, but if you figure there were about 8,000 people in that hotel, why that is only a 1 percent loss of life!"

And this is a great town for playing the percentages. I'm surprised the MGM didn't put it up in lights outside: "99-1 Chance Of Making It Out Alive. Come On In!"

"We always knew," the chief said earlier, "that one day something was going to happen like this."

Now he tells us. Funny we never saw that on billboards at the airport. We never saw anything that said: "See Las Vegas and Die."

Some people were willing to tell the hard truths after the fire at the MGM. In a front-page column, *Las Vegas Sun* newspaper publisher Hank Greenspan said it was greed that killed the 83 people, the desire to "cut corners and amass gold."

And gold was very definitely on people's minds. There was story after story about casino employees, fleeing the fireball, and being told by their bosses to go back and save the drop boxes where the money is kept.

Patricia Celline was dealing blackjack when she saw the flames race across the floor: "Somebody said, 'Get the drop boxes.' I yelled back, 'Screw the boxes, get yourself out of here.' "

The MGM will certainly reopen. Structurally it appears untouched. And the people will certainly come back. They will play the percentages.

Joe Hughes is 39 and was in the MGM Grand for a computer show. He walked down 24 flights of stairs, through choking smoke, leading his wife by the hand to safety.

"There was a guy who showed us the way, otherwise we would have died," he said.

I talked to him, hours after he had escaped, while he was flat on his back, breathing through an oxygen mask. The MGM had found him a room at the Las Vegas Hilton.

The room was on the 22nd floor and Joe thought about that good and hard.

"Oh, what the hell," he said. "Life's a gamble, isn't it?"

November 24, 1980

Putting on Gloves
for a Golden Dream

eonard Valdez stands glistening in the square of light. Sweat runs
off the hard, flat muscles of his chest. He lifts one gloved hand to
his forehead and with a leathered thumb describes a cross in the
air before him.

Outside the boxing ring there is only darkness. But in that darkness
there is constant movement, a constant mumble broken by the shouts
of the people who have come to see the fights. In the back of the high
school gym, along one wall, rows of bleachers have been set up. The
fighters, waiting for their turn in the ring, sit silent and hulking. They
cast secret, sidelong glances at their opponents and then stare down
again between their shoes. The Vaseline spread under their eyes
catches the light from the glowing ring and makes them look like
jungle cats, muscles bunched and waiting.

There is a sharp whistle and five seconds later a bell. The stool
disappears from Valdez's corner and, startled, he moves quickly to
the center of the ring. His shoulders are hunched, his right hand held
high to protect his face.

His opponent, Charles Blackwell, circles him slowly, looking for an
opening. They look like they are on a movie set, the sharp white light
from above capturing them. Valdez moves suddenly into Blackwell,
crowding him, and walks into a pistonlike right hand that snaps back
his head with an audible crack.

He falls backward as if in slow motion, his blue-black hair spraying
out in a halo around his head. His body hits the canvas with a dull
thump and a cloud of dust comes up from the mat and dances in the
light over his outstretched body.

For the first time he can hear the yells from the darkness. "Arriba.
Matalo, Valdez, Matalo. Mataloooo!" Up. Kill him, Valdez, kill him. Kill
him!

Leonard Valdez is not thinking about killing anybody just now. He
is thinking mainly about staying alive. He crawls up to his feet. The
referee grabs his gloved hands and wipes them on his shirt to remove
the rosin they have picked up from the mat. He pumps Valdez's arms

and looks into his eyes to see if they are focused. Sometimes the ref will ask them if they know where they are. If they know their names. Sometimes they do not.

But Valdez is young, 18, and has the stamina of youth to replace the good sense of age. He moves out to circle again and then charges Blackwell, windmilling punches that land without much force. Angry welts begin to glow red on the backs and shoulders of both fighters.

Two minutes after the round begins, the bell rings. Valdez, his slim chest heaving, walks to his corner where the stool is waiting. He sits down heavily, looping his leaden arms over the ropes. A green water bottle, covered in white adhesive tape, is tipped into his mouth. He spits the water weakly onto his chest to try to stop the awful burning in his lungs. "The breathing," he says, shaking his head. "The breathing."

His second, the man in the corner with him, has never seen him before and gives the only advice he can. "Keep moving," he says. "Keep your head down. Stay away from him. Cover up."

But Leonard Valdez has not come here tonight to cover up or stay away. He has come for what they all come for. More than a hundred this night, thousands across the country. Maybe it was watching the Olympics. Maybe it was the movie *Rocky*. Maybe it was a dare on the street or the taunt of a girlfriend. Or maybe it was the unexplainable thing that they try so hard to explain. The thing they call heart. "I wanted to be in the Gloves," Leonard will say later. "To fight in the Golden Gloves."

It is the last opportunity in America to go from nothing to champion. A career in professional football or basketball almost always means going to college first. A baseball career means spending time in the minors. But in the Golden Gloves any kid 16 to 25 can walk off the streets, get a quick physical, a mouthpiece, an athletic cup, and walk into the ring. Those who do usually get their head knocked off. But not always. It doesn't cost a dime to enter. Some call it organized brutality. These kids call it opportunity.

And they come from all over. Inner city, suburbs, some even from rural towns. They are not the punchy palookas of the fight movies.

Benny Bentley sits at ringside. He was once one of the best known fight promoters in America. In 1959 he sat ringside at the Golden Gloves in Chicago and saw an 18-year-old kid from Kentucky fight a guy named Jefferson Davis. "Jefferson Davis couldn't hit him with a bat," Bentley said. "He needed a machine gun that night. I looked up at the other kid and said, 'This is the best guy I've ever seen.' " The kid won the Golden Gloves that year. They called him Cassius Clay then. They don't call him that anymore.

"Take a look at these kids," Bentley says, waving his pipestem.

"Notice how good they look? Well, they all look good climbing *in.*
Take a look at them climbing *out.*

"They come off the streets, they're a big man in their gang, or they
watch Ali on television. Where else you gonna make a million dollars
in a night? So they come and they fight. They get a jacket, a medal,
and a dream."

He looked up into the ring to see Pete Morales hit Thomas Muhne
with a right hand that looked like it was loaded with brass doorknobs.
Muhne went down in a heap. "He is on that boulevard," Bentley said
with a wince. "On the Boulevard of Broken Dreams."

Leonard Valdez is not on that boulevard. Not yet. After the first
round he sits on the stool trying to understand what his second is
telling him. There is the whistle and the bell. Leonard moves out,
circling away from Blackwell's right hand. He has learned fast. He
had to. Because Leonard Valdez has never been in a boxing ring
before. He has never put on 10-ounce boxing gloves before. Or
jammed a clumsy mouthpiece between his teeth. Or gone out to hit a
stranger.

At the side of the ring, just in the fringes of the light, his father,
Wally, watches the oldest of his eight children exchange blows with
another man.

"He never trained or nothing," he says. "But he wants to fight. He
read about it in the paper. He sent in the coupon and they sent back
this thing telling him where to show up. I think he got it from
watching the Olympics. From that Sugar Ray Leonard. He thinks he
can whip anybody. He's a good boy, a good kid. He goes to school,
then he goes to see his girlfriend. He doesn't get in any trouble. His
girlfriend, she came tonight.

"If he wants to box, what can I do? It's OK. If he wants to go to
college, that's OK, too. I'll take out a loan on the house. He deserves
a chance at whatever he wants."

That is what they have come for. It is easy to laugh at the Golden
Gloves, criticize it when you see two 18-year-olds pounding each
other to jelly in front of a howling crowd.

But when you see them walk in wearing a pair of beat-up Converse
tennis shoes, a terrycloth bathrobe from home, and a bewildered
look, you learn why they are here.

Leonard Valdez, first time in the ring, will lose his fight. The judges
will decide by a two-one decision that Blackwell beat him.

Walking to the back of the gym with Wally, he sits on a stool as a
man with a long-handled pair of silver scissors cuts the tape from his
hands. "I had no strength left," he says. "But next time, I'll train. And?"
He shrugs. "Who knows?"

The movie that has brought so many of them here tonight, *Rocky,* has a simple point. A washed-up palooka is given a chance to fight the heavyweight champion of the world. Before the fight, he tells his girlfriend that he knows he cannot win. All he wants to do is to finish the fight, he says.

There are not that many winners in life. The victory circle is a small one. Most of the kids know that they will never be another Ali, they will never fight in Madison Square Garden. But all they want to do is take a shot at it. There aren't that many places where you can do that anymore.

Benny Bentley is chewing on his pipe. In the 1930s he fought in this ring. In his third bout, he was eliminated from the tournament. "But on my feet," he says. "I lost it on my feet." Forty years later that is still what counts.

A fighter comes into the locker room and stops near where Valdez is slowly dressing.

"You shoulda jabbed him," the fighter says. "You coulda won."

Valdez shrugs. "I went the distance," he says.

Sometimes, that is enough.

February 27, 1977

How to Avoid Being a Flying Wimp: Wing It!

By the time you are done reading this, you won't be a wimp anymore.

What's that? You don't think you are one now? Take this simple one-question test to find out:

You save for six months for your dream vacation. You skip lunches, you stop buying beer, you sell the kids.

Finally, you go. You check into the lovely Chez Casa Grande Hotel, which is costing you $115 a night.

The bellhop shows you to your deluxe room. Which happens to overlook the local toxic waste dump. And is situated next to the ice machine that goes ke-chunketa-chunketa at precise 27-second intervals.

The air conditioning doesn't work. The hot-water faucet yields a rusty trickle. The TV gets only Channel 38. And the bed is propped up by two telephone books.

You look around. You turn to your spouse and say:

"Well, honey, how much time are we really going to spend in the room anyway?"

That's a wimp. A wimp can be a man or a woman. It has nothing to do with manhood. A wimp is a person who has already surrendered in the battle of daily life.

A wimp never demands another room at a hotel. Or a new table in a restaurant even if the kitchen door is banging him in the head. When his bank makes a mistake and charges him a $10 service fee for it, a wimp pays without a whimper.

A wimp says things like "Why bother?" and "You can't fight city hall" and "It's not worth the fuss."

If you recognize a little bit of yourself in this, do not despair. By applying a few simple rules, you can change your life forever.

In future months, I will tell you how to deal with banks, credit card companies, the government, and other quasi-criminal agencies.

But because it is the vacation season and many of you will be flying, today I will deal with airlines.

Airlines, as you already know, are terrible. They are that way on purpose. They figure anybody crazy enough to go up in the air in a metal tube gets what he deserves.

Some weeks ago, my wife and I went on vacation to Las Vegas. I bought those advance seat selection, advance boarding pass tickets from United Airlines.

But when I got on the plane, they refused to give me the seats marked on my boarding passes. Instead, they offered me seats in the smoking section, where I was free to breathe deeply and get somebody else's cancer.

Rule One: Always complain. Be reasonable, but be firm. Keep in mind that you are paying them, not the other way around.

"No," I told the flight attendant. "I am not sitting in the smoking section. You are going to have to do better than that."

The flight attendant went up the gangway and came back with a nasty man. The nasty man grabbed a piece of luggage out of my hand. "If you don't like where we put you, you can get off the plane," he said.

Rule Two: Develop a cruel smile. Some people like to imitate Elvis Presley's sneer. Others try Humphrey Bogart's slow snarl. I like to use Richard Widmark's half-crazed smirk. You remember it. He always used it right before he smashed the guy in the teeth with his gun.

So I gave the guy my Richard Widmark smirk.

Rule Three: Speak very quietly. Almost whisper. Make the guy lean forward to catch the words as they fall from your lips like small, hard pearls.

"I'm not going anywhere, pal," I said. (I like to say "pal" to people I hate.) "And I want you to be more polite."

The guy was stunned. Polite? Someone was asking him to be polite? I guess in his last job, which was probably rounding up cattle, nobody ever complained.

He disappeared up the gangway. When he came back, guess what he came back with? No, not the cops. Not a cattle prod. Forget about all those fears you had when you used to be a wimp. The guy came back with an apology.

Rule Four: Be gracious in victory.

"I'm sorry," the formerly nasty man said. "Sometimes we make mistakes. We made one this time. Can United make it up to you by giving you seats in First Class?"

I didn't give him Widmark this time. I gave him Shirley Temple.

"Swell," I said. "That would be just swell."

Rule Five: Go for it.

When the flight attendants in First Class said they could not give us

First Class meals, I didn't complain. They were right. I hadn't paid for them.

But when they graciously offered us a selection off the ice cream sundae cart, I rose to the occasion. And I left wimphood forever behind me.

"Two scoops," I said. "With sprinkles."

July 1, 1982

The Shah of Springfield Splurges

I was almost moved to tears when I heard Jim Thompson's passionate speech last week about the needy of Illinois.

Thompson, who as governor has cut hundreds of millions of dollars from schoolchildren, the sick, elderly, and mentally ill, asked for massive tax increases to keep our state afloat.

So I decided to see how Jim, himself, was floating these days. And I found out he is doing just ducky. All at taxpayer expense.

While he is telling us to pay more taxes, he is living like the Shah of Springfield.

All the following figures are from the state comptroller's office. All the years are fiscal years.

Keep in mind that the Thompsons are a family of three. There is Jim, Jayne, and four-year-old Samantha, my favorite Thompson and the only Thompson whose ambitions do not exceed her talents.

Anyone else who lives in the governor's mansion or works in the mansion lives and works to serve them and is there at the governor's discretion.

Thompson finds it necessary to employ, at taxpayer expense, 16 persons to care for him and his family full time: two butlers, three cooks, an administrative assistant, a conservator, a fiscal clerk, a housekeeper, a laundress, three maintenance men, an operations manager, and two secretaries.

This costs us about $250,000 a year. And when Thompson throws big parties, he hires even more servants.

Thompson could, like other governors, cut back on that staff. Or he could, like other governors, refuse to live in such lavish style.

But he likes the way he lives. Just as long as he doesn't have to pay for it.

In Thompson's first full fiscal year as governor, the cost of the governor's mansion and the governor's office was about $1.9 million.

Last year, the cost was $3.8 million.

Why is this figure so high? Take a look at the mansion alone. The

Thompsons' electric bill there, a bill you pay, was $42,000 last year.

The governor must have been burning those lights late into the night figuring out how to cut funds from the old, sick, and unemployed.

And you can judge a man not only by his big expenses—Thompson's trip to Japan at state expense is now legendary—but also by his petty ones.

Jim Thompson gets a salary of $58,000 a year plus free room, board, utilities, cars, planes, etc. In addition, he gets millions in campaign contributions that he can spend any way he pleases, as long as he pays taxes on them.

So if he was going to buy something personal, something unrelated to state business, he'd pay for it himself, right?

Wrong. This is Jim Thompson we are talking about. Not Mother Teresa.

Last year, Thompson charged the taxpayers for a subscription to *Gourmet* magazine ($15), a subscription to *Cuisine* magazine ($12), his cable TV movie channel ($371), and his matches ($245).

He also charged us for the *Book of Modern Jewish Etiquette* ($19.95).

But his food bill was far from petty. The Thompsons spent $33,000 on food last year. And Samantha doesn't eat that much.

Nor was the extravagance all for visiting dignitaries. Thompson's cronies and campaign contributors feed at the mansion regularly.

In West Virginia, Governor Jay Rockefeller, a multimillionaire who lived in luxury in private life, has cut down his mansion staff to just seven full-time employees and is cutting down on such luxuries as shrimp and lobster.

But our governor has a fondness for shellfish that threatens to depopulate the oceans. In 1980—known in Springfield as the Year of the Shrimp—Thompson charged the taxpayers $1,047 for the little wrigglers. The cocktail sauce was extra. But you paid for that, too.

Last year, Thompson not only spent hundreds of dollars on shrimp, but thousands on mussels, rumaki, canapés, lobster tails, egg rolls, quiche Lorraine, and filet mignon.

When it comes to spending money on ordinary citizens, however, Thompson is much more conservative.

His policy is that if an agency can't manage its money well, there will be no bailout from him.

That's why Thompson didn't want to help out the Chicago schools until a financial watchdog board was created to scrutinize their budget.

I think that is a good idea.

So if I were a state legislator, I wouldn't vote for a dime in tax increases until a watchdog board was set up to monitor the expenses of the Shah of Springfield.

There is one expense I would investigate immediately.

The taxpayers spent $198 last year to rid the governor's mansion of pests.

But I think one got away.

February 17, 1983

MIDEAST JOURNAL

There is a saying in the Mideast: "If you aren't confused, you haven't been here long enough."

Covering the Mideast, from Saudi Arabia to Israel in 1981, and then returning for the Israeli invasion of Lebanon and the PLO evacuation from Beirut in 1982, was the hardest assignment I ever had.

It was not just the sometimes battlefield conditions, but the complexity of the story itself. You would interview this side and that side and get this point of view and that one.

And you would still end up asking yourself: Is this finally the truth? Have I really found it? Or is there such a thing in this mad place?

The Dead Aren't in Uniform

BEIRUT, Lebanon

The snow-topped mountains glowed silver in the moonlight and the shadow of the jet skipped across them, leaping up from the valleys and onto the peaks. In less than a second, the jet crossed the face of the dimpled moon itself and began its turn.

The ghostly exhaust trail followed behind it, writing across the sky like the finger of God. Beneath it in the harbor, the ships circled or lay at anchor, waiting for the warehouses to stop burning and hoping that the shelling would not resume.

Just for a moment, there was the rarest of things in this city: silence. Then the Dixie Express shattered the sky.

The Dixie Express is an Israeli Phantom fighter-bomber, but one does not say "Israel" here. Israel is to the south, so it is called Dixie. And the jets of Dixie roam at will, cracking the sound barrier to say hello.

"It is like a calling card," Dan Pattir, counselor to the prime minister of Israel, told me later. "It lets our friends know we are there."

And their enemies, too. Out near the airport, not far from where a Soviet T-34 tank was dug in up to its treads under camouflage netting, two Syrian soldiers got up from the fire where their tea had been brewing. They walked out from under the corrugated tin roof of their sandbagged emplacement.

With weary resignation, they began tracking the plane across the sky with antiaircraft fire, the twin barrels of the gun popping back and forth, throwing up puffs of smoke against the stars.

They did not really expect to hit it. But they had their duty. And they did accomplish one thing. From across the harbor and the city came the soft crump of the mortars, the sharp crack of artillery, the ragged tearing noise of heavy machine gun fire. The antiaircraft guns had served as the opening baton in Beirut's nightly concert.

Once upon a time not long ago, wars like this were fought with aging Garand rifles and ancient Springfields, with Molotov cocktails and mortars made from the exhaust pipes of old cars.

Now, the boats and trucks unload tanks, howitzers, rocket launchers, bazookas, and boxload after boxload of automatic assault rifles still in their oiled wrappings and complete with instructions.

In the Mideast today, weapons are the one universally recognized symbol of friendship, whether it be AWACS for the Saudis or rocket-propelled grenades for the Lebanese Christians. And everyone wants to make friends and money: The Soviets, the French, the British, the Israelis, the United States.

Over here, nothin' says lovin' like a tank.

"Lebanon is now the battleground for all the troubles of the Mideast," Alfred Mady, a spokesman for the Christian forces, said. "It is open land, open season, for everything. For narcotics, for weapons, for terrorism. There is no such word as *legal* in Lebanon. Anything goes."

It has been going badly. More than 500 people were killed here last month and the fighting continues. Not only fighting between the various Lebanese factions—some students of the conflict count no fewer than 39 separate militias—which is bad enough, but also fighting between the Syrians and Israelis.

The first thing that strikes one, though, is that the dead are almost never soldiers. This is a war planned by statesmen, directed by generals and fought by militiamen, but the casualties rarely wear uniforms. They wear business suits and carry briefcases. They wear dresses and carry shopping bags. They wear Moslem robes and carry farm tools. They often wear diapers and carry nothing.

An unmarked but very real "Green Line" separates the Christian side from the Moslem side of Beirut. In normal times, thousands cross the line every day. But in these times, when they can cross at all, people plunge and scuttle across. Taxi drivers lean on their horns and speed across the no-man's-land drawing sniper fire.

On the day I arrived, only 30 or 40 shells had fallen so the fighting was reported as "light" or "sporadic" much as in another city the weather would be reported as "partly cloudy" or "drizzly." So to the rest of the world it was not big news, surely not as important as threats of Soviet intervention in Poland or injuries from rubber bullets in Belfast.

But this is not a village, it is a city of more than a million people, with houses and apartment blocks and shopping areas and high rises. And the shells are not so much aimed as merely fired. The Moslems know all they have to do is turn their mortars east to hit a Christian. The Christians merely have to fire west to hit a Moslem. The targets are no more clearly defined than that.

It is not yet all-out war. The shell-pocked hulk of the Holiday Inn still looms silent and empty over the Beirut harbor, a monument to the civil war of 1975 and 1976, where Christians and Moslems blasted each other for 19 months, leaving 37,000 dead and property damage of about $15 billion.

But even though it is not full-scale war, the shells still fall from the skies like the wrath of heaven. And after they have landed and the yellow-gray smoke has been carried away by the Mediterranean breezes, the people get up and walk about again. They buy fat red strawberries from street vendors. They sit outside their shops, slapping down the markers of their backgammon games. They buy tax-free and dirt-cheap cigarettes and go to American movies.

Kramer vs. Kramer is still packing them in on both sides of the Green Line. The restaurants along the sea are still open, though the owners complain that the new practice of fishing by hand grenade sometimes disturbs the customers.

Kamal Jrab meets me at the airport. He works for the Commodore Hotel, and it is his job to see that guests get from the airport to the hotel alive. The fee is very small, considering the service.

To Kamal, as to many Lebanese, the fighting is an unfortunate but not overwhelming fact of life, something that makes the traffic bad and the electricity sometimes fail.

"A beautiful country," he says, sweeping his hand over the mountains that cup the city. "The Switzerland of the Mideast." They really used to call it that, a reference to the mountains and banks, not to the peace and quiet.

The front seat of our cab is covered by a tapestry that depicts in unpleasantly real flesh tones the heads of John Kennedy, Robert Kennedy, and Martin Luther King.

"For good luck," Kamal says, patting their faces. As we come to the first checkpoint and two soldiers with rifles fixed with grenade launchers come toward us, it occurs to me Kamal has picked three strange examples of good luck.

You cannot move more than a few blocks without going through a checkpoint, and they soon become a way of life. They are usually just sandbags, sometimes with a tin sheet on top and one or two bored soldiers inside. Few Westerners are bothered, although American diplomats must travel to and from the airport with bodyguards.

There are Syrian checkpoints, Palestine Liberation Organization checkpoints, Palestine Liberation Army checkpoints, Lebanese Army checkpoints, Christian checkpoints, and, if you go far enough, United Nations checkpoints, where you are stoped by red-faced Irishmen or blond-haired Swedes or black-skinned Nigerians or Fijians.

Slightly smaller than Connecticut, Lebanon is big enough for everyone to fight over.

The traffic grows heavy as we make our way toward the hotel. The traffic lights have not worked for years, and soon we are stopped in a massive traffic jam, with everyone blowing his horn furiously. Gridlock is not a dire prediction in this city, it is a way of life.

The problem is solved in the usual manner. A few soldiers wander over and start waving their rifles, forcing some cars to turn away onto other streets, letting others slip by. As soon as the soldiers appear, the horns grow silent.

The weakest element in Lebanon is the government of Lebanon. Many people don't bother paying taxes anymore. Law and order is provided by anyone who has a gun and enough armed friends to see that he keeps it. You can buy a hot Mercedes-Benz for $500. And you can drive it until someone steals it again.

Garbage lies in empty lots. Sometimes it is collected; more often someone will grow tired of the smell, douse it with gasoline, and try to get rid of it that way.

The harbor is controlled by Christian forces, who extract "taxes" from each cargo, but any trucks that unload the ships and cross into Moslem territory must pay again.

Some things do work. Phones, water, and electricity are interrupted only sporadically. And there is wealth here, both from traditional sources and from war profiteering.

Lebanon is a country that runs by force of habit. But that has its limits.

"The car bombs go off because nobody checks for them," an Irish journalist told me. "Have you ever been in Belfast? My God, you can't leave your car for five minutes without the police or army checking it over. Here, nobody checks and nobody cares. You can blow somebody's head off or blow up a block of flats and nobody will arrest you for murder."

On my second day in Beirut, an artillery shell came whistling into the central business district about a block from where I stood. It landed with a tremendous crack and knocked down three people. I waited for police sirens to wail, but there were none. No ambulances rushed to the scene. No fire engines clanged their way up the crowded streets to battle the small blaze that had been set off. The injured were collected in private cars and taken away.

The most recent round of fighting erupted when Christian militia forces tried to gain control of the town of Zahle in the fertile Bekaa Valley. The town lies near the road to Damascus, and the Syrians declared it vital to their own security. So they began shelling the town.

"In examining the questions of the Mideast, however, you must never rule out sheer gangsterism," a Western diplomat told me. "The Bekaa Valley is one of the great hashish-producing areas of the Mideast. We are talking about an industry that measures profits in the billions. Billions. Whatever army controls the Bekaa controls the traffic and that profit."

Whatever the reason behind the fighting, it is now getting beyond the control of all parties. Israel had an informal understanding with Syria: Syria would not operate too close to the South and would not deploy missiles. In return, Israel would limit its attacks to South Lebanon and the Dixie Express would buzz but not attack close to Syria.

But the Zahle fighting shattered the understanding. Fearing a massacre of the Christians, Israeli Phantom jets shot down two Syrian helicopters that had been firing on Christian positions. Now the Syrians have moved in surface-to-air missiles to knock out the Israeli planes.

Nobody seems willing to back down and, like it or not, the United States may become involved in the conflict.

"If the United States or Israel believes that it can undermine the steadfastness of the PLO and Syria, it is mistaken," Farouk Kaddoumi, the political chief of the PLO, said in an interview. "This would lead to a much wider war than the United States imagines—a war that would cover all parts of the world.

"Regardless of the costs, American interests would not escape the hands of the Palestinians. If the United States exposes the PLO to danger, we will not hesitate to strike at American interests wherever they are."

There seem to be no small wars anymore, nor short ones. I talked to a young Norwegian collector of handicrafts and antiques. She told me I must see the Syrian checkpoint near the American Embassy in West Beirut before I left.

"Go see the soldier there," she said with a cold fury. "Then you'll see what the fighting in this country is all about.

"He stands there every day with his Kalashnikov rifle and his hand grenades. And he stops people or he waves them by. And do you know how old he is? Do you? He is 10. I asked him. He is 10.

"When you use the children," she asked, "what do you have left?"

On both sides of the Green Line they would tell her that she misses the point. Both sides would show her the pictures in their literature, the slick, glossy pictures of small children carrying big guns.

The point, they would tell her, is that no matter how great the losses to this generation, the struggle will be carried on by the next generation. And the next. And the next. And the next.

May 10, 1981

'I'll Join The PLO . . . and Die a Martyr'

BETHLEHEM

They are too young to remember what their father will never forget. They do not know the pain. When you are young, all your pain is still ahead of you.

We sit and drink mint tea and eat spiced cakes in the living room of the large, whitewashed home. The windows are open and the birds are just finishing their evening song. Darkness begins to fall on the Jerusalem hills above us.

"Humiliation," the father says. "When I saw the Israeli tanks come to my door, it was not fear I felt. It was humiliation."

The sons do not feel it. The youngest, the 12-year-old, feels only anger. His name is Sadir. He will drive the Jews from Israel, he says.

For the 16-year-old, Souheil, life is good enough under the Israelis. Why complain?

Hatham, 17, will leave as soon as he is able. Why fight? The world is better elsewhere.

They are all Palestinians. They are the Hamad family. And although this is a story of the future, the future does not exist in the Mideast without reliving the past.

It is 1948 and, as Israel declares its independence, Arabs and Jews fight for the land. In the farming village of Rafat, 12 miles west of Jerusalem, the Hamads, well-off Arab landowners, gather together their belongings and prepare to flee the Jewish soldiers.

"I was just a child," Jamil Hamad, now 42, says. "I remember the day so well. We were the last three to leave the village. My father, my mother, and me. It was the afternoon and my father was riding his horse.

"We were crossing our fields. The crops were growing around us. Grapes, citrus, wheat. It was so quiet in the town. There used to be life in it. But now, even the birds were silent. I remember that. How even the birds were silent.

"My father said to my mother: 'In two months, we will be back for the harvest.' The next day, the Israelis came and blew up the houses."

The Hamads would never come back for the harvest. Their fields are part of Israel now. A kibbutz farms the land they once farmed.

Rafat no longer exists, except in the memories of a few Arabs. The Hamads still visit, but there is only overgrown rubble.

Like a half-million other Arabs—the figure is in dispute—the Hamads fled east. The Israelis say they could have stayed. The Arabs say they were forced to go.

The Hamads went to Bethlehem, which, like the rest of the West Bank, had been annexed by Jordan.

"We became refugees," Jamil Hamad says. "My father lost everything—money, land, everything. I remember waiting in line with my ration card, waiting for the United Nations relief people to give us flour and butter.

"My father came to us sons and said: 'I have nothing to give you. I have lost everything. It is your battle now.' "

In 1967, after a six-day war, the Israelis occupied the West Bank. Once again, the Hamads faced Israeli soldiers on their doorstep.

"My wife was beaten by the soldiers," Hamad says. "They thought we had a gun in the house. Some of our possessions were burned. Later, I admit, a hearing was held. The Israelis offered us compensation. I refused it.

"I tried not to be bitter. Many Israeli friends who were neighbors back in Rafat came to our home in 1967 with kisses and tears. Israel is a fact which I recognize. I want Israel to recognize me as a fact. I want to live side by side with Israel.

"I am not involved with the PLO, but the PLO is a symbol of our national aspirations. Let Israel run their country the way they want to. And let us run our country the way we want to."

Such talk qualifies Jamil Hamad as a moderate. But that is not an easy thing to be on the West Bank.

"Here," he says, "a moderate is someone the Arabs call a traitor and the Israelis call a terrorist."

But this night I have come not to hear him, but the next generation of Palestinians. After a while, the sons begin to speak.

"If someone has to rule the West Bank, I would like Israel to do it," Hatham, the 17-year-old, says. "Israel is much better than Jordan and the PLO. The PLO, she is created for killing and threats. That is all the PLO is. If you are an Arab, you prefer Israel."

"To be ruled by foreigners?" his father asks.

"This is not my problem," he shrugs. "It is not my job to tell the Israelis where to rule."

And your family's farm, I ask, it does not bother you that Israelis now own it?

"A little. Not much," he says. "I am born here, in Bethlehem. I wasn't born in Rafat. The problem is here, not in Rafat. It bothers me a little that the Israelis come here and build houses, because this is my land. But who builds the houses for the Israelis? It is Arab labor who builds them. Yes, we build them."

And will Arabs ever rule this land? I ask.

"No. You want me to dream and why should I? Arabs dream too much. My first ambition is to leave. To go to Britain. To learn the law. After I finish, I might come back. I would see how the atmosphere is. If it is not good, I would stay away."

"And your dear parents?" his father asks with gentle sarcasm. "What about them?"

"Come to me!" he says, laughing. "Come and live in Britain."

"But if your people needed your help, you would come?" his father asks more seriously.

"Yes," Hatham says cautiously. "Of course."

"I have in mind to see young Palestinians coming here and working hard like the Jews worked hard," the father explains. "Not sipping coffee and smoking cigarettes and being proud to be a Palestinian. A state is not a flag and a Mercedes-Benz.

"If Israel withdrew tomorrow, it would not be the end of our problems. It would be the beginning. We would have to show the world we could build a country."

"I am a son of the West Bank!" Hatham says in his defense. "But I can also imagine leaving."

His father sighs. "I think you are disappointing me," he says.

"Israel is not so bad," Hatham says. "Israel says to the Arab: 'Do whatever you want. Go where you want. Just do not do one thing. Do not carry a bomb.' If you are kind with the Israeli soldiers, they will be all right with you."

Sadir, the 12-year-old, is not kind with the soldiers. He throws rocks at them. This is not Northern Ireland, where such things are tolerated. Israeli soldiers take such attacks seriously.

"I don't like the Israelis," Sadir says. "They brought injustice. They took away my grandfather's land. I would like to go back to Rafat."

His brother, Souheil, snorts. "You have been for maybe two days in Rafat," he says. "On camping trips. There is nothing left of Rafat."

"They should leave so we can go back," Sadir says. "I support the PLO. They would liberate Palestine. Israel took our lands. They deserve. . . ." He speaks a phrase in Arabic to his father. "Hard punishment," the father translates.

"Yes," Sadir says. "Hard punishment. The PLO and the Arabs should be united. The Jews should be sent back to the U.S. or wherever else they came from."

You do not like Jews? I ask him.

"I like them," he says, "but not as invaders. They must leave the West Bank. They must leave Palestine. They must leave all of Israel. No more Jews. They have the right to live, but not on others' land."

And you would fight them?

"Yes," Sadir says. "I would fight them."

"The PLO is not so bad," Souheil says. "But they should not be the government. Israel is fine. Let them rule us."

But Sadir says he will drive the Israelis into the sea, I say to him.

"If Sadir can do it," Souheil says with a smile, "let him. Meanwhile, I will live in Bethlehem."

"I will live in Rafat!" shouts Sadir. "I will run the farm!"

"There is no electricity, Sadir," Souheil says. "There is no water."

"There is no one there, Sadir," Hatham says.

"It is my land! My homeland! My house! My school! It is my life!" he says.

"Here, we live fine," says Souheil.

"The kibbutz owns it now," Hatham says.

"I throw rocks at the soldiers and run," Sadir says, turning away from his brothers and toward me. "I do it frequently. If they catch me, they will beat me. I don't care. If I am beaten, I am defending my homeland."

"And what if they take your parents away?" his father asks him gently.

"If they take my parents away, I will join the PLO," he says. "I will join the PLO, anyway. I will do my best to die as a martyr. I will study chemistry and make bombs to destroy Menachem Begin and the Israelis and Saad Haddad [a Lebanese Christian allied with Israel]."

Sadir begins to chant: "P-L-O! IS-RAEL-NO!"

As a final question, I ask them all what they wish to be.

"A lawyer," Hatham says.

"A natural scientist," Souheil says.

"I will be a pilot for the PLO," Sadir says.

His brothers grin. "The PLO has no planes," Souheil tells him.

"In the future," Sadir says quietly, "they will."

No one laughed. And even the birds were silent.

May 12, 1981

◆

'I Didn't Want to Die'— But He Would Have

If in battle I shall fall, friend take my weapon and continue on.
—From a song by Zvi Ben-Josef, poet,
killed at Kfar Etzion, May, 1948

JERUSALEM

Not long before the end, the commander gathered them together and told them they were going to have to die for their country.

"He said the Jewish nation expected it of us," Rafi Horowitz said. "He said Masada was our history, and death was our legacy.

"Well, it was a very fine speech. There was only a small problem. I didn't want to die."

Rafi Horowitz fought at a place called Kfar Etzion. To an Israeli, that is like saying he fought at the Alamo. Every year there is a memorial service there. Rafi does not attend.

"Did you know," he said, "there is a physical pain to fear? I did not know that. But there is. We lived every day with the stink of sweat and the sour smell of blood and fear. Always the fear. I have fought in every war Israel has had. I retired a major. But I never experienced anything like Etzion."

This is a story of war, but it is not a war story. It is a story of why Israel is the way it is and why it does the things it does.

Kfar Etzion was a Jewish settlement nine miles south of Jerusalem and surrounded by Arabs. In May, 1948, during the Israeli war of independence, Etzion was attacked by units of the Arab Legion supported by heavy artillery and armored cars. The outnumbered Israeli defenders had some light arms, a few machine guns, and one mortar.

"Oh, I suppose we should have evacuated it," Rafi said. "But you see, we did not come to this country to evacuate.

"Let me tell you a funny story. One night I came in from one of the forward positions, and I lay down to sleep next to my comrades. They were stretched out on the ground.

"In the morning, I found out that I had laid down with the dead, those who had been killed that day. But do you know what was funny? All night long, I could have sworn someone was trying to take my blanket."

When Etzion finally fell, only three of the 88 settlers were still alive. The Israeli army units fighting with them also suffered terrible losses.

"During the siege I ran away once," Rafi said. "I could not stand it. The shelling never stopped. But I came back. Ben-Josef, the famous poet, was a tremendous friend. He had composed this song that we all sang about fighting on if one should fall.

"He was killed in front of me. He was destroyed from the waist down. He was singing when he died. Yes, I heard it. And someone came over and grabbed up his Sten gun and kept fighting."

The commander of Etzion, Moshe Silberschmidt, went down in

history for his "Masada" speech. "What are our lives worth?" he said. "Nothing compared with our task."

Silberschmidt had spent four years in a Nazi death camp and had come to Israel to grow fruit trees. The day after his speech, he was killed a few yards away from Zvi Ben-Josef.

"On the last morning, we knew we were going to die," Rafi said. "People were singing and telling jokes. And I was thinking, 'I am too young for this. I am 17 and I have never had a woman. And now I never will.'

"We talked about the one thing we wanted before we died. Some wanted just to eat a meal. Some to see their homes one last time. One man wanted a flower. I remember that."

"God," he said, shaking his head in memory. "I was never again so afraid and desperate. I lost most of my friends, most of my class-mates. They disappeared in 24 hours.

"I can see the whole class lined up. You know how they take pictures of school classes. Well, I can see us lined up, little boys, and I go down the row in my mind and I say: 'He is dead and him and this one and this one.'

"A good friend was badly wounded and he tried to kill himself with a grenade. But it only wounded him again. We ran over to the ditch where he lay and he said, 'Finish me, finish me.'

"I was scared, and I couldn't do it. Another man—don't use his name; he is famous now—he took out his gun and he shot him. For years I could not speak to that man.

"I remember at the end, retreating to a ditch with two friends and hiding under a small bridge. We heard the Arab soldiers march above us and the sounds of the massacre going on."

Rafi and his friends were the only survivors in their unit. They were sent to a prison camp in Jordan.

Kfar Etzion was Arab territory until 1967, when Israel occupied the West Bank. Rafi went back.

"I found the ditch where I hid," he said. "It was so much smaller than I remembered. I walked around picking out this hill and that. But all I saw were the faces of the dead. I don't go back anymore."

I asked him if there was a fear worse than the fear of dying.

"Once, during a break in the shelling," he said, "I was sitting there literally with the brains of a friend on my shirt, and I thought: 'If I die, this whole thing could end.' You see, we were a terribly young country. We were a few days old, and there was no guarantee there was going to be an Israel. My mother's family had lived in Jerusalem for eight generations, and I thought: 'Will it all be over? Will it end here?' "

It did not, of course. But the fighting never seemed to end. And in a way, men like Rafi do not want it to.

"I remember I was in New York in 1979," he said. "And I was taken to Greenwich Village. I went to one of those art gallery openings. I remember how Vivaldi was playing on the stereo and how there was smoked salmon and how people were orbiting and saying wise things. It was all very aesthetic.

"Someone introduced an author to me. He spoke about equality and freedom in America and the struggle for human rights, and I just exploded. I looked at him and said:

" 'What the hell do you know? What do you know? What did your freedom cost you? Do you know the price of staying alive? Do you?'

"I felt sick just listening to him. You see, he did not have to pay anything for his freedom. He did not have to pay with his friends, his eyes, his legs. Someone else had paid for America; he paid nothing. He just stood there with his smoked salmon and talked.

"How could I tell him of the people I knew who died for such things as freedom?" Rafi said, clutching his hands in front of him. "People who wanted beauty before they died, who wanted to eat, who wanted to make love, who wanted to have a flower. They died and they died and they died for freedom."

He unclutched his hands, but the emotion was still in his face and voice:

"Do you know what I tell my children? I tell my children, 'I live with the possibility you might die.' I tell them making a nation is not done with flowers and guitars. It is not done in Woodstock. Our life in this country is a continuous war. I want them to know that. I want my children never to say: 'Where is the danger? There is no danger.'

"I want them to fight always. Not with guns, if this is possible, but always to fight. If they are farmers let them fight for their crops. If they are authors let them fight for their ideas.

"I say to my son in the army: 'If you die, I will tell your brothers, your friends, your life had meaning.'

"So people say we are crazy? Let them. My God, look who we are here! Victims of the Holocaust, people right out of the death camps, others fleeing this persecution and that persecution. And you take these people and you put them in this pressure cooker, and you have them face constant war. We are so crazy here? I am surprised we are so sane.

"Let me tell you something. It is a message we know, and you Americans should learn. It is the lesson of Israel:

"If you have nothing to die for, you have nothing to live for."

May 20, 1981

Want a Drink?
It Means 60 Lashes

[Arab] ways were hard, even for those brought up in them and for strangers terrible . . .

T. E. "Lawrence of Arabia" Lawrence
"Seven Pillars of Wisdom"

AL KHOBAR, Saudi Arabia

He was breaking the law, he knew that. Even as he was drinking the stuff he knew what would happen if he was caught.

But there is not a lot of fun for a 26-year-old American in Saudi Arabia. There are no night spots, no public movie theaters, no discos. Local women are unthinkably out of bounds and dating even a Western woman is difficult. Riding in a car with a woman not your wife or relative can be grounds for deportation.

English-speaking television shows exist, but barely. You can watch American tapes on your video recorder, but how many times can you really see *Smokey and the Bandit?*

So there is drinking. And, he would admit, the saying is true: Repression breeds obsession. Because liquor is illegal here, many seek it like they would not seek it at home.

So he had a few drinks. Not enough to be drunk, but that did not matter. He was caught. And, a month later, as he was leaned up against a light pole on a public street and the prison guard began the first of his 60 lashes, he asked himself what a kid from downstate Illinois was doing here.

"I had been drinking sadaghy [sad-EEK-y]," he said. "It's distilled from sugar. It's white alcohol, white lightning. It means 'friend' in Arabic. It turned out it wasn't so friendly."

Many Islamic countries offer alcohol in hotels for foreigners who are not Moslems. But Saudi Arabia is different. As the birthplace of Mohammed, as the country where Islam was founded, Saudi Arabia takes its religion very seriously.

The only law here is the law of the Moslem bible, the Koran. The Koran forbids Moslems to drink. But when, many years ago, a prince who had been drinking shot and killed the British vice-consul in Jidda, the first king of the country banned booze for everyone, including Westerners.

"I had been here two years," Keith Bauer said. "And I probably could count the number of times I drank on the fingers of both hands. I didn't even go to many parties, they were so boring."

Almost all the liquor is homebrew. Even though the average American's salary here is about $50,000 per year, few are willing to spend the $85 it costs to buy a bottle of black-market Johnnie Walker Red, smuggled in by truck from Jordan.

New employees of Aramco, the Arabian-American Oil Co., which employs nearly 5,000 of the 45,000 Americans here, used to get instructions for home stills. They no longer do, but you can pretty well guess that when Westerners go to supermarkets and buy bottles of unsweetened grape juice, bags of sugar, and blocks of yeast, they have something illegal in mind. The stuff ferments in 22-liter jerry cans and can be drunk in six weeks.

"It was June 13, 1980, I won't forget that date for a while, and I was driving home at about 1 A.M. when the police pulled me over just to ask me where I was going," Bauer said. "They smelled liquor on my breath and that was it. If they hadn't smelled the liquor I would have been fine. But one whiff, and I was a goner."

As we talked, he chain-smoked Marlboro Lights. He was wearing chino slacks with an Yves St. Laurent belt, a tan button-down shirt, and Bass Weejuns. He is a big, athletic-looking guy, with an open, friendly face. He has a bushy mustache and gray eyes. You could dress him up in a kimono or a suit of armor and he would still be unmistakably American.

"My father was a businessman, upper-middle class, I guess," he said. "I went to Southern Illinois University at Edwardsville, but I hated it. I only stayed two years. Camping, waterskiing, that's what I liked. I managed a restaurant in St. Louis for a while; I worked on the Delta Queen, that riverboat. Then in 1978, a friend of mine told me he had gotten a job in Saudi Arabia. I said, 'What the hell, get me one, too.' "

We sat in his office, located not far from the prison where they had taken him, and he closed the door so his employees would not hear.

"The police asked me if I had been drinking, but I didn't answer right away," he said. "I didn't know if it was better to lie or confess. Anyway, they took a blood test and I figured, OK, Bauer, you're caught. You really screwed up and they're going to deport you.

"They took me to Thouqba Prison. They took my shoes and belt, and they opened the door and let me into the place. First off, forget your concept of a prison. Saudi Arabia is different. The guards don't look down on you. They are there to make sure no one runs away and no one smuggles anything in.

"There was no routine. You find your own way; you can pick any room you want. The rooms are square, cement-block rooms with a barred iron door, but the door is always open. The rooms are about 12 by 15 feet. There's a ceiling fan, two bare light bulbs and six bunk beds for 12 people. There are 16 rooms like that.

"We had mats on the floors or sat on carpets that people brought. You sit on the floor and get as near the fan as you can. The noise level borders on quiet.

"You're allowed a portable TV or radio and there is one TV in the central hallway. Sure it's color! In Saudi Arabia they can afford the best," he laughed. "And would I check into a place without color TV?

"The place was for people who were serving one to five years. I think the most serious offense was a guy who robbed a post office. There were Saudis, Yemenis, Pakistanis, British, everything. The Arabs and the non-Arabs were treated alike.

"There was an American, a black guy, I remember, he had been vacationing in Greece and he had been given some video cassettes by a friend as a gift. As a joke, his friend had slipped in an X-rated movie. When he got back to Saudi Arabia, they found it at the border. The poor schmuck got 30 days and 10 lashes."

It is possible that life in prisons larger than Thouqba Prison is harsher. However, a journalist I interviewed who had just visited two Americans in prison in Riyadh, the capital city, reported that conditions were "not bad." They had been in prison two months. The two worked in a hospital and had been sent to prison when a raid of their rooms revealed homebrew liquor and *Playboy*-type magazines.

"A friend brought food to me," Bauer said. "That's allowed. The prison food is chicken and rice or lamb and rice or what passes for hamburger. It's cooked by the prisoners and is certainly edible. You have to buy it, but you are given 13 riyals a day [about $4] by the prison authorities. You can buy food, cigarettes, Pepsi, underwear, soap, Kleenex, like that.

"There wasn't any fighting in the prison. Arabs don't fight. They yell. Boy, do they yell. They'll say your mother's a whore and you are the scum between a dog's toes, and stuff like that, but they don't hit each other. Once I saw a shoving match over which TV channel to watch, but that was it.

"Sex assaults? No, nothing like that. There were a couple of guys in there for being homosexuals, but I think their only crime was doing it with each other. If you homosexually assault somebody over here, I mean rape them, they kill you."

They sometimes do. On April 3, the local papers and TV carried the story of two men who had raped a man at gunpoint after shooting and wounding him. After a trial, they were beheaded. "This will be the fate of all those who disturb the peace and corrupt the land," the Interior Ministry announced.

"After about 10 days, I went to trial," Bauer said. "The courtroom was just an office. I didn't have a lawyer. I could have, but I didn't. I just had a translator. I figured I would get between 20 and 100 lashes. If I had been selling liquor, it would have been much worse. Some Westerners here make more from selling liquor than they do from their salaries.

"After 10 days in jail, I was actually hoping for lashes instead of time. Why? The heat. The heat was unimaginable. This was June, remember. It can drive a person insane, really. I had already lost 30 pounds. I'm not kidding you. The metal on the bed was too hot to touch. It would get up to 120 degrees.

"I was bathed in sweat all the time, even at night. We baked in it. The sweat would just drip off you. You could never quench your thirst. I had to put Kleenex under my neck at night to soak up the sweat. I couldn't shave, because the sweat made my face burn so badly. I really couldn't stand the heat in there.

"The judge was a religious judge, of course. He asked me, 'Were you drinking?' I told him, 'yes.'

"He read some files for a while. Then he looked up and said: 'Sixty days.'

"I said to myself, oh, God, I had already served 10 days but I just couldn't do another 50 days in there. So I asked him, 'Could I have the lashes instead?'

"The judge looked at me for a moment and said: 'Sixty lashes.' "

Bauer lit another Marlboro Light and for the first time his voice sounded other than matter of fact. "They do it with a palm stem," he said. "It's very hard. It's harder than bamboo, that I found out. I was pretty sure I was not going to be mutilated or deformed or anything. I mean, I'm not crazy. I just knew I didn't want to spend 60 days in that prison."

As it turned out, he spent 20 more, waiting for his lashing. The extra days were not subtracted from the number of lashes, however. In Saudi Arabia, a deal is a deal.

"The waiting was hard, but finally I was called out. I saw a doctor. He asked me if I had any medical problems, any back problems. I said no. He signed a paper. I signed a paper. We waited for the sheik from the local mosque to come, and then they led me out onto the street.

"Sure, there were people around. A bunch of little kids came over to watch. There were 10 of us prisoners to be lashed. I was the last. The fewest given was 10 lashes; the most was 80. I had a shirt on. You could wear as many shirts as you wanted, but I noticed when some prisoners came back from beatings, those who had worn a lot of clothes had been beaten harder. Their backs were really bloody.

"Finally it was my turn. They leaned me up against a light pole, one hand on top of the other. Two prison guards alternated beating the prisoners. They counted out loud. I probably reacted more than any of the other prisoners. Actually, I think the Arabs got hit harder than the Westerners. When I get nervous, my leg begins to twitch. It was twitching when they began."

He started talking faster.

"I started counting to myself. I had planned to try thinking of something else. I was going to think of water skiiing. But at 10 lashes, I lost my concentration. And I thought to myself: 'Hey, this *hurts!'"

He lit another cigarette and smoked it for a while. "The first guy who had done the whipping moved the lash up and down a lot. But my guy just hit me all in the same place, in the middle of my back.

"I think the embarrassment was worse, though. I mean I was standing up against a light pole in the middle of a street. People were standing all around and cars were going by. I had never been arrested before for anything. I got a speeding ticket once. That was it.

"When it was over, I was taken back to the cell. I took my clothes off. Everyone looked. I had plenty of welts. No blood. An hour and a half later they let me out.

"It affected me. More than I'm saying now. I went home and took a two-hour shower. I brushed my teeth about 10 times. I sat in front of the air conditioner. I slept.

"When I woke up I went to a travel agency and priced a ticket for New Orleans. I just wanted to get away. I wanted to eat a bunch of boiled shrimp and some raw oysters and wash it down with a couple of gallons of beer.

"But I never went. I was a . . . well, a basket case for a while," he said. "I was terrifically depressed. Finally, I got over it. I told myself it wasn't so bad. I told myself not to overdramatize it.

"I still go back to the prison and visit some of the guys. I bring them some things. I try not to be bitter. I mean the funny thing about that prison was that I didn't meet a single guy who claimed to be innocent. Nobody felt railroaded. We got caught. Period.

"Have I had a drink since? Yeah, once. About a month later I was at a neighbor's and I had one drink. Next time it will be six months and 200 lashes for me, so I am being very careful."

He got up and stubbed out his cigarette.

"Hey, what can I say? This country is their ballpark. You go to another guy's ballpark, you play by his rules."

May 13, 1981

'It's Hard to Die'
in Desert Blizzard

EL ARISH, Egypt

I t is very difficult to die in the desert," Mohamed Ustaz said. "If you
stay close to the road, the Bedouin will almost always find you."
The road had disappeared a few minutes earlier. The sand had
been slowly erasing it for hours. A gritty, crunching sound came from
under our tires as we crept along.

We had rolled up the windows against the sandstorm. The air was
thick and our eyes were burning with sweat.

Ustaz lit another Rothman cigarette. He reached over and slapped
my leg. "Even in the blizzard," he said, "the Bedouin will come."

When we left Cairo that morning, I didn't know what Ustaz meant
when he said "blizzard." The date palms along the Nile were whipping
in a stiff wind, but it was a welcome relief from the heat.

What had been a breeze in the city, however, was a wall of sand in
the desert. I cracked open a window to get some air. Along with the
stinging sand, scores of tiny black flies rushed in. I rolled it up again.

"I am Lawrence of Ar-ab-ee!" Ustaz sang, "and this is my camel."

Ustaz's camel was a prematurely old, un-air-conditioned Fiat. He
was a Cairo taxi driver who found it only slightly bizarre that I wanted
to go from Cairo to Tel Aviv by car.

"You know there is a desert in between?" he asked. "The Sinai? You
have heard of this?"

I told him I had. But others had made the trip before. It was not
uncharted territory. There were roads. If they could do it, we could
do it.

"Tell me," he said after a few hours of trying to see out the
windshield, "did they do it in a blizzard?"

Ustaz was supposed to take me to El Arish, about 160 miles from
Cairo and two-thirds of the way across the Sinai desert. El Arish has
been both Egyptian and Israeli. Now it is Egyptian again and is the
border between the two countries. From there I would take another
taxi to Tel Aviv.

From Cairo to the Suez Canal the sand lashed at us, but we could
see through it. And when we reached Ismailia, a crossing point on the
Suez, the desert gave way to orchards of mango trees. The road was
shaded by banyans and jacaranda, and women sold strawberries
from reed baskets.

The crossing point was not elaborate. The road simply sloped down to where the canal glistened a bright blue in the sun.

The ferry captain came over to us, beating dust from his clothes. He accepted a cigarette. "Much wind," he said. "Too much for the engine. We wait or we get blown away towards that." He motioned south toward the Red Sea, where Moses—with a little help from a friend—had crossed.

We stood and waited, our backs to the wind. After a while, without the wind noticeably diminishing, the captain said, "OK, we try it now."

We drove onto the ferry and it chugged across. The whitecaps dashed themselves against the boat. It was the last water we would see for a long time. On the other side, the Sinai began with a fury.

It was pure desert. Rolling dunes cuddled against one another, some smooth, some wavy, some rippled. They were beautiful at first, the curves hypnotic and unspoiled by a single footstep. But it was a moonscape. There was just sun and sky and sand.

And the tanks. Everywhere there were the blackened hulks of tanks, their treads ripped, their turrets blasted, their gun barrels pointing madly at the sky.

One of the largest tank battles in history took place here. On Oct. 6, 1973, about 8,000 Egyptian soldiers crossed the canal in fiberglass boats and attacked the Israeli Bar Lev Line, a fortification many thought was unbreachable.

By nightfall, 30,000 Egyptians had breached it. It was a stunning military achievement. But it was not a clear victory. Israeli troops counterattacked across the canal and drove within 60 miles of Cairo.

When it was over, Egypt had lost 7,700 men. On all fronts, including the Syrian front in the north, Israel had lost 2,552.

"Look, look," Ustaz said, pointing to a burned-out American-built tank. "Here we beat Israel!"

That is the official Egyptian view. The October or Yom Kippur War is viewed as a great victory in Egypt, an attitude not wholly disagreed with in Israel.

"What we lost in 1973 was the image that we were unbeatable," an Israeli military source told me. "From that time on, the destruction of Israel was feasible to the Arabs."

Ustaz stopped the car with a jerk and I swore as I grabbed for the dashboard. I turned toward him and then followed his eyes forward.

A boiling black smudge was rolling toward us, fingers of sand clawing up from the horizon into the sky. The wind rose from a howl to a shriek to a wail.

We crept along, bouncing across the road that had become a washboard of drifting sand. Every few minues, we stopped as the visibility dropped to zero. Then, like passing into the eye of a hurricane, the storm would lift a little and we would try to find the road again.

The dashboard became too hot to touch and our mouths had turned fuzzy. We came to a sign that read: "Foreigners are forbidden to leave the main road."

The only people who do dare to leave the road are the desert nomads, the Bedouin, who herd their sheep and goats from oasis to oasis.

"Praise God!" Ustaz shouted. "You see, you see, you are never really alone in the desert!"

Above us on a dune, a white-robed Bedouin watched us mournfully from his camel. I rolled down my window a little. "Salaam aleikum," I shouted. God be with you.

"Aleikum salaam," he said politely. And with you.

He shouted a few more words of Arabic and turned the camel away. "What did he say?" I asked Ustaz.

"He says the road is blocked," Ustaz said.

Around a hillock of sand was a camping point for the Bedouin. Along with tents there were shacks of scrap metal and palm branches. Ragged children clutched plastic water cans in both hands and staggered under the weight like tiny drunks. A camel lay flat on its belly, its chin stuck out on the desert floor, a picture of indescribable melancholy.

We slid sideways in the sand and Ustaz fought the wheel. Ahead of us, a depression in the road was blocked by sand. A few cars were already stuck.

As the storm lifted for a moment, we got out and stood by the car. The sun burned without rays. It seemed to have stopped in the middle of a dead white sky.

After a few minutes, a chauffeur-driven, metallic blue Plymouth Volare inched past us and halted. A tall, crew-cut man got out and surveyed the scene, hands on hips.

"U.S. Embassy plates," Ustaz whispered to me.

I walked over to where the man was standing and stuck out my hand. "It is difficult to die in the desert," I said. "The Bedouin will almost always find you."

He looked at me closely. "I think you ought to get out of the sun," he said. "Of course we're not going to die. Who's been handing you that crap?"

He was a senior U.S. military official, a colonel, attached to an embassy in the Mideast. He was on a vacation with his wife and teenage son.

Comandeering some men from the other stopped cars, he got his car pushed through the depression in a few minutes. He said I could go with him to El Arish as long as I didn't talk any more nonsense about dying in the desert.

I walked over to where Ustaz was now sitting dejectedly in his car. "Go back," I told him handing him some money. "You can have the full amount." I pulled my hand back before he could kiss it.

I plodded back to the colonel's car and squeezed in next to his wife. "Welcome aboard," she said cheerfully.

Inside, the air conditioning purred. The colonel reached into a cooler, pulled out a can of Pepsi, popped the top, and handed it to me. I held it against my forehead for a while.

He took out a folding knife, reached into the cooler again and cut off a chunk from a salami. "It's Israeli," he said. "It's pretty good."

He pulled back his hand before I could kiss it.

We talked about the war for a while.

"Who do I think won? Hell, Israel spent $328 million on the Bar Lev Line and Egypt rolled over it," he said. "The Israelis stopped 'em, of course. But you have to say it was a political victory for the Egyptians. Militarily it was a toss-up, I guess.

"Israel has a paranoia about casualties, you know. That's part of what hurt them here," he went on. "They will take five or ten deaths and it's a national tragedy. The Arabs lose thousands and they die martyrs."

Israelis don't call it paranoia, but because of Israel's small population—Israel has about 4 million people compared with Egypt's 43 million—losses are felt deeply.

"When they told Golda Meir we lost 2,500 men in the '73 war they had to pick her up off the floor," an Israeli government source said later.

"Israel was too cocky in '73, just like they're too cocky now with the Syrians," the colonel said. "If Syria, Iraq, and Jordan all went against Israel, there'd be quite a fight. The Israelis are just lucky the Arabs can't agree on anything.

"But Egypt is really the key. Without Egypt, all the Arab countries together could probably not defeat Israel. Oh, Israel would have a tough time, but in the end they'd win.

"No, there'll never be another war with Egypt. Not because of the Israelis, but because of the Egyptians. The Egyptians want peace too bad. You take my word for it."

As we neared El Arish, the Mediterranean broke into view and the desert seemed far behind us.

"I can't believe Moses wandered for 40 years in there," the colonel's wife said.

"That," said the colonel with a shake of his crew cut, "is what I call damn poor leadership."

Reality of War
Mirrors a Reel War

There is an old proverb that a girl may sleep with one man without being a trollop, but let a man cover one little war, and he is a war correspondent.

A. J. Liebling

BEIRUT, Lebanon

Each day I would go down to the bar in the Commodore Hotel, where the BBC parrot would squawk hello at me in Lebanese-accented English.

The parrot had been left there by a British Broadcasting Corp. correspondent and had been made a ward of the bar.

The parrot not only picked up all kinds of conversation in all kinds of accents, but he also reproduced the whistling sound of incoming artillery shells so realistically that drinkers have been known to dive to the floor for cover.

The parrot was not universally admired. His constant squawking sometimes disturbed the people who live in the apartment building across the courtyard.

A few years ago, a man in that building attemped to solve the problem in a typical manner: He walked out onto his balcony and began blasting at the parrot with a rifle.

He was a lousy shot—which is also typical here—and the parrot survived the assassination attempt. But regulars of the bar still avoid sitting near the courtyard windows.

The Commodore Hotel bar prides itself on being a war correspondents' bar. The reporters come here for relaxation and conversation and as anesthesia from the world outside.

They are also conscious of playing a role, of working hard and drinking hard and laughing in the face of death. In an abnormal place, they try to carry on not just with normalcy but with flair.

On this day, 63 people had died in the fighting throughout Lebanon. Or maybe it was 53.

"Well, which is it?" a reporter called out to the bar as he stood tearing through the news service wire copy that spit out of the two machines in the Commodore lobby. "Does anybody know?"

"Somebody said 63, and somebody said 53," a voice shouted back.

"Go with 'scores,' " another replied.

When I checked in at the front desk, I was told that almost all the

foreign correspondents stayed here, that a telex was available, that
the phone lines worked, and that drivers, translators and even visas
could be arranged.

I went upstairs to drop off my luggage, and I stood at the window
a while listening to the night sounds of Beirut. The antiaircraft guns
had not started yet, but every now and then there was the soft wump
of a mortar shell amid the sharper chatter of the machine guns.

Downstairs, a champagne cork popped. A *Time* magazine correspondent walked in carrying a squash racquet. The correspondents
were home from the war.

I saw a reporter I knew from Chicago, and he introduced me
around the bar. He bought a bottle of champagne, and then I bought
a bottle of champagne, and then Graham Leach of the BBC bought a
bottle of champagne. And after a while, you couldn't hear the mortars
anymore.

They filled me in on the fighting: the shelling of Zahle, the importance of the Bekaa Valley, the almost knee-jerk exchange of rocket
fire along Beirut's Green Line.

Later, we went into the dining room. A band was playing in the
corner. The steaks were rare and tender. And on the day that 63 (or
53) people died, the waiter asked if I wanted more sour cream on my
baked potato.

This happens in war. Some people die, and some people report that
fact. Both sides play their part. One part is just more permanent than
the other.

The next day, an artillery shell landed with a tremendous explosion
near where I was talking to another reporter. We went down the
street to where the thick black smoke was still rising. There was
shrapnel all over, and I picked up a piece as a souvenir. It was still
warm.

Later that night, I wrote my column from my room. I had been told
to stay away from the windows but there was only one place in the
room that wasn't near one. So I sat on the bathroom floor with my
typewriter on the toilet lid. And I knew as I was typing what a nice
anecdote it would make.

Down in the coffee shop, a videotape of the *Wild Bunch* was playing
on the big-screen TV. It would be followed by *Apocalypse Now*. The
correspondents would get a drink and sit down to watch the actors
explode into fragments of bone and blood. But only after they had
filed their stories on the people outside who had exploded into
fragments of bone and blood.

And I wondered if a reporter could reach a point where the deaths
of the people outside were no more real to him than the deaths of the
people on the screen.

The phrase that fascinated me in the stories filed from Beirut was "sporadic fighting." It had such a harmless sound to it. It meant only one or two or three people on their way to school or work or market had been killed or crippled or blinded.

Aside from measuring the level of warfare, the stories would sometimes try to convey a sense of history. They would begin, "In the worst fighting since . . ." and then you could fill in the blank: Since 1957. Since the civil war. Since yesterday.

What the stories didn't have, though, were the names of the dead. The dead were not people. They were just part of the running body count, part of the grand strategy of Syria or the Palestinians or the Christians. The dead had no real identity. Their numbers just served as a measuring stick to compare this to other wars.

I was scared all the time in Beirut but was not in much danger. I was just passing through, a quick-hitter in for a few days and out again.

I asked a correspondent who had been there a while how he stood it. "Actually it gets better the longer you are here," he said. "Every day convinces you a little more of your own invulnerability."

Western correspondents almost never have been targets here. So if a reporter were killed, it almost certainly would be by accident, by being under a falling shell or passing near a car bomb at the wrong time.

That would be big news, of course. The death of a reporter would rate a story. And he would have a name.

In early 1976, I was covering the Massachusetts presidential primary and went to dinner in Boston with a bunch of reporters who had been correspondents in Vietnam.

At the end of a long meal, the war stories began, stories of the friend who was wounded and the stranger who never returned.

"My God," the guy next to me said with real feeling, "do you know that 45 people got killed in that war?"

For a moment, I didn't understand.

"Forty-five?" I said. "Thousands died, didn't they?"

"Forty-five *real* people," he said. "Forty-five of *us*."

I never forgot that. Real people. Reporters. Us.

On my last day in Beirut, I had lunch with a young woman named Karin Linstad, whose apartment windows had been blown out by a bomb the night before. She was making plans to leave the country.

We ate in the coffee shop of the Commodore, taking a seat away from the windows. Next to us, the *Wild Bunch* was playing again. I picked at my cheeseburger and watched the movie a little.

"I hate it all," Karin said suddenly. "The bombings and the stupid movies and . . . and . . . the phony romance of it all!"

She missed the point, of course.

Without the bombs and movies, without the blood and the champagne, without the romance, war wouldn't be any fun at all.

June 4, 1981

◆

Guerrillas' Guns Fire a Last Salute

BEIRUT, Lebanon

The black truck nosed out of the sports stadium and then whipped through the shattered streets of the city.

From everywhere, from the rooftops and doorways, from the skeletal remains of the once-tall buildings, the PLO fired a last salute to itself.

The gunfire was so heavy you could feel it through your feet. There was the staccato crackling of small arms, the chatter of machine guns, the thump of mortars, and the whistling shriek of artillery.

It stopped as suddenly as it began.

"Fantazia," said the Lebanese army officer standing next to me. "Fantazia."

Fantasy. That is what they call gunfire done solely for show.

There was more than a small element of "fantazia" to this day. And a little, perhaps, to the entire war.

The trucks carrying the first of the PLO to be evacuated rolled into the port, preceded by French troops in jeeps, the tricolor snapping dashingly from the antennas.

The French ambassador preceded them all, giving his personal pledge for the safety of the guerrillas.

The PLO had been issued new uniforms, and from where I stood, they looked well-pressed. Some of the troops flashed the victory sign, while others waved palm branches. One man held a flower.

Another, his face completely swathed in a red-and-white checked Arab *kafiyeh*, held his rifle high above his head.

The trucks halted in front of the ferry Sol Georgiou, which would take the PLO to Cyprus. From there, they would go by plane to the Arab countries that had agreed to house them. By midafternoon, with about 400 men on board, the ferry churned out of the coral blue harbor and began its long, slow journey.

Both sides claimed this was the beginning of the end—of each other.

Israeli Defense Minister Ariel Sharon, the Patton of his country, strode into the port area as the ship left, even though Israel is trying to maintain a low profile here.

It has pulled back its Merkava tanks into the forest, but nobody can pull back Sharon.

Short, portly, and often compared to a tank himself, Sharon had been publicly rebuked by his own cabinet for bombing Beirut while peace negotiations were in progress.

Setting up a quick press conference in an electric company office yesterday, Sharon said, "We got rid of the terror of the PLO. We have created a historical opportunity for the Arabs and Israel to embark on a peaceful path.

"We hope the PLO does not return to terrorist activity, because terror doesn't pay."

But there remained the question: Was this war necessary? And especially: Was the bombing of Beirut necessary?

Did it accomplish the destruction of the well-dug-in, well-supplied PLO? Or merely the destruction of many civilians in west Beirut?

Jerusalem Post defense correspondent Hirsh Goodman put it this way:

"The strikes were relentless, the aircraft used ultrasophisticated, the ordnance drops highly destructive, the delivery systems the most modern in the world. Yet the 11,000 to 13,000 terrorists and Syrians under siege in the city managed both to survive and to retaliate."

The PLO is claiming victory, of course. It says it was not the bombing that brought the peace, but the high Israeli casualties.

Some are buying that. I interviewed Radwan Abu Ayyash, a West Bank Palestinian activist.

"The PLO has gained prestige from this, not lost it," he said. "The PLO showed steadfastness for more than 70 days. The Arab armies lasted only hours against the Israelis in 1967.

"For a group of 'terrorists' to last more than 70 days is unbelievable. It is a victory."

The Israelis were prepared for this. Having fought the PLO in Lebanon, Israel now is fighting what may be a tougher battle for public opinion.

"We are aware of the PLO's desire to portray its departure as a military victory," said Moshe Yegar, assistant director-general of foreign affairs. "They are talking about Beirut as their Stalingrad. They say they resisted us, and they are leaving only for humanitarian reasons.

"We hope the world does not take this seriously. The PLO as a military structure has lost all effectiveness."

If one looks at it optimistically, that is true. The PLO has been scattered. It has lost its heavy weapons. The Arab nations have been shown what happens to the capital city of a country that serves as a base for terrorism. And Israel hopes this will relieve West Bank Palestinians from fear of PLO reprisals if they cooperate with Israel.

That's the optimistic view. The pessimistic one is that this may be Israel's Vietnam. The PLO remains in the north. The Syrians remain in the Bekaa Valley in the east.

The Israelis say they will not leave until everyone else leaves. But for how long can Israel occupy Lebanon? The war has been hideously costly. Tourism is down.

And more seriously, this war is having a profound effect on the Israelis themselves. As the Sabbath ended with the news that the PLO had begun departing from Beirut, there was no wild celebrating in Tel Aviv or Jerusalem.

There is some talk—just some—about winning the battle and losing one's soul.

Even Yitzhak Shamir, the Israeli foreign minister, normally a feisty individual, seemed to be subdued.

"It was a tragic necessity," he said. "The results of this war will justify the damage done to civilians and the loss of our own soldiers."

As one PLO truck pulled into the port, a guerrilla lifted a white sign toward the reporters. Written on it in Arabic was the single word: *Victory.*

But for whom?

And at what price?

August 22, 1982

Yet Again, Simon Says It

I know a guy so mean that he goes to a Chinese restaurant and refuses to share.

◆

Has anyone ever really read the foreword to a book?

◆

People who stand at the elevator jingling the change in their pockets should be stomped by elephants.

◆

Why does everyone always take the second newspaper in the stack, even when the first one looks just fine?

◆

One of the great joys in life is not having to shave on a weekend.

◆

The loneliest people in the world are those who eat at the bar.

◆

Was Don Rickles *ever* funny?

◆

Why does it seem like all the stories on "60 Minutes" come either from California or Florida?

◆

The world is ready for a noiseless vacuum cleaner.

How come people who play loud music never play music you like?

◆

Has anyone figured out an alternative use for those fondue pots they got in the sixties?

◆

I never believe any ad that tells me something is going to cost me "only pennies a day."

◆

When public schools did away with desks fastened to the floor, they lost control.

◆

How come the phone company charges you a monthly fee *not* to publish your number? How can it be more expensive *not* to publish something?

◆

I have never met a tattooed woman I liked.

◆

Band uniforms aren't impressive without spats.

◆

Suspenders that end in little brass snaps are unacceptable.

◆

Sign of the times: Bellboys no longer thank you for dollar tips.

If we can land a man on the moon, why can't we develop newsprint that doesn't come off on your fingers?

◆

If you look right now, I'll bet you can find 12 things in your wallet that you could throw away and three keys on your key ring that are a complete mystery.

◆

The worst thing a person can say when entering your home is: "Who was your decorator?"

◆

Tell people you like their laugh and you're likely to hear it more than you want to.

◆

Whenever somebody says "to make a long story short," you know you've got at least 20 minutes to go.

◆

I don't want to know why, but I really get a big kick out of shopping for a new flashlight.

◆

A woman's compliment to another woman rarely means anything.

◆

People who threaten other people should be beaten with sticks.

◆

I hate restaurants that roll up the silverware in the napkins.

I have never known an exception: Wives determine the length of their husbands' hair.

◆

I really admire people who can de-bone a fish.

◆

There is no greater embarrassment than wearing two different color socks.

◆

Endless effort has gone into making meat loaf taste like something other than meat loaf. To date, the effort has been wasted.

◆

I'm ashamed to admit it, but self-service gas pumps still intimidate the heck out of me.

◆

I don't understand how people can like feather pillows.

◆

People who sit around and hum to themselves should be whipped.

◆

I hope I'm never too old to enjoy a good magic act.

◆

Why does it seem like everyone who wins the lottery is 64 years old and wants to keep working?

◆

Never marry a man who lets someone else shave him.

If pirates really went around with parrots on their shoulders, the backs of their jackets must have been a mess.

◆

You know you're getting old if you can remember when the knife grinder came down the street.

◆

Reading John LeCarré a second time is better than reading most spy writers the first time.

◆

I always feel terribly sad when I see someone eating alone in a restaurant.

◆

People who wear lapel pins are the strangest people I know.

◆

How come when your mother served liver you hated it, but when it comes for $17 in a French restaurant, you swoon over it?

◆

Don't you worry about what happened to Mr. Carlin from the old Bob Newhart show?

◆

People who talk very quietly into public phones for long periods of time are up to no good.

◆

Why is it that people who hate spinach love green noodles?

I don't know about these new movie seats that rock. It seems like the person in front of you always ends up in your lap.

◆

Say what you will, but there has never been a better performance than Hayley Mills's, in "The Parent Trap."

◆

I don't believe you if you claim you've never shined your shoe on the bottom of your sock or the back of your pants leg.

◆

Is there any chance that Robert Duvall will actually make receding hairlines popular?

◆

People wouldn't be so intimidated by Mike Wallace if they knew his real name was Myron.

◆

Cars that tell me I left my key in the ignition should mind their own business.

◆

Fans who wear their baseball caps backward at the ballpark are showing one sign of the classic moron.

◆

Don't you love the sound when you open a vacuum-packed jar?

◆

I never have liked anyone who has liked Ayn Rand.

Press Corps Pulls Insult Out of Hat

AUSTIN, Texas

This is a story about the press, but it is not one of those funny, boys-on-the-bus pieces. It is not funny at all. It is, I think, an ugly and sad piece and one I did not want to write.

I was going to skip it, figuring that maybe I was being overly critical or overly sensitive. Then, during a conversation with another reporter, a Washington reporter who had been covering politics for more than 20 years, he brought it up independently.

"Were you there that day?" he asked. "Did you see what happened? I've never been so ashamed."

It was at the Ted Kennedy rally in San Antonio. The crowd was huge and had waited patiently for more than an hour before the senator showed up. The crowd was largely Mexican-American and I stood near a young man named Gordon Williamson, who was wearing a United Farm Workers cap and was trying to get people to sign up to be Kennedy volunteers.

He worked the crowd, handing out sign-up slips, and was getting a good response. One man, neatly dressed in a white shirt and dark pants, looked at the slip and then shook his head, handing it back. He explained that he had been in America too short a time to be a citizen. He looked ashamed.

"That's OK," Williamson said, "it's OK to work in a campaign even if you are not registered. You just can't vote, but you can work."

The man's face brightened and he smiled broadly, taking back the slip and filling it out with a flourish. "Viva Kennedy," he said proudly. "Viva America."

It was a good campaign vignette, I had thought. It is hard not to be impressed by the commitment, political and patriotic, of the Mexican-Americans in Texas. Even though it was hot, the crowd was dressed as if it were going to church. Suits and ties were the rule for the men and dresses for the women. The children were dressed as their parents were.

Finally, their wait was over and there was a stir in the crowd. The Kennedy press corps had arrived. Laughing and joking. And wearing sombreros. And not just ordinary sombreros, but the huge tourist sombreros with enormous brims and embroidery. The shock to the people in the crowd was visible.

"When I saw it, I couldn't believe it," the reporter, who is not a member of Kennedy's traveling press, said. "My God, it was like bringing watermelon into Harlem.

"And afterwards, two of them leaned up against a wall and pulled their sombreros down to look like sleeping Mexicans."

The whole press corps was not involved, of course. But the small band of reporters who make up the inner circle on the Kennedy bus has been written about before. They have formed a special group, whose behavior, some say, goes beyond standard campaign pranks.

Practical joking and general fooling around by the press is not new. Or bad. It is a necessary insulation, perhaps, against the pressures and boredom of the road.

"But this is different," the reporter said. "Everybody plays cards and drinks too much and chases the stewardesses, but these guys have stepped over the boundary line. They are into public displays. They have become a bigger story than the candidate."

In Iowa, when a Secret Service agent called the Kennedy reporters "rowdy," they marched into a speech in lockstep to show how disciplined they could be. In Maine, they used to chant the lines of Kennedy's speech before he could say them.

I think those are harmless—although some would say juvenile— stunts. But what happened in San Antonio was not. It was at best insensitive and at worst arrogant and contemptuous.

Candidates sometimes put on exotic hats, but only when they are presented with them as a sign of solidarity and support. The press did it as a goof, a lark, a joke. They did it because they have become a small world unto themselves and they don't care anymore about the world outside.

The people in the crowds have become props to them, just furniture to fill up the hall while the candidate speaks. The people are outsiders and not part of their tight, little world.

The people who came to the speech in San Antonio had worked a full day, whether on the job or in the home. And they had dressed up and come to a political rally to show their support for a candidate and a process and a country. And, as those sombreros bobbed through the crowd, the people saw what the press thought of them. They saw that to the press, they were still the stereotyped, siesta-snoozing Mexicans.

After traveling day after day on the road, it is easy for reporters to develop a certain disdain for politics. It is easier still to develop disdain for politicians.

But when reporters start developing disdain for people, maybe it is time for them to rethink why they became reporters.

May 2, 1980

A Street with No Troubles

There is never any trouble on Main Street. When Merle Anderson walks here in the morning and again at night, she never has to be afraid.

Gas lights flicker above the cobblestones. Small groups of people look in store windows where seven cents will buy a dozen tomatoes or three pounds of green apples.

For 22 years Merle Anderson has walked here without fear. Everyone does. That is the purpose of Main Street—to remind us of the best in America, a street without violence, care, or woe.

Not surprisingly, Main Street isn't real. It sits in a museum, a beautifully reconstructed fiction. And every morning, four days a week, Mrs. Anderson leaves her home on the South Side to come here.

She walks into the Museum of Science and Industry, goes down to Main Street and sits at an old nickelodeon piano where she plays along to silent films. She is the last person in America doing this.

Hundreds of children laugh and clap and giggle while her music sounds throughout the day. When the museum closes, she leaves. Earlier this year, when she left the museum to enter the present and neared her home, she was savagely attacked by a gang of youths. They weren't much older than the children she had played for that day.

Mrs. Anderson spent 13 days in a hospital. Then she went back to work. She is 86 years old.

The day I went to see her she was playing for an Our Gang comedy about a poor boy who falls in love with a rich girl. Everything works out in the end.

"I'm the last one left," Mrs. Anderson said. "It's the only kind of job I can get at my age. I started in 1903 with the first traveling picture show in the United States. I played along to one-reel comedies. *The Rag Picker's Daughter. Tilly's Punctured Romance.* Things like that.

"You picked a good day, today. This one's a funny one. I never get sick of them. It seems like you see a little something different every time you see them."

There is a real ice cream parlor on Main Street and that is where we sat. Mrs. Anderson had a chocolate sundae and remembered that in 1911 she owned a car called Rickenbacker.

There was something else she remembered. Something she talked about with the greatest reluctance.

"There were seven of them," she said, slowly. "They formed a circle around me. One smashed me in the face and knocked me flat. Then another started stomping on my legs. Jumping up and down on my legs. He had metal cleats on his shoes or something and I was cut up pretty badly. I don't think they even wanted my purse at first."

People in the neighborhood rescued her and called an ambulance. She stayed in the hospital where they worked on her legs. After nearly two weeks, she was able to walk again.

"The bad part was the tapes," she said. "They had to run the tapes."

I told her that I didn't understand.

"The tapes—the recording tapes," she said. "When I'm not here, they have to run a recording to go along with the movie. You have to run something when I'm not here, so they run a tape."

It would be easy for Merle Anderson to stay on Main Street all the time. Not physically, of course. The museum closes at night. But she could build her own Main Street. She could move to the suburbs or stay tightly locked in her apartment like a number of 86-year-old urban dwellers do.

"Oh, no," she said. "I never play at home, you see. The only thing I enjoy, the only part I enjoy, is the audience. I love the children. They laugh and clap. Did you see them today? Did you see them clap?"

I told her I did.

"Well, then," she said. "You see what I mean. How could I leave them? How could I ever leave show business?"

June 17, 1976

Seven years after this was written, when she was 93, Merle Anderson finally left the museum and Main Street.
Not long afterward, she died.

Decor, But No Decorum, for Clark Kent's Office

So you still want to be a reporter, eh, kid? You think it's all roses and champagne and hounding presidents from office? Well, it's not. It's tough. Darn tough. Listen to this:

It was a day like any other. I was writing about truth and justice. My snap-brim fedora sat on my head like a squashed hen. My trench coat lay in a dirty heap on the floor. The trail of smoke from a burning stogie cast a shadow on my cruel smile.

The phone rang. I picked it up. "Your dime," I snarled.

It was a dame. It is always a dame. "I have a client," she said. "Mr. Burt Richmond. He would like to design your interior. He will come to your office and create a unique work space reflecting your personality and outlook. What is your current decor?"

I looked around the newsroom.

"We don't got a decor," I said. "We had a cat once, but it died."

The dame sighed a sigh. "What does your newsroom look like?" she asked. "What is the scheme of decoration?"

I eyeballed the joint. "Early Locker Room," I said. Then I smiled my cruel smile.

"If it is possible, Mr. Richmond would like to visit your work environment," the dame said. "He has done interior design for IBM, NBC, Kraft, McDonald's, Playboy, Quaker Oats, ALCOA, Levi's, Mogen David, and the City of East St. Louis."

"East St. Louis!" I said. "Boy, I wonder what it looked like before."

The next day, Burt Richmond showed up. He was smooth, real smooth. And a snappy dresser. His shoes matched. I met him in the hallway and took him into my "work environment."

"I have never been in your newsroom," he said, "but I am looking forward to . . . OH, MY LORD!"

I couldn't see what was wrong. Just a regular newsroom. About a hundred desks. People yelling and screaming, phones ringing, typewriters pounding, and pieces of paper shooting around the ceiling on little conveyor belts. And, of course, Old Pete had fallen asleep on his sweet roll again.

"Where is your desk?" Richmond demanded.

"I think you're standing next to it," I said. "It's hard to tell. Don't get your sleeve in anything."

"This . . . is extraordinary," he said. "You're packed together like cattle!"

"Moo," sez I. And then I smiled my cruel smile.

"Look at these typewriters," he said. "Nobody uses typewriters like this anymore. I would not be surprised to see people in green eyeshades and using quill pens. The first thing you need is acoustical floor covering."

"Huh?"

"A carpet," he explained. "It cuts down noise. Also, it is cheaper to vacuum than to wash and wax these floors."

"Wash and wax?" I said. "This is a newsroom, pal. Not the Betty Crocker test kitchen."

He nudged my chair with his foot. "I can't believe this," he said. "It doesn't even swivel."

"Roller Derby, we ain't," I conceded.

He whipped out a sketch pad and started drawing like mad. "What we need is individualized work space for you people," he said. "Some partitions. Some banners from the ceiling, maybe. Some supergraphics. Lighting bolts. Clenched fist symbols. Superman logos."

I was beginning to like this guy.

"And those offices must go," he said, pointing to a row overlooking the Chicago River. "They must be moved from the windows. They block the light."

"Those are the editors' offices," I said. "And the editors have got to be by the windows. Otherwise, they couldn't see the bridges go up."

"No, no, no," he said. "We must break down the status thing. You protect the underdog, right?"

"Every dog I can find," I said.

"Then your work space must reflect that. And we must get some greenery, some plants."

"Wrong," I said. "Nothing can grow in this newsroom."

"That's not true," he said, pointing to some green stuff on my desk. "That is alive."

"That's my lunch," I said.

He began to sketch wildly. In a trice or two he had whipped up something that looked like the set of *Star Wars*. It was beautiful. He drew in carpeting and little partitions and a plant and even a coat hook.

"How much?" I asked.

"$6.50," he said.

"Build it!" I yelled. "Build one for everybody."

"No, no," he said. "It's $6.50 for the coat hook. The whole thing would cost, ummmm, about $464. Let's say $335 without the chair."

Well, kid, there went my dreams. So I'm going to tell you what I told him.

"Sure a new office would be nice," I said. "Real nice. So would apple pie and a pennant for the White Sox and world peace. But things aren't always that way, see?

"You may look in here and see garbage. I look in here and see my friends. Never forget, a newspaper is more than just broken-down typewriters and broken-down desks.

"It is broken-down people, too."

Mr. Richmond grew very quiet before he spoke. "And just what color would you like us to make the carpet?" he asked.

"Blue to match my eyes," I said. And then I smiled my cruel smile.

September 18, 1977

Byrne Plays It the Old Way

I n the end, she played all the angles.
   She talked to God in the morning and the voters in the evening.
   Both work in mysterious ways.

"I would not have done anything differently," Jane Byrne said. "I ran a good campaign. I did the best I could."

She went to a subway platform in the early evening, when both her opponents had long since abandoned campaigning.

She shook a few hundred more hands, asked for a few hundred more votes.

She stood in the overpass of the Jefferson Park station for 90 minutes, her voice growing hoarse and her cough growing worse.

"No, I didn't plan to come out here today," she said. "I was not going to campaign. But I'm here because I heard it was close.

"It was tougher this time than four years ago. You remember what it was like that day. You were there."

They let me sit by her elbow behind closed doors for a while that day, because nobody expected her to win.

She sat behind a desk littered with nail-polish remover, tissues, packages of Wash & Dry, a bottle of perfume, cigarettes, and a picture of her infant daughter on John F. Kennedy's lap.

A large picture of her and Richard J. Daley in hard hats loomed behind her in the campaign office.

She had taken off her shoes and was rubbing her feet.

"I just want to see the polls close," she said that day. "I just want this to be over."

A national TV show called. They wanted her on the air the next morning—but only if she won.

"They'll all want me if I win," she said with a small laugh. "Then they'll all love me. If I win."

She had learned the essential fact of politics: Winning is next to godliness. Second is next to nothing.

The phones rang and rang. There were calls from her poll watchers.

Her precinct captains. Her husband. Everyone had a theory. Everyone had a prediction.

"I may stay in," she said that afternoon. "It's too exciting here to go out. Their minds are made up. Seeing me is not going to change things."

The man who ran the campaign, the man who got paid $3,000 for telling her exactly what she would pay a million dollars to hear four year later, narrowed his eyes and looked at her hard.

"I want you to go out, Jane," Don Rose said. "I want you back out there."

"Look at this toe," she said, turning it first to him and then to me. "Look at this bunion. You're going to have to pick a foot doctor."

Rose sighed. "Jane, what use are you here?" he said. "Go out. If you win by 373 votes, which is what I figure you'll get between now and the polls' closing, I'll get you a foot doctor."

She put her shoes back on. And went down to campaign at the subway platforms at State and then Dearborn.

Because she wanted it badly enough.

Four years later, she still wanted it badly.

"I am out here because I do not want to lose," she said yesterday. "I heard one poll showed me four points down. Well, I'm not going to be four points down."

The crowd surged around her. Most just wanted to go home. More passed than stopped to shake her hand.

Her aides were carrying all the flotsam and jetsam of a political campaign: buttons, bags, key chains, and even linen handkerchiefs in the mayor's green and white campaign colors.

"Mayor?" an aide asked. "Is it all right to give out the hankies?"

"Hand out *everything*," Byrne said. "No sense keeping anything. It's over tonight.

Daylight faded, and the fluorescent lights of the station came on. The cold came up from the floor and through Byrne's thin, gray shoes.

She stood her ground. She asked for votes, sometimes actually reaching out and grabbing the commuters by their coat sleeves.

"Have you voted?" she asked. "I need your help. Have you voted today?"

I asked her how her bunions were.

"Worse than last time," she said. "I've been to the foot doctor twice. And look at this."

She held out her hand. One finger had a half-inch long gouge in it.

"That's from handshaking," she said.

A woman passed. Byrne grabbed her hand. "I need your help," she said.

The woman did a double take and grabbed the mayor in a huge embrace. The mayor's bodyguards did not even blink. "You're gonna win!" the woman said, hugging the mayor off her heels. "But you should be home in bed."

"Tomorrow," Byrne said. "Tomorrow I'll have time for that."

Four years ago, Jane Byrne went to church and asked God to make her the mayor of Chicago.

I asked Byrne what her prayer was this time.

"I asked God to let me finish what I started," she said.

Now, He and the voters have spoken.

February 23, 1983

A few hours later, the votes were tabulated. Jane Byrne had lost.
On July 16, 1985, she declared her candidacy for the 1987 mayoral race.

The Saga of Pool Eleven

The president of the United States and I walked across the Astroturf together. Fifty-six thousand seven-hundred twenty-one people stood up to cheer.

The president stopped. I stopped. He waved. I waved. He raised both arms above his head. I raised both arms above my head.

One of his aides touched my arm lightly and whispered in my ear. "It is our belief," he said, "that the crowd is here primarily for President Ford."

I admit it. I got carried away. It is not often you find yourself as the only newspaper reporter at the arm of the president. It is not often you find yourself in the great bowl of William Brice Stadium in Columbia, South Carolina.

It is not often you get to squish-squash across the synthetic grass to shake hands with the Fighting Irish of Notre Dame. Or with the Fighting Gamecocks of South Carolina. Or with the Gamecock cheerleaders, who are called—I kid you not—the Cockettes.

Do not look for me in the pictures taken that day. At the last minute, the governor of the state jumped ahead of me to grab the president and the glory. But I do not seek glory. I seek truth. And here is the truth of that day. Call it the Saga of Pool Eleven.

The day began like any other aboard the Zoo Plane with a game of Beer Bomb. The Zoo Plane is that plane reserved for the dregs of the press corps, those judged unfit to ride with the big-time reporters. Through a tragic mistake, I had been assigned to that plane and had lived through many games of Beer Bomb.

Beer Bomb is a simple game. On takeoff, the reporters in the front of the plane take unopened cans of beer and roll them down the aisle. The acceleration of takeoff combined with the tilt of the plane causes the cans to travel at terrifying speeds. The object of Beer Bomb is to have the cans hurtle to the back of the plane, explode, and whirl around madly, spraying everyone with beer.

Once, over Seattle, I saw an NBC cameraman throw his body on an exploding beer bomb and yell, "I'm old! Save yourself! I'm old!"

If you think I am making this up, I will tell you who accidentally invented Beer Bomb. It was George McGovern on October 31, 1972. In case you forgot or blotted it from your mind, McGovern once ran for president. He was the man who dropped his running mate because he was unsure of his running mate's mental stability. Then McGovern picked Sargent Shriver to replace him. Figure that one out.

On Halloween four years ago, the press corps gave McGovern a pumpkin on board the plane. McGovern kept it on his lap until takeoff. Then he set it down in the aisle to fasten his seat belt. As the plane left the ground, the pumpkin sped backward like it had been shot from a cannon. It exploded in the rear cabin of the plane and the reporters were picking pumpkin seeds out of their hair from Portland to Poughkeepsie.

Beer Bomb was the logical outgrowth of that day. Lest you contemplate trying it on a commercial flight, remember that the sky marshals would be only too glad to shoot you out of your socks.

Anyway, as I was dodging beer cans one morning, I was tapped on the shoulder by a White House aide. He was smiling. "Hey, big fella," he said (for that is what they call me), "take a look at the pool list today."

A word about pools. At certain events it is inconvenient for all 250 members of the press corps to attend. In the old days, the White House press secretary would merely report on the event. He would say, "The president attended a private tea at which 37 million people were present. They said they liked the president a lot and that his opponent was a nasty man who would plunge us into thermonuclear war."

You had the choice in those days of accepting the White House lies or making up lies of your own.

Today, things are different. One member of each news medium is selected to make up a pool. The pool then reports back to the rest of the press. Naturally, only the best reporters are selected for the pools. Literally millions of people rely upon them. Accuracy, honesty, and fairness are essential.

I was told, therefore, that I would never be in a pool. "Well, not never," the White House staff told me. "But we have listed you somewhere after *Pravda*."

Imagine my surprise when I found myself one morning on Pool Eleven. Pool Eleven would accompany the president out to the 50-yard line at halftime of the Notre Dame–South Carolina game.

I reported to the stadium gate at the appropriate time and walked up to the White House aide. "Simon," I said. "Representing the newspapers of the Free World."

"This is going to be very easy," he said. "You walk on the field. You walk off the field. Try anything funny and we'll split you like a peach."

I did my job. I took my notes. At the end of the day, I was ready to make my pool report. The aide cornered me. "Play it straight," he said. "Don't be cute. Just give the facts. This is a grave responsibility."

I faced the press corps. I opened my notebook and cleared my throat. I began:

"Under a blazing sun, the president of the United States did not trip over the 50-yard line Saturday. . . ."

October 29, 1976

'There's No Phil Donahue Without an Audience'

A TV star knows when he has arrived when he makes the cover of TV Guide. Phil Donahue arrived with this piece.

It is hard to recall now, considering his great success, that he was not always a household word.

I must admit to liking him. He is either the most sincere man in America or one hell of a liar.

Phil Donahue laid his hands upon the woman. He stared at her with eyes as blue and innocent as a baby's. "I'll never abandon you," he said to her softly. "You'll never be alone."

It would be hard to say just how many American women have dreamed of hearing those words from this man. Just how many have stood at their ironing boards and dreamed of running barefoot through the hair that falls across his forehead like a graying snowdrift.

For Phil Donahue, 42, is one of the hottest talk-show hosts in the country. The man whose broadcasts are available to 86 percent of all TV homes. The man who reaches almost 4 million women per day. The man who has hit daytime television like a hormone injection directly into the carotid artery of the American housewife.

"I like women," he says, "and well . . . well . . ."

C'mon, Phil, say it.

"Well, this sounds kind of vain . . ."

Say it, Phil, say it!

"Well, they like me. I guess they think I'm attractive. Sexy."

You bet your three-piece suits they do, Phil! That's why they wait a year and a half for tickets to your show. That's why some drive hundreds of miles just for a look at you in the flesh.

That's why they would probably trade their husbands and mortgage the kids just to have you touch them gently on the arm, like you just touched Cathy, the lady who is going to be on your show today.

Cathy, as it happens, is nearly the perfect Donahue guest. She got pregnant, had a kid, and is unmarried. Big deal, you say? So what, you say?

But Donahue does not have one of the best production staffs in the business for nothing. They know what will sell and what will not. And Cathy will sell. Because she is an unwed mother who *wants* to be an unwed mother. She duped her boyfriend into impregnating her and then split with the kid. For a talk-show host, finding Cathy is like finding a diamond in your Wheaties.

It is now 10 minutes to show time. Donahue and Cathy are in a little room in WGN-TV's studios in Chicago, Donahue's home station. He is explaining to her what the Donahue show is all about, what makes it work. It is the best explanation you will ever get:

"Don't worry about all the consequences of what you say," he tells her. "Don't worry about what everyone will think.

"It's the first six minutes that count. We don't have Nancy Wilson to come out and do a song. You make the show. You and the audience. The audience is the most important thing. There is no Phil Donahue show, there is no Phil Donahue without the audience! Keep them warm, keep them happy. When we go to a commercial, you keep talking to the audience.

"And remember this: Even if I ask you a dumb question, give me a good answer. Make me look good. Help me out. And don't worry about coming up with the right answer. Forget the right answers. Just give me emotion."

By now, Cathy is emoting like Mount Vesuvius. Donahue's enthusiasm is as contagious as Legionnaire's Disease. Cathy is ready to go out and knock "The $20,000 Pyramid" right out of the ratings box. "This is going to be great!" she said. "This is going to be terrific. This is going to be . . ."

"Relax," Donahue says, getting up from the table. "It's not going to be *that* much fun."

Before each show, Donahue paces the hallways outside the studio like a jungle cat until his producer, Patricia McMillen, has warmed up the 200 women inside. "Avoid long speeches," she tells them. "Don't pontificate."

On cue, Donahue bursts up the aisle just moments before the cameras go on. "You look so much thinner in person!" he shouts in mock surprise. "You look so much younger in person! Who's pregnant? Who *wants* to be pregnant?" The audience ripples with laughter. "Who's Catholic?" A few hands go up. Donahue grabs the microphone by the cord and shakes it like an aspergillum, spraying the audience with invisible holy water. "Just wanted you Catholics to feel at home!" Donahue puts on his rarely worn glasses. "I don't really need these," he confides to a woman on the aisle. "I just wear them to look like a gynecologist."

The audience is by now shrieking with laughter, just as they always do. Donahue has met them and they are his. Now, just moments before the red camera light twinkles on, he makes the pitch. "Help me out!" he shouts to them. "Make me look good!"

One gets the feeling, when watching Donahue work the crowd like a stand-up comic, that the guests, the people who sit up on the little stage behind him, are secondary, a device to get the audience asking questions.

Just what kinds of guests Donahue invites is an insight into the American consciousness. Lillian Carter, the president's mother, captured it perfectly in an anecdote that Donahue loves to repeat. He had called her personally and asked her to be on the show.

"Phil," Miss Lillian replied, "I don't wear an IUD, I'm not a homosexual, and I don't smoke pot—just what am I going to talk about?"

You don't absolutely have to do or be one of those three things to get on the Donahue show—but it helps.

"We do serious subjects, issues, and we are proud of those shows," Donahue said. "But I am not going to do 'Meet the Press' five days a week. You can't serve up Watergate five days a week. What we do is provide on daytime TV a relief from the soaps and game shows. No other show does that.

"I honestly believe we have spoken more thoughtfully, more honestly, more often to more issues about which women care, than any other show."

The key to this, of course, is interpreting just what women do care about. And apparently Donahue gets it right. You could call his weekly lineup a careful mix or a hodgepodge, but whatever you call it, you have to call it successful. When Donahue mixes shows on Albert Speer and Ralph Nader with shows on whether breastfed babies make better lovers when they grow up (an actual show)—it somehow works.

Donahue started the series with one station in Dayton, Ohio, slightly more than 10 years ago. In that time it has grown to reach 142 markets, including every one of the major American cities. In New York, he leads the ratings in his time slot. And 87 percent of his viewers are women, and nearly half of those are in the magic 18–49 age bracket that advertisers drool over. Selling soapsuds on "Donahue" is like having money in the bank.

The reason for the success of "Donahue," to hear him tell it, is neither the guests nor his own talents. "Why does it work?" he said. "Well, I've got no desk and no couch and no bandleader. I don't have funny gags and a sidekick to laugh at all my jokes. It's the audience that makes it work. I'm not mock humble. I think I'm the best guy in the business with an audience."

Donahue not only uses his audience, he caters to it. At the end of every show he stands in the doorway, dripping sweat, and shakes the hand of every lady. He chats with each one, cheerfully signs autographs, poses for pictures and even tells them how to find their way back to the expresssway. "Look, I'd park their cars for them, if I had to," Donahue says.

"Donahue" revolves around its studio audience and a home audience that calls in from Chicago, where the show appears live. While the call-in technique is a standard device for radio, it is almost unheard of in television.

"Everyone told us it would not work," Donahue said. "They said that talking heads for an hour would never get off the ground. They said one guest per show would never work. I'll never forget when we started in Dayton. I had this doll, this boy doll that was anatomically correct. You know. And I held it up on the air and said, 'What do you think of this doll?'

"It was like a bomb had gone off. The phone company finally got through to say that every phone in downtown Dayton was paralyzed because everyone was calling our show. I just knew then that we had the formula.

"But we still couldn't get stars, big names. That probably was good in a way. We learned to survive without them. But we still begged them to come. For two years we begged them. Norman Rockwell would walk into the studio and say, 'What the hell am I doing in *Dayton?*'"

There was also another key moment in the early "Donahue" days that has since set the tone for the show. It once again proved what everyone already knew. Sex sells. And sex on TV sells very well.

"It was 1968 and we had just started," Donahue said. "And we were putting these kooks on the air. What 1968 Dayton considered kooks.

"We had a homosexual on the show and this was considered revolutionary. I was so scared. A gay in 1968. Well, we got hundreds of calls.

"And then it happens. A woman calls in and says to the gay, 'How does Phil look to you, hmmm?' My career passed before my eyes. I felt, oh, my gosh, everyone is going to think I am gay. That's what you were afraid of then.

"Anyway, I could never be gay," Donahue concluded. "I'm a lousy dancer." A lousy dresser, too, if the truth be known. "Yeah, it's true," Donahue sighed. "In the early days, I had Oleg Cassini on the show and he took me aside and said I looked terrible. So he dressed me, but I couldn't get it right. So finally, they labeled all my clothes. Really, with little labels. I was allowed to wear shirt A with suit B and tie C. That's the only way I could get it right."

Donahue usually shows up only about an hour before show time, carrying a suitbag into his office. His office, which will soon be remodeled, is done in sort of a Fallout Shelter Moderne. The walls are yellow cinder block, there are harsh fluorescent lights, institutional linoleum, and struggling plants. Donahue's desk bears an autographed picture of Dolly Parton, and four photos of Maryrose, his only daughter, and the only one of his five children who does not live with him since his divorce in 1975.

The staff, predominantly—and not accidentally—women, treats Donahue as both boss and errant child. While they defer to his sometimes angry decisions ("He is a shouter," one said), they feel genuinely affectionate toward him, often patting down the stray wisps of his carefully done hair.

Donahue grew up in Cleveland, the son of a furniture salesman, and was immediately immersed in what his staff now calls "Phil's Catholic thing." The Catholic church and what it did to him is an extremely serious subject to Donahue, one that has shaped his life and accounts for what he now refers to as "my neuroses."

"Life beats us up so much," he said. "We worry if our breasts are too small, or too big, or if our shoulders are not broad enough. Or you come home and your parents tell you you are a big pain to raise.

"Then you add to that Catholic theology: Life is a vale of tears that you will not get through without falling, but God will pick you up anyway.

"A seven-year-old can believe that he will stay in hell everlasting for something he did wrong. We believed that. We carried it with us. We were so busy trying to avoid sin that we could never make friends with women, never share ideas, never care how they felt. Women were occasions of sin. The Church taught us that.

"When you get right down to it, more war has been inflicted on people in the name of the Prince of Peace than for any other reason."

It is not really important whether Donahue is correct or not in his assessments—obviously a large number of Catholics and some non-Catholics would disagree with him. What is important is that Donahue cares about such things, that he has feelings on such issues, and that he does not hide them. Anyone who watches the Donahue show can sense that quality of involvement.

When Donahue was asked if there is anything he would not put on the air, he thought for a moment. "Well, we wouldn't use 'the marriage act,' as we used to call it at Notre Dame," he said. "Yes, I *would* show an execution. The sizzle like bacon, the smoke coming out of the head. Yes, I would. Women are tired of being protected. They don't want television to protect them anymore.

"If they found Hitler, I'd be the first in line to interview him."

Just who *does* get on television is largely a product of Donahue's staff, especially Patricia McMillen, producer, and Sheri Singer and Darlene Hayes, the associate producers. Donahue does 235 shows a year, and the public thirst for trends and issues and entertainment is insatiable.

"We read the papers for ideas, and magazines," Singer said. "We try to mix it up. Not all Bob Hope, but not all unwed mothers either.

"We try to be on top of trends. Pregnancy is out, marijuana is out, and breast cancer is getting that way. So are alcoholism and violence on TV and divorce unless they are really something new.

"Stuff about babies is always good, that 'Erroneous Zones' guy is good. Anything with marriage, couples, children. And sex. Sex always works. Always."

And after searching for 235 of these things a year, after shoveling shows into the maw day after day, has her opinion of public taste changed? "Oh, sure," she said. "It's gone down."

"The thing to learn is what is an issue *now*," McMillen said. "Donahue can be too new with an issue. This farm-strike thing. Donahue said that it will only be an effective show when people can't get bread on the shelves. That's when we do it.

"There are shows that Phil does not do as well as others. Vitamin therapy, biofeedback—he doesn't like those. And fashion and makeup shows. But he's learning. Before, all he could do was say how he hated blue eye shadow. Apparently he has this thing about blue eye shadow."

But if Donahue knows what he doesn't like, he also knows what he likes. And he likes being Phil Donahue these days. Like most TV stars, he kicked around on small TV and radio stations for years before the big break came.

And now he is big time. In 1977 he won an Emmy and subsequently his syndicated show was picked up for an hour in New York. From that followed a great deal of attention and an "inquiry"—although not an offer—from NBC's "Today" show. Donahue recently signed another long-term contract with his syndicator. "Don't let anybody tell you they don't like this kind of attention," he said. "Suddenly there is money [he gets a percentage of the show's gross in addition to his salary]. Women are asking me for autographs. I meet everybody. I go to lunch with Muhammad Ali. I'm enjoying it.

"But I remember, a few years ago I had gabardine pants with a shiny seat and nobody cared about me. I couldn't get arrested, let alone get magazine articles done on me."

Now, in the Chicago gossip columns he is a nearly daily item, mainly linked with Marlo Thomas. "Marlo is part of the American consciousness," he said. "She is enormously respected and admired. She also just happens to be beautiful. You don't know attention until you walk into a department store with Marlo Thomas. I sometimes ask myself, what is a boy from Cleveland doing on the arm of Marlo Thomas?"

Donahue asks himself questions like that a lot. He still seems slightly uncomfortable with fame and success. He is uncomfortable with his own efforts to overthrow what he considers a lifetime of sexism—a not unimportant problem considering how much his show depends on judging accurately the mood of the American woman. "How much am I driven by my own neuroses?" Donahue asked. "How much am I passing on to my kids? These are the kinds of things I worry about."

He may worry, but there's little apparent reason. His four sons (Michael, 19; Kevin, 18; Dan, 17; and Jimmy, 15) seem unscathed. They live with their father in a large five-bedroom home in a posh suburb along Chicago's North Shore. The three oldest kids have after-school jobs, and a live-in couple has replaced the string of housekeepers that Donahue tried out.

Donahue's syndication with Multimedia Broadcasting is so successful that he has an independence few persons in television enjoy. "No one station can kill us," he said. "They cancel us in Pierre, South Dakota, and we are still alive. They can cancel us in New York and we are still alive. Not happy, but alive. It is going to be hard to stamp out Phil Donahue."

And so he will continue. Daily searching for the newest of the new, the trendiest of the trendy, the unexpected and exciting in a world that grows quickly bored with itself.

And while his show will never be confused with "60 Minutes" and Donahue will never be mentioned in the same breath as Edward R. Murrow, he is better at what he does than anyone around. And the secret of it all is that Donahue has one quality that is almost nonexistent today.

He still cares. He still thinks that somehow, some way, it all matters. That the public still deserves something, even if that something is only a little fun, or a little help, or a little sympathy.

"Well, I really hate to say this," he said with a grin that began 10 years ago in Dayton, Ohio, and has been growing wider ever since, "but when you get right down to it, we really *are* good."

May 27, 1978

Phil Donahue married Marlo Thomas and moved to New York. Last I heard, he was still in television.

Who Does This Simon Think He Is?

People who *must* pick threads off other people are the strangest people I know.

◆

You know you're getting old when you think there's nothing wrong with taking the center-piece home from a wedding.

◆

I wish someone could tell me: When something comes on a bed of lettuce, is it OK to eat the lettuce?

◆

You know you are an adult when you call movers instead of your friends.

◆

Just when, exactly, did people stop saying, "I want to set a good example for my kid" and start saying, "I want to be a good role model for my kid"?

◆

Any person over the age of 19 who goes down the street with headphones on his ears should reassess his life. (I exclude joggers from this. They are beyond help.)

◆

Artificial bacon is an idea whose time has gone.

If they did a study, I'll bet they'd find I'm right: Couples that share one bed at home always get two beds on vacation. Couples who have separate beds at home, always share on the road.

◆

It drives me crazy when people don't fold up maps exactly right.

◆

The worst feeling in the world is to be in a restaurant and hear a sneeze from the kitchen.

◆

Cinnamon flavored dental floss? Aww, c'mon.

◆

The two words on the menu that strike the most fear in my heart are: market price.

◆

Isn't it disgusting how when smokers talk those little puffs of smoke come out with their words?

◆

Does anyone *really* have fun on those secluded island vacations?

◆

How come the salespeople in health food stores all look like they live on Pepsi and fries?

You can tell a lot about a person by whether he uses aluminum foil with the shiny side out or in.

◆

No matter how much you've been complaining about the food, as soon as the waiter asks you how things are you always say: "Fine."

◆

You know you're not young anymore when:
- You want to leave the game in the seventh inning in order to beat traffic.
- You actually care about the lawn.
- You listen to a presidential candidate and think he makes sense.
- You trade in your MGB for a station wagon.
- The only chemical you care about is zinc.
- Ronald Reagan doesn't seem that old.

◆

Let's face it, most women are disgusted by men with hairy backs.

◆

If the earth is round and has a North Pole and a South Pole, why doesn't it have an East Pole and West Pole?

◆

People who dot their I's with little hearts ought to consider therapy.

Dressing to impress other people rarely does.

◆

You will never see fancier wristwatches than on Las Vegas dealers.

◆

If they stopped making AA-size batteries, I think the world would grind to a halt.

◆

Confidential to "Baffled in Berwyn": Don't listen to your brother-in-law. Serving burgundy in a Flintstone's glass is perfectly OK. The rule is: Red wine, use Fred or Bam-Bam. White wine, use Wilma or Barney.

◆

If you really want to know about a person, play Monopoly with him.

◆

Be nice to a phone operator this week. You will be rewarded in your next life.

◆

I feel gypped if I go to a movie and don't see coming attractions.

◆

You know you're in a fancy place when the salad costs extra.

◆

You know you are lonely when you buy something for yourself and have it gift-wrapped.

The team names in the USFL are an embarrassment to sport.

◆

You can always tell a guy who's enthusiastic about the draft. He's too old to go.

◆

I wouldn't mind piano bars if it weren't for the pianos.

◆

Ladies, when is the last time your shoe store washed that Ped?

◆

Somebody wake me when "cowboy-chic" is over.

◆

I've never been in a town where the mall was worth it.

◆

I always feel intimidated when the waiter recommends something and I don't want to order it.

◆

Designer jeans commercials should not be shown during the family hour.

◆

At miniature golf, I am unbeatable on the windmill and the clown's nose.

◆

Is there anything more hypocritical than those public service ads by oil companies?

I feel rotten every week when the new magazines come and I haven't finished the old ones yet.

◆

Have you ever wondered what the people were really laughing at on those laugh tracks?

◆

People who don't reset the Xerox machine back to 1 should be beaten with sticks.

◆

If goose down is so warm, how come geese fly south for the winter?

◆

I can't believe anyone ever watched an Esther Williams movie from beginning to end.

◆

People who are always on time spend the rest of their lives waiting for people who aren't.

◆

Every time I get out of a bad movie, I feel like warning the people who are waiting to get in.

◆

Any bank that doesn't provide free traveler's checks is unworthy of your patronage.

◆

Admit it: The only reason you order escargot is for the garlic butter.

People who wear galoshes look like they should.

◆

I don't think anyone's luggage has ever been first off the plane.

◆

Stay at least one lane away from anyone who drives with his hat on.

◆

You can tell a lot about people by what they name their pets.

◆

Kicking vending machines should be made an Olympic sport.

◆

Does anyone still sell milk in glass bottles?

◆

Only really insecure people bring their invitations with them to parties.

◆

The only thing more senseless than marathons is the people who run in them.

◆

You know you've made it when no one dares put you on hold.

◆

Anyone who goes to all the trouble of cooking squab should just serve chicken.

Why, at the beginning of black-and-white movies, is there always someone in the audience who says, "Hey, it's in black and white!"?

◆

All TV shows with the words "Amazing" and "Incredible" in their titles ought to be canceled.

◆

Have Archie and Veronica ever done it? Would Betty be jealous?

◆

Men almost always keep the bills in their wallets in numerical order. Women almost never do.

◆

Memo to all those guys who went out and bought Indiana Jones hats: You look ridiculous.

◆

My favorite Trivial Pursuit question of the month: What communist country is closest to the United States? (If, like me, you said Cuba, you're wrong.)

◆

Did you ever stop and think where the world would be today without Lycra spandex?

◆

Why do car companies come up with colors like bronze, sea breeze and morning mist, when they really mean brown, blue, and gray?

To Her, Reverend King Was Simply Dad

ATLANTA

Though the day was cold, she sat at the edge of the reflecting pool in front of her father's tomb.

"He was a great joker," she said. "He told the funniest jokes I have ever heard. Most people don't know that.

"The photographers captured only the dramatic moments. It was the times, I guess. But I remember him as a very funny man."

Yolanda King, eldest child of Rev. Martin Luther King, Jr., is 29 now. She was 12 when her father was killed.

"He would come home and he would get on the floor and romp with us and roll around and Mother would come into the room and say: 'Stop, stop! You're going to break something,' " she said. "And then we'd stop for a few minutes until she left and then he'd roll around with us again.

"Do you know what I think of when I remember him? I think: He was such a kid. He taught me how to swim when I was four and how to ride a bike.

"So when I think of Martin Luther King, I think of laughter. I think of the play and the fun.

"He never spanked us, you know. He didn't believe in spanking kids. Of course, maybe if he had been around us longer, he would have changed his mind!"

She laughed and her corn-rowed hair shook. This is typical of her. Though she is an actress and director of cultural affairs for the Martin Luther King, Jr., Center for Nonviolent Social Change, she avoids dramatic moments.

Her speech, richly modulated, is often interrupted by laughter and mimicry. She does not give many interviews, but it was Martin Luther King Week in Atlanta and I caught her between seminars.

"He did spank us once, though," she recalled. "My sister and I had poured water down his ear while he was sleeping. We thought that would be very funny. He didn't think so.

"What else do I remember? I remember the things that people don't think of when they think of him. I remember him telling me and my older brother about the birds and the bees. I remember the simple and honest way in which he did it.

"He was always there for us, you see. He traveled a great deal, but he was there for us. And Mother was there, too, of course. She was there to comfort us when the other kids called him a jailbird and made fun of us."

It is easy to forget that Reverend King was not universally loved by the black community during his life. There were those who felt that nonviolence was an inadequate answer to the massive problems facing blacks in America.

"At 16, I went to Smith College in Massachusetts and that was right after the peak of the civil rights movement and all the rest," Yolanda said. "It was an era when students were making demands and many black students were closer to the teachings of Malcolm X, or what they thought were his teachings.

"And I remember when they would come up to me and say to my face that my father had been too moderate, that he had been an Uncle Tom."

Her father had been dead only four years, and she was terrified that perhaps history would judge him that way.

"At that time, he was still just 'Daddy' to me," she said. "I had never read his works. It was just someone who loved someone, and I knew he had done great things and now people didn't appreciate it."

So she sat down and read his books and studied the complex ideological twists and turns that marked the civil rights movement. After that study, she decided her father had been right all along.

"I learned, I grew, but I never doubted," she said. "And I made the philosophy of nonviolence an integral part of my life-style. I try to understand people who do violence. I try to understand what they are feeling and experiencing."

Even James Earl Ray? I asked. Even the man who killed your father? Are you saying you don't hate him?

"I do not hate him," she said quietly. "I was watching the news that day when the bulletin came on that my father had been shot. I prayed. I asked God, 'Please don't let my daddy die.' "

But later, when she knew her father was dead, she went into her mother's darkened bedroom. "Should I hate him?" Yolanda asked. "Should I hate the man who killed my father?"

"Your father would not want you to," Coretta Scott King said.

"And so I never did hate him," Yolanda said. "I never felt angry. I felt terribly hurt and sad, but never mad.

"I feel my father was sent here to do a specific job and when he was through he moved on to something higher.

"I honestly doubt he could have lived much longer. There was too much pressure. Too much stress.

"Andy Young said that, in a sense, his death was a freedom for him. And I largely agree with that."

Behind her, on the white Georgia marble of her father's simple tomb, were carved the words: "Free at last. Free at last. Thank God Almighty, I'm free at last."

The entire place, the King Center, is a shrine, I said. Your father's remains are right here and this is where you work. There is the constant reminder of his death here. Doesn't that bother you?

"No, because I don't think of him being in that tomb," she said. "He is in a better place. What is here is his spirit. His love."

She looked toward the eternal flame before his tomb, flickering in the winter wind.

One must come to grips with grief and Yolanda King has. But that does not mean she does not feel.

"Twice a year," she said, her voice growing thick, "twice a year we lay a wreath there. On his birthday and on his assassination day. And those are the only times I think of that awful day when . . . he left us.

"And then. Then, I wish very much that my daddy was still here."

Reverend Martin Luther King, Jr., would have been 56 tomorrow.

January 14, 1985

From a Foxhole, Wishing Wildcats Ill

I was cheating death on Grenada as the second most important football game of the year came crackling in on Armed Forces Radio Network.

They say there are no atheists in foxholes. And as we slogged through the murderous island terrain, past the souvenir shops, past the pubs, past the supermarkets, I mumbled a simple prayer:

"Please, God, let Illinois beat Michigan and then let me live long enough to go to the Illinois-Northwestern game November 19."

Last year, I was in Beirut but flew back to see Illinois squash Northwestern, like the bugs they are, 49–13.

And now, here I was, laughing in the face of the Grim Reaper once again as Illinois played Michigan for a probable Rose Bowl spot.

"Sure, Michigan is important," I told the top sergeant as we struggled through the living hell together, "but nothing is as important as the Northwestern game."

A screaming hiss shattered our conversation. A live grenade plunged from a tree above us. I didn't think twice. I threw myself upon it.

"Save yourselves!" I yelled to the others. "I die, but the Fighting Illini live forever!"

As I lay on the damp earth, waiting for the end, the top sergeant came up to me. He scratched the stubble of his chin thoughtfully. He removed a cigar stub from his lips.

"First, Illinois just beat Michigan 16–6," he said. "Second, you just threw yourself on top of a live coconut."

I got up and brushed myself off. A lesser man would have been embarrassed. "Coconuts have been known to explode," I said. "They can put somebody's eye out."

As luck would have it, I survived Grenada with nothing worse than a hangover. And I am back to write my annual Illini-Wildcat column.

Why, you ask, is this game so important?

Why is America important? I might ask in return. The annual

Illinois-Northwestern clash is a metaphor for the American experience.

Examine the purposes of the two schools: Illinois was built for the sons and daughters of solid, decent, prairie stock. Northwestern was built for the sons and daughters of the idle rich.

Illinois graduates go on to shape America. Northwestern graduates go on to clip coupons in their daddies' brokerage houses.

I don't wish to make too much of a mere football game. I simply point out that every time Illinois beats Northwestern it proves that America works. It is a triumph for the common man.

In fairness to the other side, I reprint below a letter I received a few weeks ago. It is from Cuthbert Simp-Willy, Vice President of Annuities, Money Market Funds, and Public Relations at Northwestern University.

"Dear Mr. Simon:

"I have received your letter asking who our starting quarterback will be against Illinois.

"Regardless of the rumors you claim to hear, Boy George of the rock group Culture Club will not be wearing the purple and white of Northwestern. We dropped all interest in Mr. George when we learned that he was ineligible under NCAA rules.

"You also ask if Richard Simmons might be filling the quarterback spot as well as leading an aerobics class at halftime. All I can tell you is what Coach Dennis Green told me: He will make that decision based on how the game is going at the time.

"I can assure you that Coach Green, whose career record now stands at 5–27 overall and 4–22 in the Big Ten, makes his decisions very carefully.

"I suppose you are making these inquiries in preparation for your annual slam against Northwestern. As I have informed your editors in past years, we no longer treat this matter as a joke.

"Your column has a depressing effect upon our entire campus. After reading your column last year, our Board of Trustees spit up their sherry.

"Football is not everything. I would like to remind you of the enormous success our students have attained in other fields of endeavor.

"Will anyone ever forget, for instance, Ann-Margret's stunning performance in *Kitten with a Whip*?

"And need I remind you that Paul Lynde was not only on 'Hollywood Squares' for years, but was the *center square*?

"As to your sneering claim that Northwestern is most famous for inventing ultrasuede, that is a foul lie. Northwestern is most famous for inventing control-top pantyhose.

"I will not, however, descend to your level. The university's official response to you this year is the same as our response to you in previous years: bounces off rubber and sticks to glue! Nyah-nyah-nyah!"

I think Simp-Willy's letter speaks for itself.

I would like to end this with my traditional address to the Fighting Illini:

Men, we have seen good times and bad times together. I have never been prouder of you than at this moment. Your victories this year have been more than anyone could have asked for.

But I must ask one more thing: Do not let down against Northwestern. You are not playing just for yourselves on Saturday. You are not playing just for a 9–0 conference record. You are playing for America.

Now, for the benefit of the defensive line, I would like to put this in simpler terms:

Pound those wimps to jelly or don't bother coming home.

November 18, 1983

Inspired by these words, no doubt, Illinois went on to crush Northwestern by a score of 56–24.

Unfortunately, I failed to write a column before the Rose Bowl, where the Illini were nipped by UCLA 45–9.

I may never forgive myself.

'Kitty Genovese Did Not Die in Vain'

Out of the steamy darkness, the elevated train rumbled and squealed into the Morse Avenue stop and let off its passengers.

Libby Skolnik, 28, hurried off the train, being careful to stay with the crowd. "An awful lot has been happening in the neighborhood—in Rogers Park," she said. "Muggings. Rapes. You know.

"I try and stay with the people. The exit on Lunt is under a viaduct and sort of recessed. If there is no crowd, I don't take that exit. I go where there are people."

Cathy Rieck, 26, also got off that train, but she did not care about things like crowds. She was the kind of person who took life as it came. Cathy and Libby did not know each other, but before the night was over they very definitely would.

And they would know certain things about their city and their neighbors. Because, for one brief moment on a night last week, a neighborhood decided that it was fed up with crime. And it was not going to take it anymore.

Cathy shifted the grocery bags in her arms as she stepped out onto the wooden platform and the train doors hissed closed behind her. She was coming from shopping and from a meeting of her world peace group, a gathering of people who pray together for their fellow men.

"I just don't worry anymore at night," she said. "I just sort of gave up worrying. I've lived in Rogers Park for more than 10 years, and it's getting rougher. But I'm used to living in the city."

The exit was down a flight of steps and ended in one of those tall turnstiles made of iron rods. The turnstile allows you only to exit. People on the other side can see you and hear you, but they cannot come in that way.

Libby Skolnik already had exited with the rest of the crowd when Cathy carefully walked down the steps, holding the grocery bags. The exit is a place of both bright lights and dark shadows, and it is a place where people do not linger.

A man stood just inside the exit, just in front of the turnstile, blocking it with his body. He was short and wore a bright green shirt and a white cap.

"He was just fiddling with that cap for too long," Cathy said. "I finally said: 'Are you going to let me by?' "

The man looked at her hard and looked up the steps. He had not waited there for nothing. He knew there were no others coming. He knew there are those who group together in the night for protection. And he also knew there are stragglers.

He spread his arms wide and blocked the exit. "I want to talk to you," he said with a hard, flat voice. "I want your money."

Cathy quickly looked behind her to see if there was anyone still left in the station with her. But there was no one. "I'm going through! You let me through!" she shouted at the man.

He gave her a hard shove and rocked her back into the wall. There was only one thing left for Cathy to do. And she did it very, very well.

Outside, Libby heard the screams. "They were the most blood-curdling yells I have ever heard in my life," she said. "My heart stopped. I got jumped once, and I know. I thought: 'Oh, my God, a girl is getting mugged at the L (elevated) station.'

"I turned back toward the station and saw a guy on the inside of the turnstile slapping this girl around. Really hitting her. The girl looked very timid, very docile. She had pale red hair and freckles. She only looked about 20.

"I started yelling: 'There's a girl getting mugged in there!' I kept yelling."

There were people around that night. A hodgepodge of the people in that neighborhood. Some businessmen, some couples, some young people from the jogging set, some others walking their dogs.

Few knew each other, for in the city we do not know our neighbors. It is often better, we believe, to keep to ourselves. And not get involved. But something happened in Chicago that night when two women started screaming. Something different.

Inside the turnstile, the man was smacking Cathy with his fists. Then he turned and looked up in panic. On the other side of the turnstile was a rolling mass of people, beating against the bars and yelling at him. "They were screaming and yelling for him to let me alone," Cathy said. "I couldn't believe it. Things like that just don't happen."

Businessmen and joggers and women and people with their dogs had come running down the street to answer a cry for help: A small thing. Nothing too heroic, perhaps. But how often does it happen? How often do people turn away instead?

Fourteen years ago in Queens in New York City, another young woman was coming home at night. As she walked to her home, a man jumped out of a parking lot and began chasing her. He caught up with her and stabbed her.

"Oh, my God, he stabbed me!" she shouted. "Please help me! Please help me!"

The police later established that 38 people—38 of her neighbors—heard that woman's cries. One, a man, threw open his window and called out: "Let that girl alone!" And then he closed the window again.

No one called the police. No one came out to help. The attacker got into his car and drove away at first. The woman, bleeding, dragged herself to the back of an apartment building.

A few minutes later, the attacker returned and stabbed her again. And Kitty Genovese, 28, died alone and afraid in a New York alley.

The police questioned those 38 people. "Why didn't you even call us?" the police asked. "Why didn't you do something? Anything."

Some of the replies are recorded for history.

"I didn't want my husband to get involved," one woman said.

"We thought it was a lover's quarrel," another woman said. "I went back to bed."

"I was tired," said a man.

"I don't know," said another.

"I don't know."

"I don't know."

"I don't know."

It was a deeply shocking thing, and the nation was gripped by the death of this young woman. People thought about it and talked about it and said, "What have we come to? What have we become?" And 14 years passed.

The man stopped beating Cathy when he heard the yells of the crowd and saw the people's faces. They could not get to him, but he was frightened. "He ran back up the stairs onto the elevated tracks," Cathy said. "I ran out the exit.

"The people gathered around me. They asked me if I was all right. They asked me if they could help. There were so many people I got scared a little."

Libby and the rest of the crowd could see the man up on the elevated platform. When no train came for him to escape in, he ran back down the steps and out the exit.

The crowd pursued him.

"There was even a guy with a German shepherd running after him," Libby said. "We had called the police, of course. But we just weren't going to let him get away.

"The crowd was made up of mostly young professional-types, I guess you could say. Some people were there just because they had gone out to get a paper.

"Two off-duty policemen joined the crowd, and finally they got him. The regular police came, and they put him in a car."

Libby stayed with Cathy, as did others, asking her if she needed anything. "At first she didn't even want to prosecute the guy," Libby said. "But I said if he gets away with it this time, he'll just do it again.

"I said that the neighborhood had helped her, and now she could help the neighborhood."

Other people went up to Cathy and gave her their names and addresses. Call us, they told her. We will testify. We will come to court. We will help.

"It was amazing. It was mind-blowing," Cathy said. "The crowd was not made up of gawkers. It was made up of people who wanted to help. Of people who wanted to help me. I was amazed. I felt so . . . so *protected.*"

Cathy was not alone in feeling good. "We were all so proud we pulled together," Libby said. "We showed strength. We showed we could stop crime. We showed we were not going to stand for it anymore. We showed that people could help other people."

On the street corner, with the crowd gathered around her, Cathy Rieck gave a little speech. It was only one line.

"Kitty Genovese did not die in vain," she said.

Everyone applauded.

August 22, 1978

Let Ferraro Enjoy
Her Pepsi Rallies

The thing I like best about Geraldine Ferraro's Diet Pepsi commercial is how it must make George Bush feel.

Can you imagine him last Wednesday night watching "The Fall Guy" on television, and right after the part where Colt and Howie go over the cliff in the stolen police car—except they don't *really* go over the cliff, of course—the Ferraro commercial comes on?

Can you imagine Bush bolting from his chair and grabbing the direct line to the president? "How come she gets a commercial and I don't?" he yells. "I won!"

"Calm down, Georgie," the president says from the ranch. "You get to go to a lot more state funerals than she does."

As I have always said, political ethics is to ethics what Cheez Whiz is to cheese.

So I was not shocked when Ferraro decided to do a commercial for one-half million quick bucks.

When I saw it on the air last week, I was even pleased. It was so low key, it was almost obscure.

It is hard to tell that it actually is Ferraro until you hear that wonderful Queens accent. And by the time the camera is finished with all its quick cuts and tricky angles, I couldn't remember whether she was selling soft drinks or shoe polish.

But it made me realize that America finally has found a way to reward its good losers.

What is happening to Ferraro is like something out of *Rocky*. Remember how in the first movie Rocky doesn't win, but he becomes a national symbol and gets a whole bunch of commercial endorsements in the second movie?

Well, Ferraro didn't win—didn't even carry her home state, though we may have to blame her running mate, Mr. Personality, for that— but now she emerges as a national symbol worthy of making commercials.

And Ferraro knows she is a symbol. She said in Atlantic City last week: "I had the chance to stand in for millions of women and together we declared that the tyranny of expectations is over. Women can be whatever we want to be."

Including Pepsi salesmen. But why not? Let us keep in mind there is not much for a failed vice presidential candidate to do. (There's not much for a *successful* vice presidential candidate to do.)

Some of Ferraro's former campaign people advised her not to make the commercial because (and get this) they feared "she will be accused of exploiting her political fame for financial gain."

Which is a little like accusing a ballerina of dancing on her toes.

Politics is the art of exploitation. You sell what you can. And what else can politicians sell except their names and notoriety?

Though I didn't realize that Ferraro was even old enough to have memoirs, she sold them recently for $1 million.

This was an occasion for celebration. Someone who hadn't stabbed somebody in prison, been convicted of a felony, or disgraced a nation actually was getting a fat book contract.

Richard Nixon sold his post-Watergate memoirs for $2 million in 1977. In some societies he would have been put in a cage and paraded in front of school children as a bad example. But in America, we threw dollars at him.

So why should we get upset at Geraldine Ferraro making dough? At least the former congresswoman didn't need a presidential pardon when she left office.

I am sure Pepsi is delighted with all the publicity it is getting, but how many extra six-packs Ferraro actually will sell is open to question.

I never have understood celebrity endorsements. Why should I buy a computer because Alan Alda likes it? I know he is so handsome and warm and sensitive and that he would make a great prom king, but what does he know about computers?

Do I care that Bill Cosby drinks Coke? Will drinking it make me as funny as he is?

And if we all sat down and ate Wheaties until the cows came home, we still would never be able to develop the thighs of a Mary Lou Retton who, someone once pointed out, has the thighs of a Dick Butkus.

On the other hand, Ferraro probably doesn't care what happens to Diet Pepsi sales. She was smart enough to get her money up front.

As one of her former advisers said: "The worst that can happen is that she got a fair sum of money."

There are, I think, worse fates. So grab for all the gusto you can, Ms. Ferraro.

You got a million for the book and one-half million for the commercial.

Keep this up and you're going to give losing a good name.

March 10, 1985

Take Henny Youngman— Please

H ey!" the man on the phone was shouting. "Doctor gave a guy six months to live. Guy couldn't pay the bill; doctor gave him another six months!"

Good morning Mr. Youngman. It's a pleasure to talk to you.

"Hey! Guy walks into a psychiatrist's office and the psychiatrist says, 'You're crazy.' Guy says he wants a second opinion. 'OK. You're ugly, too.' "

I've been a fan of yours for years, Mr. Youngman, and . . .

"I ask my wife where she wants to go for her anniversary," Henny Youngman shouts. "She said, 'I want to go somewhere I've never been before.' I said, 'Try the kitchen!' "

Your early career as part of the Swanee Syncopators and on the Kate Smith show must have been valuable training for . . .

"Say! My grandson, Larry, he's 21. He'll be 22 if I let him. That kid was so ugly when he was born, the doctor slapped his mother!"

I understand you first opened in Chicago in 1939 . . .

"Chicago! What a town. You know there's less crime in Chicago— nothing left to steal!"

That's very amusing, Mr. Youngman, but . . .

"Two guys meet in Chicago. One says: 'You look bad, what happened to you?' Other says: 'I lost three wives in three months.'

"First one says: 'What happened?'

"Second one says: 'First wife died from eating poison mushrooms.'

" 'How about the second wife?'

" 'She died from eating poison mushrooms.'

" 'What happened to the third wife?'

" 'Fractured skull.'

" 'How come?'

" 'She wouldn't eat them.' "

Very, very funny, Mr. Youngman. Now I understand you've been married to your wife, Sadie, for 50 years and . . .

"Take my wife—please! First told that joke on Kate Smith and for some reason it caught on. Don't know why. Today, I'm working like crazy. Do 200 shows a year. Banquets, trade meetings, sales shows, conventions, outdoor fairs, concerts, colleges.

"They love me at colleges. They don't know it, but I'm a legend in my own mind! Busy as hell. Always adding jokes. Went to a doctor. Doctor says, 'Take your clothes off.' I say, 'Take me out a few more times first!'

"College kids treat me like a joke hero, I mean folk hero. Got an album doing sensational. Called 'Take My Album—Please!' You've got to let people know you're in business constantly. Got to have publicity all the time."

The reason I'm calling, Mr. Youngman, is . . .

"I loaned my brother, Lester, money to start a business. He opens a tall man's shop in Tokyo. Brought back a thousand cameras that go 'Crick!' "

When you first started, didn't you say that the places were so small that the band played "Tea for One"?

"I'll tell you something," he said. "It's harder than it looks. It's all in the timing. If you're blessed with it, you do it. Say! Mention Dave Romaine, he's from Chicago, he's a fiddle player. And mention my son, Gary, he's making a movie called *Rush-It*. You don't mind, do you?"

No, not at all. But I was wondering . . .

"Guy goes to a psychiatrist. Says, 'Gee, it's tough for me to make friends—you big, fat slob!' "

How long can you keep this up, Mr. Youngman?

"As long as they want me," Henny Youngman said quietly. "As long as they still want me."

December 13, 1978

500th Column:
For All Those Gawkers

This is my 500th column. I didn't sit down and count them, but a very kind reader told me that this was going to be the one.

I should point out that 500 columns is not quite the milestone it seems. There are columnists in this country who passed the 500 mark sometime during the Korean War.

But still, it is one of those round numbers that weighs heavy on the mind and makes you feel as if you should do something about it.

In commemoration, I was going to write something glib about the practice of journalism. Somehow, it didn't turn out that way.

This is a strange thing to do for a living. In some ways it is a lot like juggling or balancing things on your nose: It takes a knack. It looks harder than it is. It impresses people.

Unlike juggling, however, we use other people and not Indian clubs or rubber balls to do our act. We use the stuff of other people's lives to fashion our work. And we do it, mainly, whether they want us to or not. And we don't think about it all that much.

I am always fascinated that people want newspapers to be better than they are. People stand in the freezing cold at the scene of a mass murder to catch a glimpse of a body bag, but they also complain that the press is filled with too much violence.

I'm not saying our motives are that much higher than yours. Curiosity and the thrill of covering a story are probably bigger motivations for what we do than the fancy explanations that we dream up in our speeches on free press.

We live in a society that has combined extraordinary laws protecting free speech with the extraordinary technology to carry that speech.

We live in a country that has an insatiable appetite for information, gossip, news, tidbits, rumors, hints, and downright lies.

We live in a country that, above all things, wants to *know*. About everything.

We are all gawkers at the train wreck.

Newspapers are going to tell you what you want to know and a few things that you don't. We are going to give you the facts and the commentary and the cartoons and the coupons. We are going to tell the truth as best we can determine it, which means that sometimes we won't tell the truth at all. When we don't, we'll probably say we're sorry.

We are not going to be on the cutting edge of social reform in America. I can't remember any newspaper kicking off the fight for civil rights or the fight against the war in Vietnam.

You're going to have to do those things yourselves. Once things get going, the newspapers will cover the story. Editorial pages will offer comfort and support and advice and maybe change a few minds.

And, on rare occasions, a newspaper will stand up on its hind legs and take on everybody and everything. Those are the times that make us proud of our profession.

I once read that the motto of the old *Chicago Times* was: "It is a newspaper's duty to print the news and raise hell." I don't know if that really was the motto, but if I ever own a newspaper, that's the motto I'd want.

I think newpapers, in general, do a hell of a job. We don't like to say that much. We are a very nervous industry. Anyone who claims to speak for the public is usually nervous about just how isolated from the public he really is.

So during Spiro Agnew's famous attack on the press, some of the media did a lot of soul-searching and then decided to roll over and play dead. Some fought back.

The press didn't turn out to be right and Agnew wrong just because Agnew was a crook. Agnew was wrong because he dreamed up cozy conspiracies to describe how the press operated.

I don't know many reporters who sit down and worry about the great issues of a free press when they write a story. They go out to the story and they grab it and they write it and they build it up to the city desk.

They scream when the story ends up on Page 50 with the last paragraph cut off and they bask in the warmest glow in the world when it's Page One. Somehow it all works. Truth, justice, and the American way somehow get served.

It's a simple profession with simple joys. I still remember what it felt like to get my first by-line. In college, the Associated Press would send you a check if it used one of your stories on the wire. I've still got my first one. I remember what it felt like when a newsman named Ward Just, who was my first boss in Waukegan, sent me a note saying that if I wanted to try a column, it was OK with him. I remember that when I left his paper to come to the big city that I was scared and he said not to be. "It's just a newspaper," he said.

Reporters always end up quoting other reporters when they talk about journalism. The following was written by Stanley Walker, a famous editor and author. It has been quoted before, but it's worth repeating:

"What makes a good newspaperman? The answer is easy. He knows everything. He is aware not only of what goes on in the world today, but his brain is a repository of the accumulated wisdom of the ages.

"He is not only handsome, but he has the physical strength which enables him to perform great feats of energy. He can go for nights on end without sleep. He dresses well and talks with charm. Men admire him; women adore him; tycoons and statesmen are willing to share their secrets with him.

"He hates lies and meanness and sham, but keeps his temper. He is loyal to his paper and to what he looks upon as his profession; whether it is a profession, or merely a craft, he resents attempts to debase it.

"When he dies, a lot of people are sorry and some of them remember him for several days."

February 9, 1979